Group's® Best JR. HIGH MEETINGS

VOLUME ONE

Edited by
Cindy Parolini

Group® Books

Loveland, Colorado

Group's Best Jr. High Meetings, Volume 1

Copyright © 1987 by Thom Schultz Publications, Inc.

Ninth Printing, 1994

Designed by Judy Atwood
Illustrations by Jan Knudson on pages 37, 78, 88, 142, 160, 176, 196, 290, 320, 321
Illustrations by RoseAnne Buerge on pages 18, 21, 55

Scripture quotations in this book are from the Good News Bible, the Bible in Today's English Version. Copyright © American Bible Society 1966, 1971, 1976. Used by permission.

Library of Congress Cataloging-in-Publication Data

Group's best jr. high meetings.

Selections from Group's jr. high ministry magazine.
1. Church work with youth. I. Parolini, Cindy, 1960-   . II. Group's jr. high ministry.
III. Title: Group's best junior high meetings.
BV4447. G695   1987   268'.433   87-8591
ISBN 0-931529-58-1 (pbk.)
Printed in the United States of America.

Contents

SECTION SIX: VALUES AND DECISIONS

SECTION SEVEN: SERVICE

SECTION EIGHT: SEASONAL AND SPECIAL EVENTS

How to Use This Book

Welcome to the first collection of the best meetings from Group's JR. HIGH MINISTRY Magazine!

Welcome to the adventure of sharing meaningful growth experiences with junior highers!

We all know that leading young teenagers to Christian maturity is a challenging task. Junior high kids are just beginning to move from concrete thinking to abstract thinking. And, generally speaking, faith speaks an abstract language.

Here's help. These faith-stretching meetings start where junior highers are. They connect Christian principles with everyday, concrete moorings. These meetings effectively:

● challenge young people to live their Christian faith—and they show them how;

● channel junior highers' energy to involving and creative activities; and

● give you step-by-step guidelines for successful learning experiences with junior highers.

Each meeting specifically spells out what it's designed to accomplish ("Objectives"), and gives a detailed list of everything you need ("Supplies"), preparation hints ("Before the Meeting") and handouts (which you have permission to copy). Some even add special notes on things to watch for as the meetings unfold ("Notes to the Leader").

Junior high leaders across the country contributed these meetings. And thousands have used them with junior highers. They find that the programs work well for both Sunday school sessions or weekly fellowship meetings. Some even adapt the meetings to accommodate weekend retreat schedules.

So, join the crowd. Let your junior highers enjoy the world of relational, experiential learning about faith.

Choosing Which Meetings to Use

Where to start? Begin by asking kids what their needs are right now; do an informal phone survey or a full-blown written survey. Where do your junior highers want help? In areas of self-image? Getting along with family? Keeping friends? Standing up to peer pressure? Let them tell you.

Map out your plan for meetings two or more months in advance. Include meetings on the topics your junior highers name. (If they name a topic you don't find in this volume, send us a note so we can cover it in

Group's JR. HIGH MINISTRY Magazine!) Also include meetings that recognize life events (such as graduating into high school or dealing with death). And throw in some seasonal meetings at appropriate times to remind kids you do keep track of the calendar.

Aim for balance. Realize that while the meetings in the "Faith" chapter have faith issues as their starting points, *all* the meetings apply faith to life.

Once you've mapped your plan, be flexible. You may carefully prepare for the "Be My Valentine" meeting and then discover that your junior highers are quietly panicking about tests they're facing at school. Switch gears. Do the "Getting an 'A' " meeting. You'll give kids a stronger message of love by caring enough to meet their needs—even when it's inconvenient—than by following through on your original plan. The "Be My Valentine" meeting can wait for another appropriate time.

Adapting the Meetings for Your Group

Make these meetings your own. Adapt them to fit your group and your own style. For example:

● If you always begin your junior high meetings with a game of volleyball, by all means begin these meetings with volleyball. Or singing. Or announcements. Or (yes, even) refreshments. Ritual is important.

● The meetings generally mention name tags when they specially relate to the themes. But you know your group: If your group is large and often has visitors, include name tags every time you get together even if they're simply names on plain pieces of paper, pinned on. Or if your group is small and everyone is familiar with each other, you may not want to spend time on name-tag activities.

● If your group is especially close, you may opt at times to omit the crowdbreakers or opening activities and spend more time on the learning activities.

● The meetings use both large groups and small groups. If your group is large, it's important to divide it into small groups for discussions and projects. But if it's small, you're all set—just ignore the notes to create small groups. And you won't be at a disadvantage for large group activities, either.

● Adapt the supplies as necessary. For example, the meetings often list newsprint, markers and masking tape (to tape the newsprint onto the wall). Save money by using a chalkboard. In nine cases out of 10 it would be fine (some meetings require each person or small group to have a sheet of newsprint). Or maybe you have the newsprint but not enough markers to equip your kids. Crayons are cheaper and work just as well.

Planning for the Meetings

Some nuts-and-bolts tips to help you plan for smooth-running meetings:

● Always familiarize yourself with the scripture passages used in the meetings. Choose easy-to-understand Bible translations. (The Bible passages quoted in this book are from Today's English Version unless otherwise noted.)

● Remind yourself why you've chosen to do a particular meeting with your kids. Imagine the impact it can have in specific junior higher's lives. Pray for a meaningful, growth-filled time together.

8

● For excitement, choose a variety of meeting places. Do the "Dealing With Death" meeting in a cemetery. Do the "Shoplifting" meeting in a shopping mall, after hours. Do "Good Things Come in Family Packages" in a junior higher's family room at home.

● Recruit adult sponsors to attend the meetings. Generally, one sponsor for every four to six junior highers is a good ratio. Meet with adult sponsors and discuss the meetings' topics. Also review with them the "Notes to the Leader" sections and exactly what you'll need from them during the meeting, such as leading small group discussions.

● Get adult sponsors and leader-type kids involved in preparing for the meetings. Meet together to divvy up responsibilities such as collecting supplies, doing "Before the Meeting" tasks, setting up the meeting area, distributing items during the meetings, and so on.

● Plan specific time slots for the activities. Jot the times down on a 3×5 card or right in this book to help keep you on track. The meetings generally fit nicely into either a 60-minute or 90-minute time slot, depending on how much time you spend on the games and crowdbreakers.

● Don't underestimate prizes. It's amazing how hard junior highers will work for even a small reward. Many meetings suggest prizes for game winners. Some don't. Build excitement by presenting prizes to the winners. Why not keep a prize box hidden away somewhere, and add items as you come across them: coupons, trinkets, gum—you get the idea.

● Remember refreshments. Again, meetings generally don't include snack ideas unless they relate to the theme or incorporate a needed break. But you

know junior highers.

Running the Meetings

Meeting time. The supplies are in order, the kids and adult sponsors are arriving. Go for it—keeping these things in mind:

● Greet everyone with a positive attitude and an upbeat setting. Some meetings say to have contemporary Christian music playing (especially when it relates to the theme). Why not get set up to easily play Christian music at the beginning of all get-togethers? (All of the albums suggested are available at local Christian bookstores.)

● When dividing the group into small groups for discussion, include an adult sponsor in each group. Meetings on difficult topics such as sexuality or dealing with temptation remind you to have an adult in each group.

● Use adult sponsors to fill in or sit out as necessary when you divide the group into partners.

● In all discussions, remain open and honest with junior highers. You can only expect your kids to be honest and vulnerable if you and other adults show the way. On the other hand, don't try to force sharing or get too intense too fast.

● Be on the lookout for any kids who don't receive their share of affirmation notes (or whatever) in an activity. Have a couple of adult sponsors or leader-type kids watching too; they can take action themselves as well as encourage others to fill in the gaps.

● Rearrange your time schedule if necessary. You may find kids seriously dealing with an activity you'd expected to be a simple, quick crowdbreaker. Rather than stop the learning, change your time slot from five minutes to 15.

● And, yes, when the worst happens and an activity flops, don't fret. In the first place, you may never really know what the kids got out of it. And in the second place, every "failure" has learnings in it. Seek them out with your group members. Analyze why something didn't work like you had in mind. Change it a bit and try again. Turn a disappointment into an adventure.

Following Through

One benefit of meetings that use concrete objects to carry the messages is that the learnings continue long after the lessons end. Every time your junior highers see a raw potato after experiencing the "Brothers and Sisters" meeting, they'll remember to be thankful for their brothers or sisters just the way God custom-made them; or every time they see a burning candle, they'll reflect on how Jesus is their "Light in the Darkness."

Here are some deliberate things you can do to also help the meetings' impact remain in your kids' lives.

● Encourage junior highers to take the meetings beyond the (church) walls by taking home handouts or creations. Ideally, kids' bedrooms could be decorated with remembrances of youth group meetings: handouts taped to dresser mirrors; "contracts" to themselves about behavior changes propped on desks; theme-related name tags hanging from the walls.

● At times you may want to keep for yourself worksheets that you feel would give valuable insight about particular kids. (Don't make any kids expose answers if they don't want to.)

● Set times to meet with kids who express special needs or concerns during the meetings. Get together for Cokes after school and talk.

● Meet with adult sponsors after meetings like "Facing Fears" or "Think Before You Drink" to swap insights about kids.

● Refer back to specific meetings in the weeks and months beyond them. Reinforce the learning by keeping the meetings alive. ■

Section One:

SELF-IMAGE

1 Am I Growing Up . . . or What?

By Barbara Nelson

" **A**m I growing up . . . or what?" one of my junior high guys asked me recently. Most young teenagers face the reality of a rapidly changing body, and emotional peaks and valleys as well. You can help them recognize their sexual thoughts and feelings are normal, acceptable and not weird.

Use this meeting to help your group members learn to express these feelings in healthy, wholesome activities.

OBJECTIVES

Participants will:
- examine ways television, movies, music and magazines influence them in sexual matters, especially feelings and emotions;
- look at the messages of popular songs of the past 30 or 40 years, with particular emphasis on today's music; and
- assess for themselves some music, TV shows and movies, using biblical guidelines.

SUPPLIES

Gather six small prizes such as candy or coupons; paper; cassette tapes or records of one song from each of the past three or four decades, and at least three current popular songs; lyric sheets for these songs, if available (duplicating lyrics without permission is illegal); a cassette player or turntable; newsprint; masking tape; a marker; a Bible; a large tray of assorted orange rinds, coffee grounds, eggshells and other table garbage; a large tray of fruit juices and healthy munchies such as apple slices, grapes and cheese cubes; for every five or six group members, an envelope containing 12 cut-apart words (each on a separate piece of paper) for the complete Proverbs 4:23 verse: "Be careful how you think; your life is shaped by your thoughts"; and, for each person, a "Who and What Influences Me?" worksheet and a pencil.

BEFORE THE MEETING

Read the meeting and collect supplies.

Recruit enough adult sponsors to have one for every five or six group members.

If you think it's best to pre-choose small groups because of the topic, do so now and plan how you'll get kids into those groups.

Ask a sponsor to make sure the two trays for refreshment time are kept out of sight during the meeting.

NOTES TO THE LEADER

Young teenagers often wonder if they're weird for having sexual thoughts and feelings. Some reassuring guidelines from you, and the opportunity for group discussion, will help them see the relationship between what they *do* and who they *are* in these formative years.

Because of this meeting's topic, you may feel uncomfortable presenting it. If that's the case, find someone in your congregation—a nurse, doctor or perhaps a junior high teacher—who could lead while you assist.

THE MEETING

1. *Small group scramble*—Begin by dividing the group into small groups of five or six with one adult in each small group. Give an envelope with the scrambled Proverbs 4:23 verse to each adult. At the word "Go," the adult empties the envelope, and the kids try to be the first group to put the words in order. Give each member of the winning group a prize. Have

the winning group members proclaim, all together, this Bible verse.

2. *Who and what influences me?*—Get everyone together in a circle. Explain: "All of you are taking some giant steps toward adulthood. We're going to be talking about some of those steps during our meeting."

Mention you have a short worksheet about some of the influences in their lives, especially television and movies. Say: "Just as your bodies are changing and maturing, your thoughts and feelings are becoming more grown-up too. Guys and girls are curious about each other's bodies. Fantasizing about the opposite sex is normal at your age. Today we're going to think and talk together about what influences us in these thoughts and feelings. Now let's get started!" Hand out a "Who and What Influences Me?" worksheet to each person. Ask kids to fill them out by themselves. Tell them they don't have to put their names on the worksheets.

3. *Recording and reporting*—Have kids get back in their small groups to compile answers. Hand out paper. Each group should pick one person to be a "recorder/reporter" and write down the group's thoughts. After 15 minutes, or when the groups appear to be finished, have kids get back into one group again. Ask the recorder/reporter of each group to share the worksheet results. Ask: "What are the most common answers?"

4. *Messages in the music*—Play parts of selected songs (keep lyric sheets handy for reference if you have them). Say: "As you listen to these songs, think about the 'sexual' messages they give. Are they good, positive, loving messages, or hurtful, negative, destructive messages?" Play a portion of each song you've collected from past decades. Then play portions of at least three songs currently popular on the radio.

5. *Putting it all together*—Across the top of a sheet of newsprint, write this portion of Philippians 4:8: " . . . fill your minds with those things that are good and that deserve praise: things that are true, noble, right, pure, lovely, and honorable." Make two vertical columns: "Yes" and "No."

Say: "Now let's list the songs we listened to by putting each title in the column that best describes that song's message. Ask yourself this question about each song: 'Is it good and deserving

14

Who and What Influences Me?

Answer each statement according to how you feel. Place an "X" on either the "Yes" or "No" line to indicate your response.

	Yes	No
1. Magazine ads and TV commercials that picture great-looking people of the opposite sex often get my attention.	_____	_____
2. Some TV commercials are embarrassing because they talk about personal stuff too much. (If yes, please give examples.)	_____	_____
3. When watching television or movies, I'm usually aware they don't show life as it really is.	_____	_____
4. I really enjoy watching the romantic or sexual relationships shown on television or in the movies.	_____	_____
5. I find myself wanting to have similar romantic and sexual experiences in my own life.	_____	_____
6. I watch more than eight hours of television per week.	_____	_____
7. I know the words of many popular songs.	_____	_____
8. I find it hard to understand why parents and other adults get so upset about the use of sexual terms in some of today's music.	_____	_____

9. How many hours a week do you watch television? _____ hours

10. List six of your favorite TV shows you never want to miss:
    - ●
    - ●
    - ●
    - ●
    - ●
    - ●

11. Think about how these TV shows present sexual relationships. (For example, are males shown as tough, strong, macho, gentle, bossy? Are females shown as manipulative, soft, emotional, nurturing?) Write brief comments about your favorite shows.

12. Do you sometimes daydream about characters portrayed on television? List one or two you'd like to meet.

13. Violent sexual activity is often portrayed on television. Give an example you've seen recently.

14. What are the two *best* TV shows you've seen?

15. What made these shows good?

of praise, according to God's Word?' "

Next, do the same thing with the favorite TV shows kids wrote on the "Who and What Influences Me?" worksheet. Ask: "Which column do they fall under?" Let kids decide.

Next, ask: "What about movies?" List those in the same way. You'll be amazed at how many ideas pop up *and* how kids assess these various influences. Give everyone an opportunity for input.

6. *Briefly biblical*—Quickly summarize the results of your time together. Make the point that as sexual beings, we have bodies, minds and emotions to express ourselves, and we can make good and healthy choices in using these God-given gifts. Have someone read Ephesians 4:13-16. Discuss how it applies.

7. *Goodies or garbage?*—Say: "Snacks are now being served." Then turn kids loose. After they've crowded around the serving table, which has been bare, bring out the tray of table scraps. You'll get lots of complaints.

Ask: "What's the problem?" They'll respond with exclamations such as "This is garbage!" or "Do you expect us to eat that trash?"

Then bring out the tray of good stuff. Place it beside the tray of scraps. The kids will help themselves to the good food. As they are munching, ask them: "Why do you think we did something like this?"

After they've guessed, tell them: "We gave you a choice—goodies or garbage. Just like the choices you have when it comes to your sexuality. So why settle for garbage when you don't have to?"

They'll get the message. ■

2 *Being Popular*

By Paula Mott-Becker

Junior highers dream about being well-liked and well-known—being popular. Acceptance is a major issue in their lives. Being popular means you always have someone to be with; it means you feel important; it means you are liked.

But popularity can be dangerous: when it becomes a driving force; when it dictates decisions and actions; when it lets people be treated as objects; when it causes people to forget values and faith.

Use this meeting to help your junior highers choose a healthy perspective on popularity.

OBJECTIVES

Participants will:
- explore what makes popular people popular;
- identify positive and negative aspects of popularity;
- discover the role popularity played in Jesus' life;
- examine how popularity or the lack of it affects them; and
- be encouraged to be genuinely themselves and act as God's people regardless of whether it means being popular.

SUPPLIES

Gather newsprint; tape; markers; Bibles (preferably ones with paragraph headings such as the Good News Bible); a sheet of newsprint with these popularity traits written on it: wears brand-name clothes, has money, has great hair, uses alcohol, uses drugs, gossips, smokes, is fun, smart, friendly, musical, a snob, two-faced, kind, caring, cute, tough, loyal, easygoing, a star athlete, a class president, a cheerleader, the teacher's pet; for every three or four group members, "The Popular Jesus" discussion sheet; and, for each person, a 3×5 card, "The Popularity Circle" worksheet and a pencil.

BEFORE THE MEETING

Read the meeting and collect supplies.

THE MEETING

1. *Everyone knows them*—As kids arrive, direct them to a wall with a large sheet of newsprint on which you've written "Popular TV, Movie and Music Stars." Provide markers and ask group members to list people in these categories.

Gather the whole group together in front of the newsprint. Spend a few minutes talking about the people listed. Discuss:

● What are some things that make these people popular? (List these on newsprint.)

● Are the people popular for the same reasons? Explain.

● How are the people different? How are they the same?

● Do you think popularity is good or bad for them? Why?

2. *Popularity profile*—Say: "We've been talking about people who are popular all over the country. Now let's bring our discussion closer to home. Don't say any names or consider people in this group, but think about one or two people you know who you think are popular. Think about their personalities, the clubs or extracurricular activities they're involved in and any other things that help make them popular."

Have group members sit together in small groups of three or four. Give each group a large sheet of newsprint and markers. Tape the newsprint list of popularity traits onto a wall, and draw everyone's attention to it.

Say: "Each group will build a popularity profile. Draw a large stick figure in the middle of your sheet of newsprint. Then fill in your stick person's body by using words or symbols you think describe someone who'd be popular at your school. Use the popularity traits you see on this list or any others you think of."

18

Give some ideas to help the kids get started (see the "Popularity Profile Example").

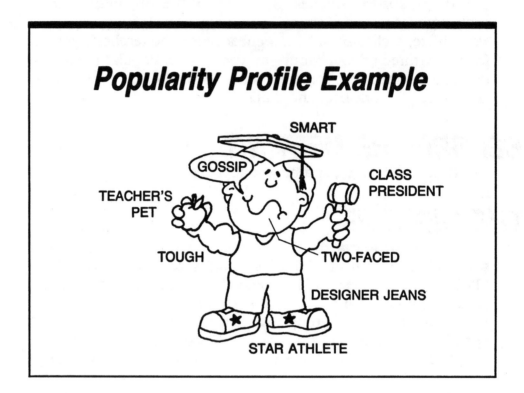

Popularity Profile Example

SMART

GOSSIP

CLASS PRESIDENT

TEACHER'S PET

TOUGH

TWO-FACED

DESIGNER JEANS

STAR ATHLETE

When they're finished, have each group one at a time tape its profile onto the wall and explain it. Discuss:
- What popularity traits appear most often?
- How are the profiles different?
- Are any of the popularity traits hurtful to the person or others? Explain.
- What are the traits that unpopular people tend to wish they had?
- What feelings do unpopular people often have toward the popular?
- What feelings do popular people often have toward the unpopular?
- What are good things about being popular? Explain.
- What are hard or bad things about being popular? Explain.
- Is it possible for popular and unpopular people to have relationships with each other? If so, how?

Summarize: Popularity isn't something people naturally have; it's something others give them. Sometimes we make people popular because they're nice, honest and fun to be around. Other times we make people popular because they dress great and have lots of money or because they have or do things we'd like to have or do. Being popular isn't bad or good by itself: Popularity is bad when it causes those who are popular or those who would like to be popular to say and do hurtful things to themselves and others.

3. *Jesus and popularity*—Say: "Jesus was very popular on Earth. Many people followed him and wanted to be near him. Let's look at the role popularity played in Jesus' life."

Divide the group into two groups. Give each group a large sheet of newsprint, markers and Bibles. Instruct each group to go through the Gospels and list all the things they can find that Jesus said or did that helped make him popular. Examples for the lists: feeding the 5,000, raising Lazarus, walking on water. They don't need to write the references. Allow 10 minutes.

Then, display the lists and count the items on each. The group with the longer list may stand and bow as the other group applauds and cheers. Have group members return to the small groups in which they created the popularity profiles. Have an adult sponsor in each group. Give each group some Bibles and "The Popular Jesus" discussion sheet. Allow about 10 minutes for discussion.

The Popular Jesus

1. What kinds of things did Jesus do that made him popular?

2. Look over the lists carefully. If you didn't know anything about Jesus except what you see on the lists, would you describe him as a friend to many, a glory seeker or a magician? Why? How else might you describe him?

3. What are some things Jesus did that he probably wouldn't have done if all he wanted was to be popular? Look in your Bibles for these; for example, telling a rich man to sell his belongings or telling people to love their enemies and be kind to persecutors. Name as many as you can.

4. Imagine that Jesus came only to be famous, popular and loved. How would his life have been different? Make up an ending that would be suitable for such a Jesus.

Get group members back together in one large group and summarize: If Jesus had let his popularity determine his actions, he'd probably still be here today doing miracles—and you and I couldn't know him personally. Being humble and meek, telling people what they needed to hear instead of what they wanted to hear, and dying a shameful death are *not* popular things to do. Jesus didn't let popularity control his life. We too have a similar decision to make about popularity.

4. *Personal popularity*—Give everyone a 3×5 card and pencil.

Say: "In the upper left-hand corner, write two words that describe you right now in terms of your relationships to other people. For example, you might write: good listener, friend, helper, caring, sensitive. Choose just two words that fit the way you see yourself and write them now. (Wait a minute or so.) Now, in the middle of the card, write a sentence or two that you hope others would use to describe you when you finish junior high. No one else will see your card, so please be honest. Hold on to the cards because we'll use them a little later."

Hand out "The Popularity Circle" worksheets. Allow five minutes for group members to complete them.

Briefly discuss:

● What things in the circle are easy to do without thinking they'll hurt yourself or others? Why?

● What things in the circle should you try to do anyway, whether or not you become popular by doing them? Why?

● Compare what you wrote on your 3×5 card to what's on your worksheet. How do your hopes match up with the way you're willing to act right now? Explain.

5. *Closing worship*—Have all group members place their 3×5 cards and worksheets face down on the floor in the shape of a cross. Then have them form a circle around the cross.

Have an adult sponsor read: "We are here, Lord, in a circle facing you and each other. We all want to be accepted and loved—that's why being popular can be so important. Help us remember that what we are and what we hope to be can be shaped by you, and we can reflect your love to others. Give us courage to be your people, no matter what the consequences. Help us always look to you for guidance and to each other for support. Amen."

Ask the young people to pass in the 3×5 cards and worksheets and dispose of them. Encourage group members to continue thinking about their personal approach to popularity. ∎

The Popularity Circle

1. Being popular means being accepted by a certain group of people. Check which group you'd most like to be popular with.

Athletes _____   Intellectuals _____   Beautiful people _____   Rebels _____   Other _____

2. How important is it to you to be popular? Place a star at the point on the continuum that best describes your response.

I'm not interested. |_____| I'd do anything.

3. What would you do to enter the popularity circle? Draw a solid line from "you" to the various points on the circle that are things you'd feel okay about doing. Draw a broken line to the things you'd be tempted to do if they meant being popular.

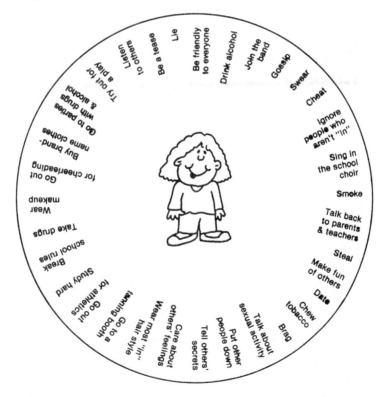

3 *Getting an "A"*

By Cindy Hansen

Junior highers face lots of homework, tests and grades. Fifty-eight percent of them worry about their school performance, according to a national study by Search Institute. And how they do in school affects how they feel about themselves.

Use this meeting to help your junior highers practice simple but effective study skills.

OBJECTIVES

Participants will:
- grade themselves on study skills of memory, listening, taking notes and using the dictionary;
- play games that exercise and improve these study skills; and
- receive "A+" affirmation from each other.

SUPPLIES

Gather posterboard with this message written on it: "Homeroom—Study Skills 101"; a large chalkboard and chalk; masking tape; glue; an instant-print camera and film (or an ink pad); scissors; for every row of chairs in your meeting room, a bowl filled with slips of paper, each with one of these "teacher features" written on it: eyes, nose, mouth, ears, hair, neck, shirt, pants, shoes, hands, hat; "academic awards" such as pencils or erasers; a bed sheet with a 4-inch hole cut in the middle of it; tacks; five 3×5 cards, each with news about an upcoming junior high event written on it (see the example in activity #6); paper; a dictionary for every two group members; and, for each person, a 3×5 card, a straight pin, a pencil, a chair, a "Report Card" handout, a Bible, a brown paper bag containing a candy bar taped inside of a slip of paper on which is written Proverbs 2:10, Proverbs 4:13, Proverbs 8:10 or Luke 2:52.

BEFORE THE MEETING

Read the meeting and collect supplies.

Arrange your meeting room like a classroom. Set chairs in rows and place the chalkboard and chalk up front. Tape the "Homeroom" sign above the chalkboard.

Set a bowl filled with "teacher features" at the front of each row of chairs.

Tack the bed sheet over an open doorway.

THE MEETING

1. *Making school IDs*—As junior highers arrive, give them each a 3×5 card, straight pin and a pencil. Make glue available. Ask kids to each create a school identification card by writing "School ID" at the top of the card and their name at the bottom of the card. Gather kids together and, using an instant-print camera, take a group photo. Cut out the individual faces from the photo and give them to the individual kids to glue to their school ID. (If you don't have an instant-print camera, find an ink pad and have kids each make a thumb print on their card.) Ask the junior highers to pin their IDs to their clothing and wear them for the rest of the meeting.

2. *Drawing the teacher*—Direct everyone to sit in the chairs; each row makes up one team. Tell the junior highers that the bowl at the front of each row contains several slips of paper with "teacher features" for them to draw on the chalkboard. On the word "Go," the first student in each row runs to the bowl, chooses a piece of paper and draws that feature on the chalkboard. The relay continues until all the slips have been chosen and each team's teacher is completely drawn. Give "academic awards" for best picture, funniest illustration and first team done.

3. *Studying school skills*—Say: "This meeting will help you practice study skills like memory, listening, taking notes and using the dictionary." Give everyone a "Report Card" and have

kids grade themselves now and again later in the meeting in the following manner for each skill:

A—Fantastic
B—Better than average
C—Could be better; could be worse
D—Passing, but just barely
F—Don't tell anybody

Report Card

	Memory	Listening	Taking Notes	Using the Dictionary	
At the start of the meeting					Comments:
Later in the meeting					Comments:

---

4. *Trying to remember*—Give group members each a piece of paper and have them write on the paper the numbers from one to four. Tell the kids the first study skill they'll practice is memory. Choose four people to stand behind the bed sheet that's tacked to the doorway. Have each kid, one at a time, stick a facial feature (such as nose, eye, mouth, lips) through the hole. The other kids will strain their brains, search their memories and try to guess whose feature it is. Have them record their guesses on their paper. Afterward, ask the four people to tell who went first, second, and so on. Ask: "How many correctly guessed who all four features belonged to? three? two? one? none?"

Choose four different kids and try again (this way everybody can test their memory). Ask: "How well did you do? What tips can you give each other that will help you remember things? What have you learned from this activity that will help you with schoolwork?"

5. *Learning to listen*—Get kids into pairs; have each pair choose a person to do the talking and a person to do the listening. Give the talkers 60 seconds to tell the listeners everything they can about their experiences in the second-grade: teacher, favorite sport, best friend, town in which they lived, name of school. After one minute, have the listeners report back as many of the facts as they can. Then switch—listeners become talkers; talkers become listeners. Ask: "How many of you remembered most of the facts you were told? What was difficult about listening? What things interfered with listening? How can you improve your listening skills? How will this activity help you at school?"

6. *Taking notes*—Members will practice this skill by taking notes of short skits. Divide the group into five groups. Give each group a 3×5-card announcement of an upcoming junior high event. Give each group three minutes to prepare an announcement to give to the rest of the group. All members must be involved in the presentation. For example, one group could be given this announcement:

3×5 Announcement Example

Next week's meeting is on
PEER PRESSURE.
Meet at Don's house at 7:00 p.m.
Guys bring pop, girls bring
popcorn.

The group members could act out the announcement by having one person lie on the ground and the others pile on top of him or her. The person experiencing the "pressure of his or her peers" could announce the details of the junior high event.

Give everybody a piece of paper, and ask the "audience" to take notes on all the information. After each group presents its announcement, discuss what the others saw and heard. Ask: "Did everyone record the correct information? What methods of note-taking did you use? How many of you wrote down key words? How many of you tried to write down the announcement word-for-word? Which method worked best? How will you apply what you learned in this activity to taking notes in school?"

7. *Digging into the dictionary*—Divide the group into pairs; give each pair a dictionary, a piece of paper and pencil. Say: "You get to practice your dictionary-usage skills by playing the following game. When I call out a word, one person in each pair will find the word in the dictionary and the second person will write down its first definition. The first pair done stands and reads the definition." Use words such as examination, concentration, cafeteria and memorization. After a few words, switch partner tasks, then continue. Ask: "What was difficult about using the dictionary? What was helpful? What suggestions do you have for writing papers and giving school reports?"

8. *Reflection*—Get everyone back in the rows of chairs one more time. Ask the junior highers to reflect on the activities and re-evaluate their study skills. Ask them to use the same grading scale and update their report cards. Ask: "How many of you improved your grades? Were you surprised? What study skills do you need to practice?"

9. *"Extra credit" card*—Gather the kids' IDs and redistribute them so the group members have names other than their own. Say: "This exercise is for extra credit; you'll receive an 'A+' affirmation from another group member." Ask kids to each look at the name on their card, then think of this person's special qualities and gifts. On the back of the IDs, have kids complete this sentence, "I'll give you an 'A+' for . . . " For example, "I'll give you an 'A+' for your friendliness. Your smile and willingness to talk always make people feel welcome." Ask the members to give the IDs back to their owners.

10. *Brown-bag goodies*—Distribute a brown-bag snack and a Bible to each person, then ask the kids to find a partner. Tell the junior highers that inside their bags are sweet rewards for practicing their study skills, and Bible references for verses that talk about knowledge and wisdom. Ask the partners to open their bags and find the Bible references. After they read the verses in their Bible, have them discuss these questions:

● What does this verse mean to you?
● How does this verse apply to you at school?

Once they've shared answers, let the junior highers munch on their candy. Have the kids put their IDs and report cards in their brown paper bags. Encourage them to keep the bags as reminders of the importance of studying to increase ". . . in wisdom and in stature, and in favor with God and man" (Luke 2:52, RSV). ■

4 How Do You Picture Yourself?

By Don Schatz

Wondering about themselves is at the heart of junior highers' maturing. Occasionally there's pain and uncertainty as kids grapple with their view of themselves. But God offers good news.

Use this meeting to help your junior highers look at what they think of themselves. They'll also see how God views them, and join the two views into one complete picture.

OBJECTIVES

Participants will:
- form a picture of themselves by combining their view and God's view;
- uncover God's response of love in spite of their failings; and
- take part in a celebration of being God's children.

SUPPLIES

Gather markers; masking tape; magazine pictures of babies, elementary-age and junior-high-age kids, each attached to a piece of paper; a shallow box to hold photographs; paper; newsprint; a sheet of newsprint with the "Speech Choir Parts" from activity #5 written on it; and, for each person, a blank nameplate made from 2×9-inch posterboard glued to a construction-paper "frame," "The Whole Picture" handout, a Bible and a pencil.

BEFORE THE MEETING

Read the meeting and collect supplies.

Well in advance, tell kids to each bring three photographs of themselves: as a baby, at age 6 to 8, and present.

THE MEETING

1. *Who am I?*—As kids come in, collect the three photographs from each person. Have kids each use a marker to write their first name on a nameplate. Tape the nameplates onto a wall, chest level to eye level.

If some kids don't bring photographs, display the magazine pictures of babies, elementary-age and junior-high-age kids. Have the kids without photographs each pick three pictures—one from each age group. To personalize them, on the paper attached to the baby picture, have them write where they were born; on the elementary-age picture, have them write the elementary school they attended; on the junior-high-age picture, have them put their junior high school. Put these and the real photos into the box.

Gather group members in a circle in front of the nameplates. Have one person draw a picture from the box and tape it below the name he or she thinks it matches. While that person's matching, the next person draws a picture and matches it with a name, and so forth. Continue until each nameplate has three pictures next to it. Everyone should have matched three pictures with names.

2. *The right match*—Get everyone in the circle and have each person in turn correctly match his or her name and pictures. Encourage kids to tell which of their three pictures they like best and why.

When the kids finish, say: "During this meeting you'll be looking at two views of you. One is the picture you have. The other you'll discover. Our goal is to bring the two views together into one."

3. *The whole picture*—Distribute "The Whole Picture" handouts. Make sure each person has a Bible and a pencil. Have each person individually complete the ''Your View'' sections.

When they're finished, divide the group into small groups of four to six. Have small group members read the Bible verses and answer the questions in ''The View From Above.''

4. *Getting into focus*—Give each small group a piece of paper. Have one person divide the paper into horizontal thirds, one third for each section on the handout. Say: ''Write 'Your View' on the top left side of your paper and 'The View From Above' on the top right side. Have each person in your group write one response under each heading from each of the three sections on your handouts.''

While the kids are working, put up three sheets of newsprint, one for each section of the handout. When groups finish, have a representative from each group tell what's written. List responses on the newsprint. Note repeated responses with an asterisk (*).

Discuss: ''Are you surprised at the number of similar responses in 'Your View'? What does this say about how people view themselves? What do the verses say about the views expressed in 'Your View'? How can we help one another see what God sees in us?''

5. *Speech choir fun*—Say: ''To take a closer look at God's view, we're going to paraphrase parts of Genesis 1 and 3.'' Divide kids into four groups to form a speech choir. Display the ''Speech Choir Parts'' on newsprint. Use yourself or another adult leader as director, giving cues to each small group. Give each group its part.

Before beginning the speech choir, allow each group a few minutes to practice its words and actions in a four-beat rhythm. Practice your cuing. Then have fun performing.

6. *A picture of love*—Get kids in a circle on the floor. Have someone read aloud Genesis 1:27-28, 31. Discuss: ''Which group's part reflects this Bible passage? Think of times when everything seemed good and life was great. Describe those times. How are those times like God's feeling at the end of creation's sixth day?''

Have two kids read aloud Genesis 3:1-13 by alternating verses. Ask: ''Which group's part reflects this Bible passage? How does what Adam and Eve now know about themselves compare to Genesis 1:31? When was a time you 'blew it' like

The Whole Picture

Your View
Three to five words that describes me are . . .

The View From Above
In 1 Peter 2:9, what words does the Lord use to describe
you?

Your View
In order to be liked by others, I must . . .

The View From Above
In Romans 5:6-8, what does the Lord say about what you
have to do before he'll like you?

Your View
Something I have to offer the world is . . .

The View From Above
In Galatians 5:22-23, what does the Lord say you have to
offer the world?

32

Instructions for the Speech Choir Director

Give each group its cue by pointing when it should start. Keep the pace moving in a steady four-beat rhythm. Start slowly and increase the tempo as kids catch on.

1. Cue Group 1 to start the continuous background sound.

2. Cue Group 2 to start on the first group's fourth repetition.

3. Cue Group 3 to start on the second group's fourth repetition.

4. Cue Group 2 to join Group 1 ("Ba-doo-ba-doo-wop!").

5. Let Group 3 repeat its part three more times.

6. Cue Group 3 to join Groups 1 and 2, all repeating "Ba-doo-ba-doo-wop!"

7. After all three groups have joined the background refrain, cue Group 4 to start.

8. Let Group 4 repeat its part five times, then cue Group 4 to join the others for one final repetition of Group 1's phrase.

Speech Choir Parts

Each group says and does its part in a steady four-beat rhythm.

Group 1: (This group provides continuous background.)
Words: Ba-doo-ba-doo-wop!
Actions: Snap fingers on "wop!"

Group 2:
Words: It's cool! It's good! I'm satisfied!
Actions: Clap once on "cool," "good" and "satisfied."

Group 3:
Words: We've sinned. We're bad. We're doomed. Oh no!
Actions: Throw hands in the air on "Oh no!"

Group 4:
Words: You've sinned. You'll die. I'm love. You'll live.
Actions: Clap twice on "live."

Adam and Eve? Did you want to hide? Why or why not? How did you expect your parents to react? your friends? Were those expectations met?"

Have another young person read aloud Genesis 3:14-24. Ask: "Which group's part reflects this Bible passage? How does God react to Adam and Eve's disobedience? How does God react to their needs (see verse 21)? How does that make you feel?"

Finally, ask: "Did God ignore Adam and Eve's sin? Did he abandon them as a result of their sin?" Pause for the answer. Then continue: "Just as the answer to both questions is 'No,' God doesn't ignore your sin or abandon you when you sin."

Read aloud Romans 3:23-24; 1 John 4:10. Say: "In Jesus, God comes to us as one of us to rescue us from sin. What does God's willingness to die on the cross say about his love? What does that say about his view of you?" Encourage kids to share their feelings about this.

To help kids understand what God *did* and still *does,* namely, forgive sins and give his love, have a young person read aloud 1 John 1:9.

7. *Children of God*—Close by having group members stand in a circle with their backs toward the center. Have them hold hands. Begin by saying of the person on your right: "Thank you, Lord, for Mari. She is your child." Then turn to face the center and retake the hands you were holding. Mari then says of the person to her right: "Thank you, Lord, for Calvin. He is your child." Mari then turns to face the center and retakes the hands she was holding. Calvin then continues the prayer. The prayer is complete when everyone faces the center.

Say: "God declares, 'Don't worry, I've come to your rescue. I call you by name. You are mine.' Amen."

Give kids their "photo album" nameplates from activity #1. Encourage group members to put them up in their bedrooms, along with "The Whole Picture" handouts. ∎

5 I'm So Self-Conscious!

By Katie Abercrombie

Feeling self-conscious is part of being human. At times we all are concerned with how others see us and what they think of us. But for junior highers, these feelings of self-consciousness intensify.

Junior highers are concerned about the changes they're undergoing—physically, emotionally and intellectually. But, worse, they assume that everyone else is just as concerned and is watching them! David Elkind, in his book **All Grown Up & No Place to Go** *(Addison-Wesley)*, calls this assumption the "imaginary audience." Junior highers feel as if they're on stage and everyone's watching everything they say and do.

Use this meeting to help junior highers express some of their self-conscious feelings as well as realize that others have them too.

OBJECTIVES

Participants will:
  ● explore and discuss situations and events in which they feel self-conscious;

- test the reality of the imaginary audience;
- discover ways to cope with self-consciousness;
- experience the consistency of God's love; and
- praise the good characteristics in one another.

SUPPLIES

Gather a pair of dark sunglasses; sheets of 11 × 14 construction paper—four only of any color, but enough sheets for each group member to have one; scissors; markers; a large pair of sample construction-paper spectacles with blank lenses to allow room for writing; newsprint; a Bible; a sheet of newsprint with the two incomplete sentences from activity #6 written on it; masking tape; and, for each person, a "Here's Lookin' at You" handout, a pencil and a "Spectacle Continuum" handout.

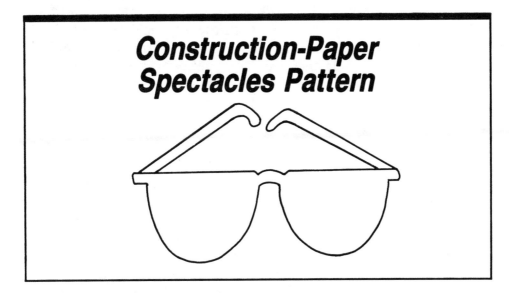

BEFORE THE MEETING

Read the meeting and collect supplies.

Spend some time remembering what it was like to be a self-conscious junior higher.

THE MEETING

1. *Spectacle game*—Introduce the topic by saying: "Everyone feels self-conscious sometimes—about what they do, how they look or what happens to them. These feelings are especially

strong during junior high years. It's normal to feel that everyone's watching you. It's normal for almost anything to make you feel self-conscious or even embarrassed."

Say that the meeting will begin with a game. Have everyone sit on the floor in a circle. Tell group members you'd like them to each tell a story about a time when they made spectacles of themselves—when they wanted to disguise themselves because they felt so self-conscious or embarrassed. You begin by putting on the dark sunglasses and telling a story about yourself. Then choose the next storyteller by handing him or her the sunglasses. That person should put on the sunglasses, tell a story and then pass the sunglasses on to the next storyteller. And so on. Continue until everyone has had a turn.

2. *Here's lookin' at you*—Give each group member a ''Here's Lookin' at You'' handout and a pencil. Explain the handout and go over what each symbol means. Have kids each fill in the incomplete sentences with the appropriate symbols.

When everyone's finished, have group members get into pairs and discuss their answers. Then get everyone back together and ask group members whether they noticed any particular trends such as parents mostly seeing them one way or friends another.

3. *Spectacle continuum*—Give each group member a ''Spectacle Continuum'' handout. Make sure everyone has a pencil. Have kids complete the handout.

When everyone's finished, ask kids to stand. Designate one end of your meeting room as ''Not at all self-conscious'' and the other end of the room as ''Embarrassed to tears.'' Read each statement, and have group members line themselves up on the imaginary continuum approximately where they placed themselves on their handouts. Discuss any items that seem appropriate or that the kids have strong feelings about.

4. *Spectacles spectacle*—Give each group member a sheet of construction paper. Make scissors, markers and pencils available. Show the kids your sample spectacles and tell them you'd like each of them to make a similar pair. Say they may be as creative as they like as long as their spectacles are as large as yours and have a blank space on each lens to write on.

Tell kids to write on the right lens of their spectacles 10 things they're self-conscious about—things they think people no-

Here's Lookin' at You

Here are symbols for different kinds of "glasses" people may see you through. For each situation, complete the sentences with the symbols to indicate how you think other people see you.

(Mirror) People can't see you; they tend to only see and think of themselves.

(Scratched-up glasses) People can't see clearly; they don't always notice what's around them.

(Magnifying glass) People see and examine every detail.

(Microscope) People critically examine everything; they notice every imperfection.

(Rose-colored glasses) People see only good things.

(God's glasses) People see all that you are, good and bad, and love you as you are.

1. When I have a piece of food stuck in my teeth and don't know it,

● people who don't know me see me through . . .
● my parents see me through . . .
● my friends see me through . . .
● God sees me through . . .

2. When my pants rip at a youth meeting,

● people who don't know me see me through . . .
● my parents see me through . . .
● my friends see me through . . .
● God sees me through . . .

3. When I have a stain on the front of my shirt,

● people who don't know me see me through . . .
● my parents see me through . . .
● my friends see me through . . .
● God sees me through . . .

4. When everyone in the room hears me say something embarrassing,

● people who don't know me see me through . . .
● my parents see me through . . .
● my friends see me through . . .
● God sees me through . . .

5. When I drop my hymnal with a "bang" during the prayer in worship,

● people who don't know me see me through . . .
● my parents see me through . . .
● my friends see me through . . .
● God sees me through . . .

38

Spectacle Continuum

For each situation, mark an "X" on the spot on the continuum that indicates how self-conscious you'd be.

1. You're new in town and you walk into your first youth group meeting.

Not at all self-conscious |————————————|————————————| Embarrassed to tears

2. You drop your tray in the lunch room and everyone cheers.

Not at all self-conscious |————————————|————————————| Embarrassed to tears

3. You have to give a report in front of your class.

Not at all self-conscious |————————————|————————————| Embarrassed to tears

4. You wear jeans to a party and everyone else is dressed up.

Not at all self-conscious |————————————|————————————| Embarrassed to tears

5. You trip while crossing the parking lot at the mall.

Not at all self-conscious |————————————|————————————| Embarrassed to tears

6. You go to the movies with your parents on a Friday night.

Not at all self-conscious |————————————|————————————| Embarrassed to tears

7. The youth group goes out for ice cream and you don't have any money.

Not at all self-conscious |————————————|————————————| Embarrassed to tears

8. You sit alone for lunch in the cafeteria.

Not at all self-conscious |————————————|————————————| Embarrassed to tears

9. You fall down on the sidewalk between classes.

Not at all self-conscious |————————————|————————————| Embarrassed to tears

10. You're assigned the cutest guy or girl in school as your project partner.

Not at all self-conscious |————————————|————————————| Embarrassed to tears

11. A person no one likes at school comes up and greets you like an old friend.

Not at all
self-conscious

Embarrassed
to tears

12. You aren't developing physically at the same rate as your friends.

Not at all
self-conscious

Embarrassed
to tears

13. A member of the opposite sex gives you lots of attention.

Not at all
self-conscious

Embarrassed
to tears

14. You walk by a group of kids and they burst into laughter.

Not at all
self-conscious

Embarrassed
to tears

15. You don't have time to take a shower after gym.

Not at all
self-conscious

Embarrassed
to tears

16. You discover that you have a large pimple on your chin.

Not at all
self-conscious

Embarrassed
to tears

17. You forget your gym clothes and the teacher yells at you in front of the whole class.

Not at all
self-conscious

Embarrassed
to tears

18. You get to school and discover that your socks don't match.

Not at all
self-conscious

Embarrassed
to tears

19. Your youth leader asks you to find a partner during an activity.

Not at all
self-conscious

Embarrassed
to tears

20. You're the only person at one end of the continuum.

Not at all
self-conscious

Embarrassed
to tears

tice in a critical way about them; for example, "the way I walk" or "when my clothes don't match." Tell them to write on the left lens things they notice or watch critically about other people.

When everyone's finished, ask group members to stand and hold their spectacles in front of them. Give them a few minutes to wander around and read one another's spectacles. Then have kids sit where they are. As a whole group, discuss the differences, if any, between the right and left lenses. Suggest that we tend to notice many things about ourselves that other people don't see.

5. *Spectacle solutions*—Have kids get into small groups of four by finding three other people who have the same color spectacles and sitting down together. Ask small groups to each choose a situation from one of the handouts or make one up that they think would make them feel especially self-conscious. Give groups newsprint and markers. Have them spend five minutes brainstorming and listing ways to cope with those self-conscious feelings.

Get everyone together in a circle. Have the groups of four each tell about their situation and solutions. Conclude by emphasizing that in all embarrassing situations we can do something to help us feel good about ourselves.

6. *Through eyes of love*—Read aloud Luke 12:22-31. Remind the group that God sees us through eyes of love and loves us even when we drop our tray in the cafeteria or forget to prepare for a speech in English class.

Ask the kids to return to their groups of four. Display the sheet of newsprint with these two incomplete sentences:
● When I think of God's unconditional love for me, I . . .
● The next time I feel self-conscious, I'll . . .
Have small group members discuss how they'd complete the sentences.

7. *Rose-colored glasses*—Ask kids to find their own spectacles and write their names on the backs of them in large letters, then tape them onto the wall with their names showing. Provide markers or pencils and masking tape.

When the spectacles are on the wall, say: "Now I want you to put on your 'rose-colored glasses.' When you look at one another, you will see only the good, positive characteristics.

Write one good, positive thing about each person on his or her spectacles. Remember, you're wearing rose-colored glasses—so only good comments are allowed. When you finish, sit back down in a circle.''

8. *Closing*—When everyone's back in the circle, close the meeting with a prayer to see one another through eyes of love. Remind kids to get their spectacles to take home. ■

6 *It Hurts to Compare*

By Mike Gillespie

A junior higher can't help but compare. Mark has a great bike. Sue has all the brains. Don can do anything he wants. Rock stars have wonderful lives.

And it hurts.

You can help. Use this meeting to explore with your young people the dangers of comparing—and the good news that God loves them just the way they are.

OBJECTIVES

Participants will:
- identify things other people have that they want;
- hear about and discuss dangers of comparing themselves to others and envying others;
- read Bible passages showing God's love for them;
- listen to and discuss a story about being themselves; and
- experience God's message that they don't need to compare themselves to other people.

SUPPLIES

Gather markers; enough red 1-inch-wide circle stickers for each girl to have five and enough blue 1-inch-wide circle stickers for each guy to have five; sheets of newsprint with these phrases written on them: fabulous clothes, super looks, neat friends, fantastic freedom, great popularity, good athletic skills, gifted intelligence, mucho money, great humor, terrific talents, beautiful looks, always a winner, personality plus; masking tape;

a sheet of newsprint with the discussion questions for activity #2 written on it; blank newsprint; scissors; a cassette tape or record of Billy Joel's song "Just the Way You Are"; a cassette player or turntable; and, for each group member, a plastic-covered name tag attached to a straight pin, two pieces of thick posterboard, two 1 × 12-inch strips of posterboard, a "Scripture Treasures" handout, a Bible, a pencil and a "Letter From God" handout.

BEFORE THE MEETING

Read the meeting and collect supplies.

Tape onto the wall the sheets of newsprint with the phrases written on them.

THE MEETING

1. *Welcome*—As kids arrive, greet them. Give each group member a plastic-covered name tag attached to a straight pin. Provide markers. Tell kids to write their names and pin on their name tags. Hand out five colored 1-inch-wide circle stickers to each group member—blue to guys, red to girls. Tell kids to initial their circles and stick them on their name tag covers.

2. *What other people have that I want*—Point out the sheets of newsprint on the walls. Tell kids to each choose five of the qualities listed that they think about when comparing themselves to others. Have them stick their initialed circles on those qualities.

If any qualities were chosen more by guys or by girls, mention that and ask why. Discuss answers.

Divide the group into two groups: guys and girls. Make sure there's at least one adult sponsor in each group. Display the sheet of newsprint with the following questions for the guys and girls to discuss separately:

● How will the items you want make you a better person?

● How are people who have these things better than you are?

● How do you feel when you compare yourself to someone else?

● What makes comparing so dangerous?

Say: "Comparing *is* dangerous! It hurts ourselves and others if we keep trying to be just like someone else. Here's what hap-

pens when you compare yourself to someone else."
Write this diagram on newsprint as you explain it:

Comparison ▶ Envy ▶ Jealousy
Anger/Ridicule/Depression

Keep kids in their separate groups of guys and girls. Tell them to each think about three people they compare themselves to. Ask them to discuss qualities those people have that they envy. Hand out a sheet of newsprint and a marker to each group, and have the sponsor list the qualities the group names.

3. *Graveyard of envy*—Provide pieces of thick poster-board, scissors and markers. Tell group members to each get two pieces of posterboard and cut them into the shape of tomb-stones. Tell them to write on each one a quality they wish they had. Or, to help them think, have them complete "I envy people who . . . " or "Here lies . . . " on the tombstones.

Tombstone Example

Hand out the 1 × 12-inch strips of posterboard. Show kids how to make stands for the tombstones by cutting two 2-inch-high slits about 5 inches apart at the base of the tombstones and then inserting the strips (see the illustration).

When your graveyard is constructed, have kids sit in a circle around it.

Discuss: "Why is it so hard to really 'bury' comparisons like this? Why do comparisons sometimes haunt us, like ghosts from a grave-yard?"

Say: "Sometimes we compare ourselves to others because we're not sure about our own worth. But God's given each of us great value. Let's see how we can know that."

4. *Scripture treasures*—If you need more space, move aside the tombstones. Divide the group into small groups of four to six, each with an adult sponsor.

Distribute the "Scripture Treasures" handouts, Bibles and pencils. Have small group members work through the handouts together.

When small groups are finished, have everyone get together in one circle. Go through the handout's answers. Emphasize:

- God created us good.
- God created us in a position of high importance.
- God looks at our hearts, not visible qualities.
- Nothing can separate us from God's love.

Say that God's unconditional love for each person means we don't need to compare ourselves to others.

5. *Real vs. unreal*—Read aloud the excerpt from *The Velveteen Rabbit* by Margery Williams (Heinemann Publishing).

Ask: "What does this story say about being real? If being real grows from love, how does God's love for you help? What does it mean that 'Once you are Real, you can't be ugly, except to people who don't understand'? What can you do to show you are real?"

Scripture Treasures

Read the Bible verses listed. Then write your answers.

1. Read Genesis 1:4, 10, 18, 21, 25, 31.
The writer tells us God said creation was_____.
Since each of us is part of that creation, we were created _____.

2. Read Psalm 8.
The psalmist says God created us _____.
That means each of us is in a position of_____.

3. Read 1 Samuel 16:1-7.
In this story, Samuel discovers that God sees_____.
That means for God the most important part of each of us is_____.

4. Read Romans 8:28, 38-39.
Paul was sure everything works _____ when we love God.
Paul also says that _____ can separate us from God's love.
The good news for each of us is that_____.

46

The Velveteen Rabbit

Nursery magic is very strange and wonderful, and only those playthings that are old and wise and experienced like the Skin Horse understand all about it.

"What is Real?" asked the Rabbit one day. "Does it mean things that buzz inside you and a stick-out handle?"

"Real isn't how you are made," said the Skin Horse. "It's a thing that happens to you. When a child loves you a long, long time, not just to play with, but really loves you, then you become Real."

"Does it hurt?" asked the Rabbit.

"Sometimes," said the Skin Horse, for he was always truthful. "When you are Real you don't mind being hurt."

"Does it happen all at once, like being wound up," he asked, "or bit by bit?"

"It doesn't happen all at once," said the Skin Horse. "You become. It takes a long time. That's why it doesn't often happen to people who break easily, or have sharp edges, or who have to be carefully kept. Generally, by the time you are Real, most of your hair has been loved off, and your eyes drop out and you get lose in the joints and very shabby. But those things don't matter at all, because once you are Real, you can't be ugly, except to people who don't understand."

Excerpted from *The Velveteen Rabbit* by Margery Williams. Reprinted by permission of William Heinemann, Ltd.

Say: "Being yourself and being loved by God makes you real. Comparing yourself to others and envying them makes you unreal."

6. *Just the way you are*—Have group members close their eyes and listen while you play the song "Just the Way You Are."

Have kids keep their eyes closed. Tell them: "Think about ways you try to change to please other people. Think about the fact that God already loves you. He looks at the inside you, not at how you try to please other people. Be happy that God loves you just the way you are. He doesn't compare you to other people. And nothing can take away his love for you."

7. *Closing*—Have kids find partners. Distribute the "Letter From God" handouts and pencils. Tell kids to fill in the blanks.

Letter From God

Dear_____:

    I want to let you know how much I believe in you.

_____, I've noticed you sometimes feel you're left out in some ways. I've noticed you compare yourself to _____ because he/she has _____. I've noticed the way you envy _____ because of _____. And even those times when _____ gets on your nerves because he/she always seems to have _____ _____.

    Please believe in yourself, _____. I believe in you very much. You can do many good things such as _____, _____ and _____. I want you to feel good about the positive things you do for others when you ____ _____. You don't need to compare yourself to anyone. You're lovable and capable and very special to me just the way you are.

Forever,

God

Have partners read their letters to each other as a closing prayer.

Encourage kids to each take their "Scripture Treasures" handout and letter home and tape them onto their dresser mirror or bedroom wall. Tell them you'll dispose of the tombstones to help get rid of envy. ∎

7 Me!

By Ben Freudenburg

Fragile *is a good word to use when talking about self-image. A wrong word, look or action sends junior highers into a tailspin.*

Experts in early adolescent psychology agree there are three major areas that affect self-image: (1) intellectual ability, (2) money—affording to look like and act like other junior highers, and (3) physical appearance.

Use this meeting to help junior highers examine things that affect their image of themselves.

OBJECTIVES

Participants will:
- learn how self-image is affected by intellectual, physical and money factors;
- learn from studying the Bible that each person is valuable to God; and
- experience giving and receiving affirmation.

SUPPLIES

Gather tape or a stapler with staples; a sheet of newsprint with the two discussion questions from activity #4 written on it; a recloseable bag; a "Study Questions" handout for every three to seven group members; and, for each person, a Bible, a "Self-Image Score Sheet," a pencil and a 2×18-inch strip of paper on which is written a word or phrase to be the object of a compliment—such as eyes, hair, ears, hands, shoestrings, earrings, piano playing, sports ability, good grades, common sense, sense of humor, suntan.

BEFORE THE MEETING

Read the meeting and collect supplies.

Recruit enough sponsors to have one for each small group of three to seven.

THE MEETING

1. Compliment game—Staple or tape a paper-strip "hat" on each kid's and adult's head as people arrive. Don't let a person know what his or her hat says. Have everyone mingle and read each other's hats.

After reading another person's hat, group members are to each give three carefully worded compliments to make it difficult to guess what's being complimented. For example, if the hat says "eyes," a group member might say "It's nice yours are so perfectly matched" or "The color matches your shirt" or "How lucky you are that they're exactly the same size."

If the hat-wearers guess what's being complimented, they remove their hats and watch the fun or continue to play as they choose.

2. Additional opening suggestions—If there's time, use these ideas.

Back rubs: Have group members make a circle holding hands, then let go of hands. Have group members turn so their left shoulders are inside the circle. Tell them to place their hands on the shoulders of the person in front of them and give that person a good, caring back rub.

Lap sit: Have group members form a circle the same way as in "Back rubs" or begin this at the end of that activity. Have group members turn so their right shoulders are inside the circle and take one step sideways toward the center of the circle. Repeat as necessary until the circle is tight, with little space between people.

Tell group members to each look behind them to spot the lap of the person behind them. Tell everyone to slowly sit down on the count of three. The object is for everyone to remain sitting for another count of three, then stand up again. Keep trying until it's successful.

3. Bible study—Divide the group into groups of three to seven, each including one adult. Give a Bible to each person. Give a "Study Questions" handout to each adult leader.

Explain: "Listen to this story about Jesus' followers who asked him, 'Jesus, if we follow you, how will we eat and where will the money come from to buy new clothes?' "

Have one person read aloud Luke 12:22-34, while the rest follow along in their Bibles.

Instruct small groups to discuss the questions on the leaders' handouts.

Study Questions

- What things were the disciples anxious about?
- Why do you think Jesus used the illustration about ravens and lilies? What does it mean?
- What does this story tell about God's love for us?
- What does this story tell concerning worries about self-image?
- What kind of treasure is Jesus really talking about in verse 33?
- What does verse 34 mean? Explain it by using different words from the words in the Bible.

Urge the small groups to deal with all the questions, but remind them when it's time to move on to the next activity.

4. Self-image score—Say: "This exercise helps you discover certain things that affect your self-image. You'll discover which areas affect you more than others. The three areas we'll examine are: intellect, physical appearance and money. The score tells only how *you* feel about these things. There are no right or wrong answers. Your friend's feelings won't help you. The only feelings that count in this exercise are your own."

Give a "Self-Image Score Sheet" and pencil to each person.

Self-Image Score Sheet

2 = greatly affects my self-image
1 = somewhat affects my self-image
0 = has no affect on my self-image

Intellect	Money	Appearance
1.	1.	1.
2.	2.	2.
3.	3.	3.
4.	4.	4.
5.	5.	5.
6.	6.	6.
7.	7.	7.
*Total:	*Total:	*Total:

*Note: The higher the total, the more this area affects your self-image.

Explain: "I'll read each statement twice. Write the score in the appropriate spot on the score sheet. A 'two' means this situation greatly affects your self-image. A 'one' means this only somewhat affects your self-image. A 'zero' means this has no affect on your self-image."

Read the statements and have kids write their scores.

Intellect statements:

1. I bring home a report card with two D's.
2. I get a D on a major test.
3. I'm not chosen to be in an honors class.
4. I give the wrong answer in class.
5. My best friend gets a better test grade than I do.
6. I can't understand how to use the computer in class.
7. I ask a question in class and everyone laughs at me.

Money statements:

1. At a special event, all the other kids have $30 to spend

and I have only $10.

2. My parents drive an 8-year-old car that's dented and needs paint.

3. My clothes are nice, but they're hand-me-downs.

4. My friends find out I didn't go to camp because my family couldn't afford it.

5. A group of my well-dressed friends from school see my mom and me buying my clothes at a thrift store.

6. On a bike hike, I show up on my one-speed; everyone else has a 10-speed.

7. I can afford the movie, but I pretend I'm not hungry afterward because I don't have enough money for pizza.

Physical-appearance statements:

1. Someone at the pool party asks, "Why are you wearing that T-shirt over your swimsuit?"

2. The teacher in health class says, "Today we're going to measure and weigh each other."

3. After I come home from a haircut, I look in the mirror and discover my hair is way too short.

4. Right before the first big school dance, I break out with a bad case of acne.

5. I go to my first gym class of the year and in the locker room I discover I haven't physically progressed as fast as the others.

6. The school nurse sends a note to my parents saying I need glasses; I'd rather have contacts, but my family can't afford them.

7. On the first day of school, I discover I'm the tallest girl/shortest guy in my class.

Say: "Add your scores in each column. Circle the column with the highest total. The highest total shows that this area affects your self-image the most. How many are surprised about your scores? How many are pleased about your scores?"

Display these questions on newsprint and have small groups discuss:

● What would happen if your scores show you have an unrealistic source of self-image? For example, if physical looks affect you the most and you're not an attractive person.

● What are ways God's love helps you with your self-image?

After a short time, have group members each turn over their score sheet and complete the following: "God, I know you should be the greatest influence on my self-image. The thing I need your help on the most is . . . ''

When everyone finishes writing, collect the pencils. Have group members each fold their paper one time with the score sheet on the outside.

5. Closing—Have group members hold their folded papers and form one large, close circle. Now have them keep refolding the papers until they're as small as possible.

Place your folded paper into a recloseable bag, pass it to the person to your right and say: "Pray for God to help me with this need." That person places his or her paper into the bag, passes it to the next person and repeats the same phrase. Continue around the circle until the bag returns to you.

Close the bag and say: "God, this bag is filled with needs, *our* needs. Jesus promised us you'd care for all of our needs. Please help us learn that you're the main source of our positive self-image. Amen."

Discard the bag to ensure the group members' privacy. ∎

8 *Mirror, Mirror*

By Katie Abercrombie

*J*unior highers are "mirror watchers," observing their own physical images and constantly checking out the human "mirrors" of others for reflections of their own self-images.

Use this meeting to help junior highers see how others have helped form their self-images and how God's Word reflects his grace and love for them.

OBJECTIVES

Participants will:
● discuss things they like and dislike about their mirror images;
● explore and evaluate how reflections from others influence their self-images;
● discover what God says about them in the Bible; and
● experience positive reflections from themselves and each other.

SUPPLIES

Gather a full-length mirror; a large sheet of newsprint with a mirror frame drawn on it, so it looks like a mirror; masking tape; markers; scissors; a sheet of newsprint with the "Three-Way Mirror Example" in activity #4 drawn on it; a sheet of newsprint with the "Reflective Writing Example" in activity #7 drawn on it; for every two group members, a Bible, a 3×5 "scripture-reflections" card on which is written one of these Bible references: Genesis 1:26, Psalm 8:4-9, Psalm 23, Psalm 139:1-6, Psalm 139:13-16, John 3:16, 1 John 3:1-2; and, for each person, a reflective symbol (see preparation notes in "Before the Meeting"), a "Reflections of Myself" handout, a pencil and two sheets of newsprint. Optional: extra mirrors of different sizes and a carnival mirror.

BEFORE THE MEETING

Read the meeting and collect supplies.

Set up the full-length mirror against a wall in the meeting room. Onto the wall next to it, tape the sheet of newsprint with a mirror frame drawn on it. Place markers on a table nearby.

Prepare reflective symbols from construction paper by drawing and cutting out a symbol for every person. Cut out the symbols in pairs and draw on them so they'll be mirror images of each other. Use symbols that fit the theme such as different kinds of mirrors (hand, round, rear-view, silvered sunglasses) or different things that reflect or shine (stars, moon, diamonds).

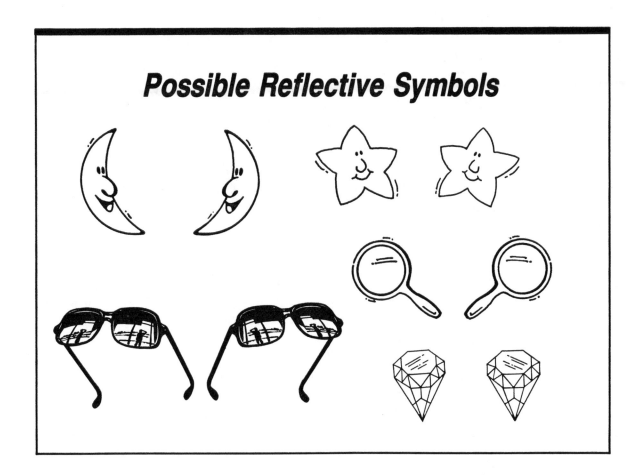

Possible Reflective Symbols

For fun, decorate the room by hanging extra mirrors of different sizes at different levels. Another option: Borrow carnival mirrors that distort images; the kids could have fun with these as they arrive for the meeting.

THE MEETING

1. *Mirror images*—As kids arrive, ask each one to stand in front of the full-length mirror for a few seconds and write a one- or two-word reaction on the newsprint mirror.

2. *Reflective symbols*—Hand out reflective symbols and markers. (Hand out both symbols from each reflective pair.)

Ask junior highers to think about the time they stood before the full-length mirror. On the back of the reflective symbols they're now holding, have them write their names, two things they *liked* about their individual mirror image, and one thing they *didn't* like about it. Have them each find their "mirror partner" by finding the person whose symbol is the mirror image of their own.

When mirror partners find each other, have them stand facing each other. Ask one member of each pair to be the leader and the other to be a "mirror." The leader, without moving away from where he or she is standing, moves his or her hands, arms or entire body and makes faces while the person being the mirror acts as the reflection of those movements. Allow partners to play for 60 seconds, then have them switch roles. After they play for another 60 seconds, ask them to sit facing each other and discuss what they wrote on the back of their reflective symbols.

3. *Reflections of myself*—Explain: "Just as mirrors affect how we feel about our physical images, other people act as mirrors to affect how we feel about our whole selves or our self-images. Both what people say to us and how they act toward us reflect how they feel about us, and they help us form images of who we are. People can be mirrors that are just as important to us as mirrors hanging on a wall."

Give each person a "Reflections of Myself" handout and a pencil. Ask junior highers to mark their answers.

Allow a brief discussion for each situation. Ask: "Does someone else's putdown really make someone a less important person? Why or why not?"

Reflections of Myself

Mark an "X" on the space on each line that best represents your answer.
This is how I feel about myself when . . .

● a friend says: "Thanks for listening to me. I know I can talk to you when I feel bad."

"I'm worthless." └─────────────┴─────────────┘ **"I'm the best!"**

● my parents say: "Hey, you really did a nice job on the car. You really helped me out!"

"I'm worthless." └─────────────┴─────────────┘ **"I'm the best!"**

● a teacher says: "So you have the lowest grade in the class. What else is new?"

"I'm worthless." └─────────────┴─────────────┘ **"I'm the best!"**

● my mom says: "I'm tired of picking up after you. When are you going to stop being such a slob?"

"I'm worthless." └─────────────┴─────────────┘ **"I'm the best!"**

● my friend says: "That dress looks pretty good on you, even if it is way out of style."

"I'm worthless." └─────────────┴─────────────┘ **"I'm the best!"**

● my little sister says: "Thanks for fixing my doll. I love you!"

"I'm worthless." └─────────────┴─────────────┘ **"I'm the best!"**

● a neighbor says: "Will you take care of our cats while we're out of town? We need someone like you we can depend on."

"I'm worthless." └─────────────┴─────────────┘ **"I'm the best!"**

● a friend ignores me in the hall at school.

"I'm worthless." └─────────────┴─────────────┘ **"I'm the best!"**

● my teacher writes "good job" at the top of my paper.

"I'm worthless." └─────────────┴─────────────┘ **"I'm the best!"**

● my dad says: "You never do anything right! That was really dumb!"

"I'm worthless." └─────────────┴─────────────┘ **"I'm the best!"**

4. *Three-way mirrors*—Hand out sheets of newsprint. Make markers available. Ask each group member to draw a mirror with three sections. Encourage them to be creative, but to leave plenty of room to write in each section. Have kids label each section with one of the following: ''Family,'' ''Friends'' and ''Teachers.'' Display your newsprint example. They should then write words in each category that they think their families, friends, or teachers would use to describe them. Encourage them to write a minimum of three positive things in each category. Next ask kids to circle all the words they agree with.

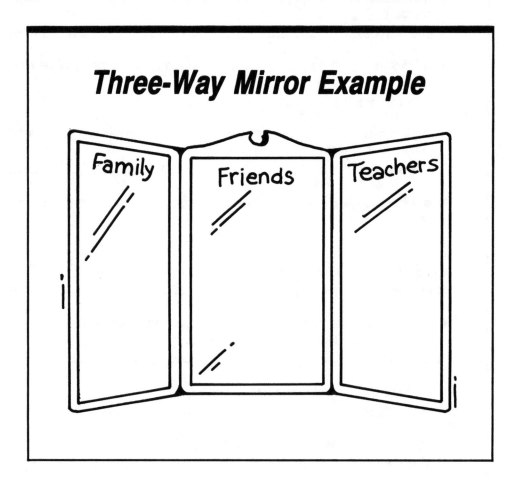

After they've finished, ask group members to sit facing their mirror partners. Have partners tell each other one item they circled from each category and why. When everyone's finished, tape the mirrors onto the wall.

5. *Reflection break*—Have mirror partners sit back to

back. Tell kids to each change one thing about their appearance such as removing a piece of jewelry or untying a shoe. When partners have changed something, have them turn around and guess what changed.

6. God's image—Give each pair a Bible and a scripture-reflections card. Ask each pair to read the verse and determine the most important thing God is saying about them in that verse. Have them decide how that affects how they feel about themselves and then have each pair develop a short mime or charade to communicate that to the group.

When they've had sufficient time to create their mimes, bring the group members together and have all the pairs, one by one, present their mimes. Have the group members guess what they mean, and then have the pairs read their scripture reflection and explain their mimes. Encourage the group to guess each mime's meaning and applaud after each presentation.

7. Reflective writing—Give group members each another sheet of newsprint and ask them to draw another mirror with a vertical line down the center. Beginning at the center line, have them each write their first name on their paper. Beginning at the center line again, going the other direction, have them each write the "reflection"—a mirror image—of their name. Display your newsprint example.

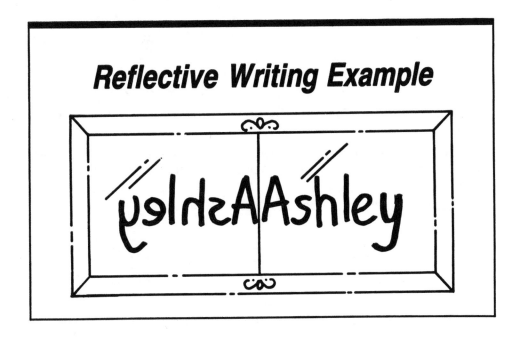

On the right-hand side of their paper mirrors, ask junior highers to write five to 10 things they like about themselves. Because this may be difficult for many junior highers, give some examples such as "I like the way I feel when I help my sister with her homework," "I like the way that it's easy for me to like different kinds of people," or "I like my talent in swimming." Tell kids it's important to be able to see positive qualities in themselves and it's okay to say good things about themselves.

Have group members tape their mirrors onto the wall. Ask them to go around the room and write on the left-hand side of each person's mirror something they really like or admire about the person. Even if they don't know a person well, encourage them to find something as simple as a hair style or a friendly smile to compliment. Emphasize that what they write should be positive and complimentary, but also sincere. Model this by writing compliments on all the mirrors yourself.

8. *Reflective prayers*—Have mirror partners sit on the floor facing each other again. Explain: "I'll say a short introductory prayer. When I finish, I'd like you to pray for your mirror partner in your pairs. One of you should start by thanking God for three things about your mirror partner. Then the other member of your pair should do the same. All the pairs can pray at the same time and you may say more than just three things if you wish. When all of you have finished, we'll say the Lord's Prayer *reflectively*; I'll say a line and you'll repeat it."

Begin the reflective prayers like this: "Heavenly Father, you created us in your image, so we can reflect your love and grace to your world. Thank you for the gift of many mirrors you've given us in our parents, friends and your Word. Help us remember we're your people and that even though we're imperfect, your love shines on us. Enable us to shine and help others to shine."

Allow time for mirror partner prayers. Then lead the group in the Lord's Prayer, in which you say each phrase and have them repeat it in unison.

Close with group hugs and individual hugs. ■

9 Rave Reviews

By Kevin Miller

Ask junior highers to list things they don't like about themselves. You'll get a list as long as two Nike tennis shoes: I'm too short; my nose is too big; I'm too flat-chested.

Ask junior highers to list things they like about themselves. You'll get a list as long as a worn pencil eraser. Search Institute conducted a major national study of early adolescents and found that kids' desire to "feel good about myself" jumped dramatically as they moved from sixth- to ninth-grade.

Kids (and all of us) need to be reminded they're special just the way they are. The best reminders come in the form of praise from parents, youth leaders, friends and God.

Use this meeting to give your kids plenty of praise reminders.

OBJECTIVES

Participants will:

● run a relay and discuss the importance of being who they really are;

● create posters publicizing who they are;

● receive positive comments from peers and give positive comments in return; and

• cheer the fact they're super because they're loved by a super God.

SUPPLIES

Gather masking tape; newsprint; 1-inch-wide self-sticking colored circles, at least one for each person, with a positive word or phrase such as nice to be around, cute, neat, fun-loving or caring written on each; markers; Christian cassette tapes or records; a cassette player or turntable; for every four or five group members, a small prize for each, glue, scissors, old magazines; and, for each person, a 3×5-card name tag with only the word "is" written in the middle of one side (see the example), a straight pin, a ½- by 2-inch slip of paper, a pencil and a deflated balloon.

Name Tag Example

BEFORE THE MEETING

Read the meeting and collect supplies.

Place the 3×5-card name tags, written-on colored circles, markers and straight pins near the entrance.

Clear the center of your meeting area.

NOTES TO THE LEADER

Some junior highers have trouble giving genuine praise to

others, especially kids they don't like. This meeting gives an opportunity to help junior highers praise others. Watch that kids don't give confusing compliments such as "You're not bad for being a total geek."

THE MEETING

1. *As they arrive*—Have Christian music playing. Ask each person to write his or her first name above the word "is" on the name tag, and then select a sticker to place beneath the word "is." If some kids have difficulty, offer to select one for them, but gently urge them to select one for themselves. Tell everyone to pin on his or her name tag.

2. *"Let Out the Real Me" relay*—When everyone has arrived, divide the group into small groups of four or five, each with an adult sponsor. Explain that they're going to run a wild relay called "Let Out the Real Me."

Give each person one of the small slips of paper, a pencil and a deflated balloon. Say: "Write on your slip of paper a phrase that completes this sentence: 'One neat thing about me that people don't see is . . . ' " (For example: I like to read, I love animals, I visit my grandmother once a week.)

Have each person fold his or her slip of paper, stuff it inside the balloon, blow up the balloon, tie it and hold it.

Next, have kids each think of one thing that others think about them that is *not* true about what they're really like. (For example: class clown, superbrain, party king or party queen, Mr. or Ms. Athlete, Joe or Joan Religious.)

Tell the kids to use markers and carefully draw these untrue or partly true images on the outside of their balloons. If some have trouble drawing them, let them write the words. Have kids each tell what they drew (or wrote) and why to the other members of their team.

Here's the relay: Each team lines up single file on one side of the room. Place one chair for each team on the other side of the room. At the signal, the first person from each team runs to the chair and sits on his or her balloon to pop it, grabs the small slip of paper that falls out, stands on the chair and yells the "real me" statement from the paper. The person races back to the team and tags the next runner, who repeats the process. Encourage yelling by modeling it yourself. Give the first team to finish a title such as "The Big Bubble Busters" and award prizes.

3. *Getting into the theme*—Have the kids sit in the same small groups. Say: "In order for another person to find the real you, you had to break your balloon. What does breaking the balloon represent? Why? (Whenever you try to live up to some false image, you can't be your true self.) Why do some people act one way, when that's not who they really are inside? What are some of the false images kids project? Sometimes we get scared that people won't like us the way we really are, deep down inside. We try to live up to some image we think they *will* like. But those images are full of air, like a balloon.

"You're going to find out that it's okay to be who you really are, because important people already love you just the way you are."

4. *"The Real Me" publicity posters*—Give each person a sheet of newsprint. Have glue, scissors, markers and magazines for each group.

Explain that sports stars, actors and actresses and rock musicians use posters to advertise and promote themselves. Say: "Now you're each going to make a poster advertising yourself, the real you. First, write your name across the top of your poster."

To spark creativity, ask the kids to include on their posters at least one good thing about themselves in each of the following areas: my body, my family, my talents. Write these three categories on a sheet of newsprint and tape it onto the wall. Help kids think of their positive qualities. Praise each person's efforts.

Tape all the posters onto the wall. Have kids clear away all supplies except for the markers. Place markers near the posters.

5. *Rave reviews*—Gather kids together in one large group. Say: "What nice things do you wish people would say about you?" Or, "What things do you admire in other people?" Brainstorm positive qualities and list them on newsprint. The list might include thoughtful, friendly, athletic, fun to be with, doesn't tell secrets.

Explain that top sports stars, actors and actresses and rock musicians get rave reviews. Say: "You're going to give and receive rave reviews. Walk around and write at least one positive comment, a rave review, on each person's poster. Be honest and be sure you say only positive things. If you have trouble thinking of something to write, use ideas from the list."

Check the posters to be sure comments are positive. Also

have sponsors and some kids write on those posters with only a few comments.

Gather kids together again in one group. Ask volunteers to show their posters and read their rave reviews.

Point out the variety of positive comments. Remind the group: "Each person is created with certain special qualities, not like anyone else's. That's okay—it's part of being the 'real you' each person is created to be."

6. Rave reviews from God—Ask: "Suppose God wrote a rave review on your poster. What do you think he'd write?" Pause to let kids think. There may not be a response. Say: "Most of us aren't sure what God would write, or are a little afraid he wouldn't say anything nice about us. But God loves each of you, just as the 'real you' he created you to be."

Have group members form a circle. Explain that the entire group will share in a responsive prayer; however, it will also be like a cheer. First you'll read a rave review from God, then the entire group will respond with the line: "I'm super because a super God loves me!" Then you'll read another rave review, the group will respond with its same line, and so on.

Ask kids to *yell* the line louder each time they respond. Also read louder each time to get the kids in the spirit of the cheer. Add fun to the cheer by having kids take one step forward every time they say it. Here's the "Prayer Cheer," based on Psalm 139; Genesis 1:27, 31; and Romans 8:28-39.

> **Leader:** *God says: "I loved you before you were born."*
> **Kids respond:** *I'm super because a super God loves me!*
> **Leader:** *God says: "I chose you to be someone special for me."*
> **Kids respond.**
> **Leader:** *God says: "I know everything about you. And I love you."*
> **Kids respond.**
> **Leader:** *God says: "There is nowhere you can hide from my love. And you don't need to. I want what is best for you."*
> **Kids respond.**
> **Leader:** *God says: "I love you when nobody else loves you and you aren't even sure you love yourself."*
> **Kids respond.**
> **Leader:** *God says: "I love you. The real you."*
> **Kids respond.**

If you sense the group is really responding, consider this option. Say: "God says, 'I love (the name of one of the kids).' " Then have the group respond: "You're super because a super God loves you!" Do this for each person in the group.

Have kids move closer and closer until the circle becomes a lump. Close with a big "lump hug."

Here are options for making the meeting's impact extend throughout the week: Have kids take their posters home and ask their family members to write rave reviews on them. Or hand out sheets with the days of the week marked on them, and a passage or two from Psalm 139 or Romans 8 listed for each day. Suggest that kids read the passage listed each day during the next week and experience a daily rave review from God. ■

10 Your Body, Your Self

By Kristine Tomasik

What we think of our bodies, we think of ourselves. Having a positive body image is especially hard for a junior higher, whose body changes and grows at a breathtaking pace.

Use this meeting to help kids experience their bodies as whole, powerful, creative and attractive—just as God sees them.

OBJECTIVES

Participants will:
- enjoy using their bodies to move, relax, create artistic expressions and eat;
- express feelings of acceptance of their bodies; and
- experience God's loving acceptance of their bodies.

SUPPLIES

Gather cassette tapes or records of popular energetic and meditative music; a cassette player or turntable; pitchers of lemonade and cups to serve it in; masking tape; markers; brightly colored chalk; hairspray; refreshments such as fruit, nuts or popcorn; a dark crayon for every two group members; and, for each person, a body-sized sheet of newsprint. Optional: male and female body images cut from current teenage magazines.

BEFORE THE MEETING

Read the meeting and collect supplies.

Ask yourself: "How do I feel about my own body? Do I accept it and love it as part of God's creation? How has my body

68

image been wounded by the world's values?'' Meditate in God's presence to experience healing and empowering of your own body image.

NOTES TO THE LEADER

Be prepared for some giggles and strange comments. Kids may express their uncomfortableness by telling jokes or clamming up.

THE MEETING

1. *Everybody move!*—Play energetic music. Lead aerobic exercises to the music: jump, run, skip, hop, do jumping jacks and arm circles, kick up your heels! The point is to get kids moving and experimenting with many different ways their bodies are equipped to move.

When you're all thoroughly pooped, sit down and do this cool-down and relaxation activity: Form a circle. Have each person turn to the right and rub the shoulders of the person in front of him or her.

For a third pleasurable bodily experience, offer kids a refreshing drink of lemonade.

Then say: ''Through our wonderful bodies, we experience many pleasurable things. We can run. We can jump. We can get a backrub. We can give one. We can taste lemonade. God gave us a terrific gift when he gave us our bodies.''

2. *Body outlines*—Have junior highers each pair off with someone they feel comfortable with. Give each person a body-sized sheet of newsprint. Give each pair one dark crayon. Have the pairs take turns tracing each other's body outline on the newsprint. Kids will have to spread the paper on the floor and lie down to do this. Have each person write his or her name on the body-outline sheet. Tape the body outlines onto the walls all around the room.

3. *I like my body*—Ask kids how it felt to get the backrubs. Most will probably say it felt great. Say: ''Getting a backrub is like getting a pat on the back. Today we're going to give ourselves spoken pats on the back. We're going to list all the things we like about our bodies. For instance, you could say, 'I like my body because it can run.' Or, 'I like my body because it can climb trees.' Or, 'I like my body because it can see beautiful sunsets.' "

Give kids markers and have them write on their body-outline sheets. Watch for anyone who's having trouble thinking of things to write; help out with suggestions that focus on the body's wonderful capacities—seeing, hearing, tasting, touching, smelling, moving, making, building.

Have a "body cheer" when kids finish writing. Get the group together and shout "Hip-hip-hooray for my body!" Or adapt an old cheerleading cheer. "Give me a B!" and so on, to spell "body."

4. *Body pains*—Gather group members together in a circle. Say: "We don't always feel happy about our bodies. Sometimes we feel unhappy about them." Ask kids to close their eyes and *think* about, not speak, how they would complete the following sentences. Slowly read the sentences.

● Sometimes I wish my body were less . . .
● Sometimes I feel ashamed of my body because . . .
● Sometimes I wish my body were more . . .

Give kids a moment of silence. Then have them open their eyes. Say: "What you've just experienced are body pains. There are several reasons we might feel dissatisfied with our bodies.

"Sometimes we compare our bodies with unrealistic ideals. (Mention current media stars or show pictures from girls' fashion magazines and guys' sports magazines.) Not too many people look like this. It's okay to be human.

"Secondly, your bodies are changing from children's bodies into adult bodies. It's okay to be on the way. You don't have to be all grown up all at once.

"And finally, maybe you're not taking care of your body as much as you could. Poor diet, no exercise and little sleep can keep your body from looking, feeling and doing its best."

5. *Created in God's image*—Form groups of no more than four and give each a marker and newsprint. Assign kids each one of the following roles: reader (who reads the scriptures); note-taker (who records the group's ideas on newsprint); reporter (who shares the group's ideas with the whole group); and encourager (who make sure everyone contributes to the discussion).

Assign groups one or two scripture references from the following list: Genesis 1:26-27; Matthew 10:29-31; Romans 6:11-14;

1 Corinthians 6:12-17; 1 Corinthians 6:19. Have readers read their passages. Then have group members summarize the theme of their passages in one sentence. Have groups brainstorm ways that theme is reflected in the creation of our bodies. When note-takers have listed their groups' ideas on the newsprint, have the reporters share their conclusions with the whole group.

Ask: "Why is it important to recognize that we were created in God's image? How does that affect how we look at ourselves? What do Jesus' teachings tell us about the importance of our bodies? How can we honor our God-created bodies in everyday circumstances? What are some positive characteristics we've each been given by our creator, God?"

6. *A few good words*—Form a circle. Stand in the center of the circle holding a mirror. Say: "In our body-conscious world, people often focus on outward appearance. But God focuses on the person inside. I'm going to walk around the circle and pause at each person. When I hold up the mirror in front of you, listen to the words from Genesis 1:27 and 31 and see yourself as God sees you."

As you stop at each person, read aloud Genesis 1:27, 31. Ask kids to join you in repeating the verses. If you have more than 12 students in class, show the mirror to two or three kids at a time before you say the verses.

When each person has had a chance to look in the mirror, have volunteers close in prayer, thanking God for creating us with unique and positive physical traits and personalities. ∎

Section Two:

FRIENDSHIP

11 *Building Bridges*

By Lee Hovel

*J*unior highers need to celebrate, have fun and
develop skills in cooperation and working
together.

Use this meeting to build a sense of community
among the kids while they learn skills that help
them build bridges in relationships.

OBJECTIVES

Participants will:
- experience opportunities for fun and celebration;
- complete activities that call for cooperation;
- hear that God's bridge to people is Jesus; and
- understand that they are bridges of God's love to each other.

SUPPLIES

Gather a box approximately 12 inches deep and 12 inches
wide; three bricks or objects of a similar weight; newsprint; a
marker; a sheet of newsprint with "Words in Action" phrases
from activity #4 written on it; for every three to six group members, a "Friendship-Building" handout, an 18-inch-high stack of
newspapers, a roll of masking tape; and, for each person, a
"Pyramid Possibilities" handout and a Bible. If you'll be indoors, collect mats and rugs for cushions for "Pyramid Possibilities"; otherwise, use a grassy area.

BEFORE THE MEETING

Read the meeting and collect supplies.
Review the "Pyramid Possibilities." If some look dangerous

to you, caution your group so kids don't try anything beyond their capabilities. The key to this activity is cooperation—not competition. Kids must work together to make sure no one gets hurt.

Tape a large, blank sheet of newsprint onto the wall for use in activity #4.

THE MEETING

1. *Relationship bridging and building*—Divide the group into small groups of three to six, with an adult sponsor in each group. Give a "Friendship-Building" handout to each group, and allow time for group members to complete its tasks.

Friendship-Building

1. Each find something that's totally unique about yourself—something not common to anyone else in your small group. (For example, I've gone helicopter skiing.) Keep checking out your uniqueness until everyone in the group has one unique statement.

2. Together discover something "unique" that everyone in your group has in common. (For example, everyone in our group is left-handed.)

3. Decide on a group name and a group cheer.

4. Be ready to share your group's uniqueness, name and cheer with the other groups.

When everyone's finished, invite all the groups to share three things: uniqueness, name and cheer.

2. *Bridge-building*—Next give each small group an 18-inch-high stack of newspapers and a roll of masking tape. Say: "Each small group is to build a free-standing bridge, high and wide enough for this box to fit underneath it (show the box). Make your bridge strong enough to support these three bricks (show the bricks). When I place these bricks on your bridge, it should hold them up. The newspapers and masking tape are your only materials. You have 10 minutes to plan your strategy. You may not touch your newspaper or tape. You may not measure the box or touch the bricks. You may only look at them. After 10 minutes of planning, you'll have 10 minutes to build your bridge. You now have 10 minutes to plan. Begin!''

After 10 minutes, call time. Tell groups to begin their bridge-building. You might have to extend the 10-minute time limit, but push the groups to finish in the allotted time. At seven minutes, call out each minute to inform the groups how much time they have left.

When you call time, go to each group's bridge and see whether the box fits underneath it and whether the bridge supports the bricks. Most groups will succeed, but if they don't, be positive about how group members worked together.

After you've tested all the bridges, celebrate the successes with applause and another round of group cheers. If you want group members to share their feelings about the activity, keep it light. Focus on building relationships, fun and a chance to work together.

3. *Pyramid-building and people bridges*—Give each person a "Pyramid Possibilities" handout. Say: "We're going to build pyramids with people bridges. You'll need to cooperate and work together. Each person is important. You'll need to support each other to make it work. Start with the pyramids for two and gradually move on. It's important to use correct and careful placement of your feet on the 'base' person when you do supporting stunts. For example, place your feet on the strong parts of the body such as thighs or shoulders, rather than on a weak part such as the hollow of the back." Demonstrate this so everyone understands.

Circulate throughout the group to offer assistance if necessary, and to point out completed formations to the entire group. If the kids make all the designs on the sheet, have them create "originals."

4. *Worship celebration*—On a large sheet of newsprint taped to the wall, print the following: "God's bridge of love is Jesus." Have group members discuss this statement. Help them see how the activities they've been doing relate to this statement.

Hand out Bibles and have junior highers read 2 Corinthians 5:17-21. Have kids name ways they can be bridges of love for each other in the group. List their ideas under the newsprint statement, "God's bridge of love is Jesus."

Choose one or two ideas for your group goals. Do something specific to act on them.

Divide the group into five groups. Tape the "Words in Action" statements on newsprint onto the wall. For the worship celebration, assign each group one of the "Words in Action" statements paraphrased from 2 Corinthians 5:17-21.

Ask each group to give life to its phrase with action, song, rhythm or dance. For example, one group could come from all corners of the room and stand in the shape of a cross for "People who are in Christ." Or another group could create a rhythmic cheer for "Are a new creation." Allow three to five minutes for planning, then gather group members together. Have each group present its phrase for the others.

As a closing celebration, have the groups present their phrases in order several times. ■

Words in Action

1. People who are in Christ
2. Are a new creation
3. The old is gone, the new has come
4. Changed from enemies into friends
5. Called to be a bridge of God's love

Pyramid Possibilities

For Twos:
For Threes:
For Fours:
For Fives:

12 The Pressure's On

By Cindy Hansen

We hear a lot about how tough peer pressure is for kids. But peer pressure isn't necessarily bad. Friends can help one another do what's right—not just what's wrong.

Use this meeting to help your junior highers identify negative peer pressure in their lives and see how they can support one another in doing what's right.

OBJECTIVES

Participants will:
- define peer pressure and how it can be positive and negative;
- identify and discuss things they feel pressured to do and how others would respond;
- study Daniel 3's examples of both negative and positive peer pressure and demonstrate how they apply to life today;
- be applauded for times they did what was right; and
- discuss ways to support one another in what's right.

SUPPLIES

Gather a chalkboard and chalk; a sheet of newsprint with the three questions from activity #3 written on it; masking tape; refreshments; for every four to six group members, a Bible, a concordance, a "Who Says?" handout, about 10 pieces of paper, a cassette player, a blank cassette tape, a microphone; and, for each person, a "Pressure Cooker" handout and a pencil.

BEFORE THE MEETING

Ask several junior highers to help you publicize the meeting during the announcements at a church service. Have one kid sit on a chair at the front of the worship area. Have several others enter and proceed to "squeeze" him or her. The first junior higher stands on the chair (so he or she can see over the others' heads) and says: "The pressure's on! All junior highers come tonight [or whenever the meeting is] and learn about peer pressure." Then all the others pick up the individual and carry him or her away.

Read the meeting and collect supplies.

Place the chalkboard and chalk at the front of the meeting room.

THE MEETING

1. Leading the followers—Play "Follow the Leader." Choose a junior higher to be the first leader. Tell all others to do exactly what the leader does. Encourage the leader to lead activities like jumping and skipping and also activities kids feel pressured to do in everyday life, like combing their hair a certain way, listening to the radio, dancing with the latest moves, jogging or lifting weights. Let several kids have turns leading.

You be the last leader and lead everyone to the front of the meeting room. Gather them around the chalkboard, and discuss the game. Ask: "How did it feel to lead and have others follow? How did it feel to follow no matter what the leader said or did?"

2. What's peer pressure?—Say that this meeting is about pressure to follow along with a crowd; peer pressure, that feeling that you have to do what others do in order to be liked and accepted.

Ask the kids to help you define peer pressure. Definitions could range from "blindly following another" to "being afraid to be different from your friends" to "not thinking for yourself."

Draw a line down the center of the chalkboard. At the top of the left half of the board draw a "-"; draw a "+" at the top of the right half. Ask kids to shout out all kinds of negative, not-so-good things they sometimes feel pressured to do; for example, cheating on tests, lying, gossiping, ignoring kids who don't fit in, drinking, smoking. List these on the "-" side of the chalkboard.

78

3. *Pressure points*—Give each person a "Pressure Cooker" handout and a pencil. Have kids each complete the handout.

Pressure Cooker

For each activity, shade in the column to indicate how much pressure you feel to do it. The higher you shade, the more pressure you feel.

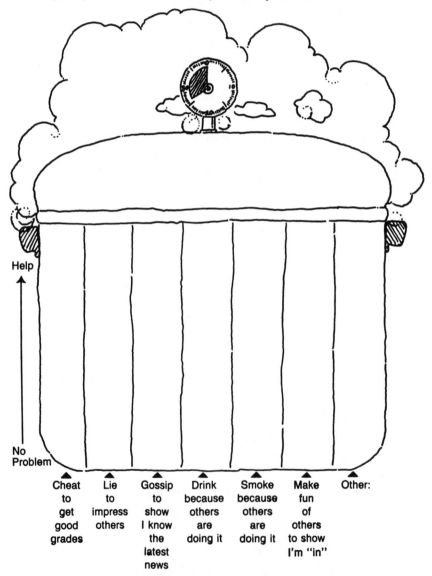

Have kids get in small groups of four to six to discuss their answers. Make sure there's an adult sponsor in each group. Display the sheet of newsprint with these questions:
- What activities do you feel the most pressure to do?
- Why do you feel pressured to do these activities?
- How do you know what's right and what's wrong?

4. *Who says?*—Give each small group a Bible, a concordance and a "Who Says?" handout. Assign each small group a pressure point from the "Pressure Cooker" handout. Say: "There are several ways we can know what's right and what's wrong. We can listen to our parents, the pastor and good friends, we can read the Bible, and we can think of how we feel. In your small groups, discuss your pressure point and complete the 'Who Says?' handout. Use the Bibles and concordances to look up scripture verses and figure out what the Bible says."

Who Says?

Write the pressure-point situation your leader gives you. Then discuss and write how you think your parents, pastor, best friend, the Bible and you would respond to it.

The "pressure-point" situation: _____

- My parents would say:

- My pastor would say:

- My best friend would say:

- The Bible says:

- I say:

Permission to photocopy this handout granted for local church use. Copyright © 1987 by Thom Schultz Publications, Inc., Box 481, Loveland, CO 80539.

When small groups finish, have each small group present its findings.

5. *Positive peer pressure*—Get everyone back together

around the chalkboard. Say: "So far, we've only talked about negative peer pressure. Not all peer pressure is negative. Some is positive. For example, good friends can help each other do the right thing—such as say no to drinking or be friendly to a new person at school."

Have junior highers brainstorm some positive pressures; for example, studying for a test to get good grades, telling the truth, apologizing. Write them on the "+" side of the board.

6. *A hot example of pressure*—Say: "Daniel 3 tells a story that describes both kinds of peer pressure: positive and negative. Shadrach, Meshach and Abednego are pressured to bow to the king's statue. The three friends help each other stand straight and tall and not give in to the pressure to worship the statue. The friends help each other through a burning situation."

Ask for volunteers to read aloud Daniel 3. Then discuss:

● How do you think Shadrach, Meshach and Abednego felt about going against the king's rule?

● Do you think it was hard for them to be different and not go along with the others? Why or why not?

● What are examples of negative pressures in this story?

● What are examples of positive pressures in this story?

7. *Recorded stories*—Have kids return to their small groups of four to six. Give each group paper, a cassette player, blank cassette tape and microphone. Make sure junior highers still have their pencils. Tell kids they have a chance to record a modern-day version of the Bible story. Challenge each small group to translate the Bible story, setting and characters to today. Read this modern-day "translation" as an example:

Sidney, Michele and Abner went to Central Junior High. One week the principal decided to make a rule that all students should bow to her picture as they passed it in the hallway.

The principal made bowing a very "in" thing to do. Kids could letter in the activity if they bowed to the picture daily. They could win a T-shirt for the best bower if their bow-style was outstandingly unique. All kids could receive extra credit for bowing to the picture.

But Sidney, Michele and Abner thought this was ridiculous. No picture should be bowed to. So they refused to do it. Some kids told the principal that Sidney, Michele and Abner wouldn't follow the new rule. The principal placed the trio on detention until they would decide to give in to the demand.

Stay tuned for next week. Will Sidney, Michele and Abner give in to the pressure to bow to the picture, or will they refuse—together—to cooperate?

Give small groups 15 to 20 minutes to write and record their modern-day versions of Daniel 3.

Get everyone together in a circle. Let small groups take turns playing their stories for each other. Then discuss:

● Do any of the modern-day versions describe situations you've had to deal with in school? If yes, explain.

● How does it feel to not want to do what everyone else is doing?

● Have you ever faced a situation when you've helped a friend do the "right" thing? Explain.

Go around the circle and let everyone tell about a time when he or she helped a friend do something that was right. After each person shares, have everyone else stand and applaud.

8. *Support from friends*—Tell kids this is a game that lets everyone support each other in accomplishing a task. It's called "Climbing the Walls" from *Building Community in Youth Groups* by Denny Rydberg (Group Books). Get kids into groups of six to 10. Give each group a piece of masking tape. Tell the junior highers they may only use the wall and each other for support, and they have eight minutes to see how high they can place the tape onto the wall. Be sure groups use "spotters" to soften the landing if someone takes a tumble. Afterward, discuss:

● What part did you play in this exercise?

● How did it feel to work as a team to accomplish a task?

● How does this compare to supporting each other, and helping each other do what is right every day?

● How can we continue to support friends and help them do what's right?

9. *Refreshments*—Remember the commercial that publicized this meeting? Do instant replays: Have kids take turns standing in the center of a circle and being squeezed by everyone else to symbolize being supported. The last person to be squeezed gets carried over to the refreshment table and is first in line. How about serving fresh-squeezed orange juice or lemonade? ■

13 Psst . . . Did You Hear?

By Cindy Hansen

"Did you hear about Rob? He skipped class all last week and will be suspended from school."

"Don't tell anybody I told you, but Steve's gonna ask Sharon to the dance. Why would he ask her?"

Gossip tidbits travel with ease. Everyone has experienced gossip. We've gossiped to others, or we've been gossiped about by others. Nobody is immune!

Use this meeting to help your junior highers understand gossip and find positive ways to respond.

OBJECTIVES

Participants will:

● discuss the nature of gossip—what it is, how it starts, how it feels to be gossiped about, why we do it;

● play games that show how gossip develops and how it affects everyone;

● think of ways to stop gossip; and

● praise others' positive qualities.

SUPPLIES

Gather newsprint; masking tape; one handout for each of the three case studies in activity #6; a piece of green yarn, long enough to go across a large bulletin board; a large bulletin board; for every four to six group members, a piece of paper, a piece of paper with a simple hand-drawn picture of an object such as a house, cat or car; for each person, a chair, a pencil, a Bible, a copy of "The Telltale Tongue" handout, eight 4-inch leaf shapes cut from green construction paper, a marker, three tacks, an unruled 3×5 card, and a 2-foot piece of green yarn. Optional: a cassette player and a cassette tape of "I Heard It Through the Grapevine" by Marvin Gaye or Gladys Knight and the Pips, and "Grape, Grape Joy" by Amy Grant.

BEFORE THE MEETING

Publicize the meeting with posters that say "Psst! Did you hear the latest? All junior highers come to the next meeting to hear the scoop about gossip!"

Read the meeting and collect supplies. Set up chairs in a circle.

Make a "gossip column" graffiti area for use in activity #1 by taping newsprint along one wall of the meeting room. Place markers nearby.

THE MEETING

1. Gossip column—If you have a recording of "I Heard It Through the Grapevine," play it as kids arrive. Direct them to the gossip column and tell them: "Write on our gossip column some examples of the 'juicy' gossip you hear around school. We don't want to hurt anybody, so *don't use names* or any real gossip that's floating around your school right now. Just make up some typical examples. An example of gossip: 'Did you know that _____ got kicked out of school for three days for cheating?' "

2. Neighbor game—After everyone has written on the wall, have kids come to the circle of chairs and sit down. Ask one person to stand in the middle of the circle. Remove extra chairs so everyone has a chair except the middle person who's "It."

"It" approaches a person and asks, "Who are your neighbors?'' The person must say the names of the people sitting next to him or her on each side. If the person *can't* name his or her neighbors, ''It'' exchanges places with the person. If he or she *can* name the neighbors, ''It'' asks ''How is (name of one neighbor)?'' If the person says ''All right,'' everyone in the circle must move one chair to the right. If the person says ''All wrong,'' everyone must move one chair to the left. If the person says ''You should hear about my neighbor,'' everyone scrambles anywhere in the circle for another chair. ''It'' tries to get a seat during any of the scrambles.

3. *What is gossip?*—Have group members move their chairs to make a semicircle facing the gossip column. After they've sat down, say: ''We're going to rate the gossip you've written. As we go over each example, if it's good gossip, give me a 'thumbs-up' sign and stand up; if it's bad gossip, give me a 'thumbs-down' sign and stay seated; if it's neutral, cross your arms and sit on the floor.''

After the ratings, ask: ''What makes certain information gossip?'' Point to the gossip column and ask them how they decided what was ''juicy'' gossip. Say: ''It's easy to see gossip is rarely good or neutral. It's almost always bad or hurtful.''

4. *Back art*—Divide the group into teams of four to six. Instruct each team to sit in a line, one person behind another, and take a vow of silence for the game. Give the first person in each line a pencil and a piece of paper. Then give the last person in each line a simple hand-drawn picture of an object such as a house, cat or car. That person must use his or her finger to draw the object on the back of the person in front of him or her, and so on. When the drawing reaches the first person in line, he or she must draw it on the piece of paper. Have judges determine which team's picture most resembles the original.

Ask: ''How did the picture get so scrambled? Explain. How is this like gossip? How do messages get scrambled when they pass from person to person?''

5. *Gossip game*—Get everyone in a circle. Whisper the following into one person's ear: ''Did you hear that Susie went out with Sam last Friday night? They stayed out until 3 a.m. Her parents won't let her see Sam again!''

Have the kids pass the gossip around the circle until the last person tells you what he or she heard. Discuss: ''Were some

Case Study #1

A friend catches you in the hallway between classes. She says: "Did you hear about Sandy and John? Last Saturday, they told their parents they were going to a friend's house to watch television. They didn't get home until 4 a.m. They said they fell asleep during a boring show. Sure!"
- What would you say to your friend?
- How would Sandy or John feel if they knew they were being talked about?
- Why do you think the friend is passing along this story?
- How could you stop this talk from going further?

Case Study #2

A rumor is floating around school that one of your friends is pregnant. You know this isn't true.
- What would you do or say if you heard this?
- If the story isn't true, why would somebody make it up?
- How could you stop it from going further?

Case Study #3

You overhear two friends talking about you. They're saying you failed a math test they thought was really easy. The truth is, you *did* fail the test.
- If something is "the truth," is it okay for people to talk about it? Explain.
- How would you feel if you overheard someone talking about you?
- What would you do?

facts exaggerated? How did the story change? What caused the change? What causes inaccurate gossip?''

6. *Why do it?*—Divide the group into three groups. Give each group one of the case studies.

Have the groups discuss these. Then gather as a large group and go over each case study. Focus on why people gossip. Discuss: ''Is it a need to know something others don't? Is it a need to hurt others?''

7. *Tongue types and tongue control*—Distribute a pencil, Bible and copy of ''The Telltale Tongue'' to each person. Have the kids work in pairs to complete the worksheet. Number the partners ''one'' and ''two'' in each pair. (You'll use the numbers for the discussion after the activity.)

Say: ''With your partner, you have 10 minutes to complete the first part of 'The Telltale Tongue,' called 'Tongue Types.' We'll then discuss the questions following it.'' Read the instructions to get them started.

After 10 minutes, have kids explain the kinds of gossip they discovered. They can show their illustrations too. Say: ''Now, ones, you have 20 seconds to tell your partner a time you witnessed *flattering* gossip.''

Go through each gossip type, alternating the partner who tells and the one who listens. For example, the next time you say: ''Twos, you have 20 seconds to tell your partner a time you witnessed *proud* or *boastful* gossip.'' Continue through sharp, lying, deceitful, mischievous, back-biting, deadly and fiery gossip.

When you've completed this, say: ''The Bible also tells us what to do with our tongues. Complete the second part of 'The Telltale Tongue,' called 'Tongue Control,' and you'll see what the Bible says.''

After five minutes, discuss the questions following the verses.

8. *Grapevine guidelines*—Say: ''Now think of ways to individually stop gossip. For example, one good way is 'Don't start it!' Or, 'If you hear it, don't pass it along.' What are other ideas?''

Distribute three construction-paper leaves and a marker to each person. Tape a long piece of green yarn horizontally across your bulletin board. Tell group members this is a ''grapevine,'' and, in case they don't know the expression, ''I heard it through

The Telltale Tongue

Tongue Types

1. Check what the Bible says about gossip. Read each verse, then draw a picture that illustrates the "tongue type."

   Psalm 5:9
   Psalm 12:3
   Psalm 52:2
   Psalm 109:2
   Psalm 120:2
   Proverbs 17:4
   Proverbs 25:23
   Jeremiah 9:8
   James 3:6

2. Answer these questions:
   ● Describe times when you've witnessed these types of gossip.
   ● Why does the Bible warn about these uses of the tongue?

Tongue Control

1. The following verses also refer to the tongue. Read each verse, then draw a picture that describes it.

   Psalm 141:3
   Proverbs 10:19
   James 1:26

2. Answer these questions:
   ● What does God want us to do with our tongues?
   ● How can we "bridle" our tongues and watch what's said?
   ● Read Matthew 22:36-39. What is one of the best ways we can "love our neighbors"?

the grapevine," explain it. Ask the kids to each write one guideline to avoid gossip on each leaf they have. When everyone's finished, ask the kids to say, one at a time, their guidelines and tack them to the yarn "grapevine" on the bulletin board. Discuss the finished product.

9. *The "great-vine"*—Give the group members each an unruled 3×5 card and five more green construction-paper leaves. Have each person write his or her name on the index card and then tape it onto the gossip column. Then have the kids each attach a 2-foot piece of green yarn to their 3×5 card and tape their five leaves to the yarn.

Tell everyone: "Let's make this a *great*-vine, for only positive, good things about people! Go to each person's vine, and on one of the leaves, write something positive about that person. Leave room for other people's comments." Watch for people who can't think of enough good things and help them out. Also, be sure everyone's vine gets plenty of positive comments on its leaves! You can help by writing a positive comment on each person's vine.

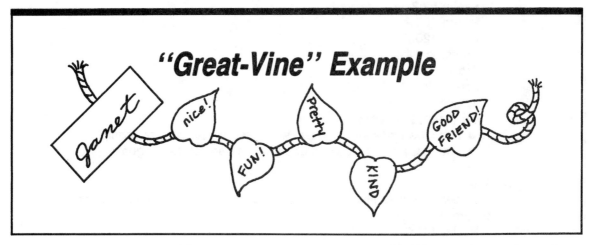

10. *The human grapevine*—End with a prayer asking for God's help to stop gossip. Give thanks that God doesn't listen to gossip.

Following the prayer, form a human grapevine. Have everyone join hands in a straight line. Have one end curl around tightly like a cinnamon roll. On the count of three, have everyone hug and join in a yell: "Squeeze the gossip out of the grapevine!"

11. *Having a grape time*—Treat kids to theme refreshments. Try grapes, grape juice, grape fruit bars! If you have it, play Amy Grant's "Grape, Grape Joy." It'll be a truly grape ending to a fruitful meeting! ■

14 The Secret of Friendship

By Randy Carter

Junior highers need friends. Yet few junior highers know how to be good friends. They're afraid to make sacrifices or become vulnerable. They don't always put true friendship into action.

Use this meeting to help your junior highers learn a secret of lasting friendships.

OBJECTIVES

Participants will:
- tell about their best friends and probably realize how little they know about them;
- build a spirit of friendship through a progressive relay;
- experience John 13:1-17 by washing each other's feet;
- discover Jesus' example of being a servant-friend; and
- write personal reminders of ways to improve as friends.

SUPPLIES

Gather two identical sets of 3×5 cards, each with one relay instruction written on it (see the "Possible Relay Instructions" in activity #3), enough so that the total number of cards equals at least the total number of kids you expect will attend; two chairs; two paper bags; enough small prizes for the relay's winning team members (half of the group members) to each get one; three Bibles; newsprint; masking tape; markers; a basin of water and a towel for every two group members; and, for each person, a "Best Friend" handout, a "Letter to Myself" handout, a pencil and a stamped envelope. Optional: cookies and a mirror and comb for the greeters to use.

BEFORE THE MEETING

Read the meeting and collect supplies.

Plan two places for your meeting: a large non-carpeted room for the relay (activity #3) and a more intimate room for everything else.

Ask two or three junior highers and adults to be "servants" who will greet kids. Coach them on "servant" ideas: As people enter, they could hang up their coats, offer a mirror and comb to fix their hair, escort them to the meeting area, offer a cookie.

Set up the relay area. Place two chairs about 10 feet apart at one end of the room. Place one set of 3×5 instructions in each paper bag and place the bags on the chairs. Double-check that (1) each bag has the same amount of cards with the same instructions, and (2) the combined total of cards at least equals the number of people at the meeting. If your group is small, make more cards than the exact number of people. This will make the game longer and crazier.

THE MEETING

Best Friend

Tell your best friend's . . .
- name
- phone number
- favorite sport
- place of birth
- mom's first name
- career goal
- #1 priority in life (God, sports, family)
- most embarrassing moment
- worst childhood memory
- biggest fear

1. *Servant-greeters*— Have predesignated kids and adults come early to greet and serve junior highers as they arrive. Make sure each person who enters feels welcome and "given to."

2. *Insight time*—Have group members find partners and sit facing each other. Give each person a "Best Friend" handout. Allow five to 10 minutes for partners to tell each other the answers to "Best Friend." Say that if they know an answer, but it's too personal, they don't need to share it.

Then have junior highers tell their partners things about their best friends.

Get everyone together and say: "It's great to have friends and talk positively about them. During this meeting we're going to discover what will help us be better, more dependable friends."

3. *Progressive relay*—
Move to the room that's been arranged for the game. Divide the group into two teams. Have teams line up in single-file lines on the side of the room opposite the chairs. When the "start" signal is given, the first person on each team will run to the chair, take one 3×5 card out of the sack, follow the instructions, tag the chair, run back to the team and lock arms with the next person in line. *Both* of them will run back to the chair, take one 3×5 card out of the sack, fol-

---

Possible Relay Instructions

- Sing "Jingle Bells."
- Do five jumping jacks.
- Run around the room.
- Take off your shoes.
- Run backward to your team.
- Get a drink of water.
- Hop to your team.
- Run around the chair two times yelling your school's name.
- Kneel and say "(your school's name) rules."

---

low the instructions together, tag the chair, lock arms again, run back to the team and lock arms with the third person. And so on. This continues until all team members have been included, finished the instructions, run back to their starting line and sat down. Award prizes to the first seated team.

4. *Bible time*—Move back to the intimate meeting room. Have kids sit in a circle and take off their shoes and socks. Bring out basins of water and towels. Have kids face partners to listen to the scripture passage. Have three good readers take turns reading the verses in John 13:1-17.

Say: "Jesus was so committed to us that he made himself *look* like a servant, then he got down on his knees and washed his disciples' dirty feet. Now let's wash each other's feet. It might feel awkward and uncomfortable, but let's do it anyway. Remember your feelings during this experience so we can talk about them later. In your pairs, have one wash and dry the other's feet; then switch roles."

When everyone's finished, say: "Jesus washed the disciples' feet because he knew the main ingredient of true friendship: the willingness and desire to serve one another. He reminded them that if they wanted to be happy, they would serve one another too."

5. *Tying it all together*—With group members still sitting in the circle, discuss: "Which was more comfortable for you—washing feet or being washed? Why? Which is easier for you in a friendship—to give or receive? Why? What are ways you 'serve' your friends? (List these specific ideas on newsprint for later reference.) How much did you know about your best friend in the earlier exercise? Were you surprised? Why or why not? What did you learn about yourself through that? From Jesus' example, what is the most important ingredient of friendship?"

Say: "Even though friendships are important to us, many times we want to 'get' from friends rather than 'give' to them. If everyone did this all the time, no one would ever get. Jesus is the perfect friend who wants to be your friend—your best friend. He wants to give his love to you. Jesus will never leave you and by following Jesus, you can serve others better."

6. *A letter to myself*—Give a "Letter to Myself" handout, a pencil and a stamped envelope to each person. Tell group members to each complete the handout by writing specific, measurable ways to be better friends. For example, not simply "serving," but "letting Joey use my skateboard when he asks." Refer them to the newsprint list of ideas made earlier.

Have group members put the finished letters in their envelopes, seal them, address the envelopes to themselves, and turn them in to you. Assure them the letters won't be read, and you'll mail them in about four weeks. Be sure to follow through and mail the letters!

7. *Closing*—Have kids bow their heads, close their eyes and pray silently for the person they talked with at the beginning of the meeting. After a few moments, say "Amen." Before dismissing kids, say: "Remember, when everyone gives, everyone gets. For instance, you weren't praying for yourself, but everyone was being prayed for. Although you must pray for yourself too, giving to others is the secret of being a good friend." ■

Letter to Myself

Dear _____,

   Have you been doing everything you can to be a true friend lately?
If not, remember what you learned at church not long ago:

You can be a better friend by:

15 *Stamp Out Putdowns!*

By Phil Baker

Putdowns are the #1 enemy of junior highers. Why? When a pre-adolescent becomes an adolescent, one of his or her greatest concerns is to be perfect.

Any putdown—word or act—that questions this perfect self-image is magnified and accepted as true.

Use this meeting to help junior highers explore what a putdown is, what it does to a person's self-image, and alternative ways of acting.

OBJECTIVES

Participants will:

● identify what putdowns are, where they come from, and how they make people feel;

● be introduced to a Christlike way of treating other people; and

● practice treating others in a Christlike way by giving compliments.

SUPPLIES

Gather cassette tapes or records of upbeat Christian music; a cassette player or turntable; newsprint; masking tape; a 3×24-inch black construction-paper strip; and, for each person, a marker, two 3×5 cards, a straight pin, a Bible, a pencil, a piece of paper, a crayon and a balloon.

BEFORE THE MEETING

Read the meeting and collect supplies.

Tape a couple of sheets of newsprint onto a wall to create a graffiti board. Write across the top: "Putdowns: Words and Actions That Hurt." Draw a large sad face (☹) on the board.

Read Matthew 25:31-45 for personal preparation. Think of the kids your youth group overlooks. For instance: the ugly girl, the shy boy, a bratty sister, the class klutz.

THE MEETING

1. *As they arrive*—Have Christian music playing. Have kids use markers to print their names on 3×5 cards, then use straight pins to pin the name tags on. Have them go to the graffiti board.

Tell group members to write putdowns they hate the most on the graffiti board. To help them get started, print two or three putdowns such as "dummy" or "klutz" on the board.

2. *Identifying putdowns*—Have kids sit in a semicircle facing the graffiti board.

Ask group members to read the putdowns written on the board. Add any additional words they think of.

Discuss: "Why do putdowns upset you? Why do people use putdowns? Since putdowns are actions as well as words, what kind of actions make you feel bad (for instance: giggles, frowns or pulling away from a touch)? Since putdowns aren't always true, why do they hurt so much?"

To help identify sources of putdowns, say: "Look at the graffiti board. Which of the words, phrases or actions are most likely to come from your parents?" As kids name them, write a "P" by parent putdowns. Add new putdowns they think of while they're talking.

Continue the discussion using the following categories in the same way: brothers/sisters (S), teachers (T), friends (F), other kids (K), other adults (A).

3. *Bible search*—Divide the group into small groups of three to five. Have an adult sponsor in each group. Give each person a Bible. Say: "The opposite of a putdown is a compliment or a thoughtful act. The Bible tells us to be kind and thoughtful to each other, even to strangers and enemies. One story in Matthew 25:31-45 shows this.

"Read this story. Find out what Jesus means when he uses the phrase 'the least of these.' Who is he talking about? When your small group has read this story, discuss who 'the least of these' means."

When kids finish discussing, hand out 3×5 cards and pencils and say: "On your 3×5 card, write a time you felt like one of the least of these, a time you really hurt. Don't put your name on it. When you're finished, hand it in to me." Collect the cards. Have a sponsor sort through the cards and choose six or 12 to read in the closing prayer.

Continue: "Our scripture search taught us to be concerned about others. Most likely none of you have visited a prison or fed a hungry person. But you can reach out to people every day. There are people in our lives right now who hurt just like 'the least of these.'"

4. *Compliment game*—Explain: "It's easy to give putdowns, to hurt someone. It's more difficult to say nice things to others, especially to people our own age. Let's practice complimenting each other as we play the next game."

Hand out pieces of paper, crayons and masking tape. Have kids help each other tape a blank piece of paper onto everyone's back. Tell them to write sincere compliments to each person on that person's piece of paper. Say: "Giving compliments is serious stuff. Compliments build up rather than put down. So let's build each other up by writing good things about each other—no putdowns allowed!"

Begin the compliment game. Play upbeat Christian music. Make sure kids write on everyone's back. Watch to see no one is left out.

After a while, call time. Let kids read their own pieces of paper. Ask: "How did it feel to give sincere compliments? How did it feel to receive sincere compliments?"

Challenge junior highers to compliment others outside the youth group—to reach out with words and actions that make others feel better about themselves.

5. *Stamping out putdowns*—Hand out balloons. Have each person blow up and tie one balloon.

Say: "Use a marker to write the putdown you hate the most

on your balloon. Write the word or use a symbol or picture.

"Hold the balloon carefully when you finish writing. Form a semicircle facing the graffiti board."

When everyone's in position, hold the black construction-paper strip and say: "This strip of black construction paper is a symbol that means putdowns hurt.

"Signs that have this bar across them mean to stop doing whatever the sign pictures. A bar across a picture of a lighted cigarette means no smoking. A bar across a picture of people walking means to stop walking in that place. This bar will cover putdowns on our poster. It says: Stop it. They hurt. No more putdowns. (Tape the strip diagonally across the sad face.) Place your balloon carefully on the floor in front of you, but don't move from your place. Join hands and close your eyes."

Have the sponsor who sorted the 3×5 cards read them during the closing prayer. Do the prayer like this:

> ***Leader:*** *I was hungry.*
> ***Adult Sponsor:*** *(Reads one or two cards.)*
> ***Leader:*** *I was thirsty.*
> ***Adult Sponsor:*** *(Reads one or two cards.)*
> ***Leader:*** *I was a stranger.*
> ***Adult Sponsor:*** *(Reads one or two cards.)*
> ***Leader:*** *I was naked.*
> ***Adult Sponsor:*** *(Reads one or two cards.)*
> ***Leader:*** *I was sick.*
> ***Adult Sponsor:*** *(Reads one or two cards.)*
> ***Leader:*** *I was in prison.*
> ***Adult Sponsor:*** *(Reads one or two cards.)*
> ***Leader:*** *God, putdowns hurt. And you've just heard what hurts us. Use these balloons as symbols of our hurts. Help us stamp out putdowns. Help us do good things for our friends and for "the least of these." Let Jesus be our example for loving others. Amen.*

Say: "Now break your balloon as together with God's help we stamp out putdowns."

Have junior highers help clean up the balloons.

Encourage kids to hug at least five different people before they leave. ∎

16 *Such Good Friends*

By Cindy Parolini

" " **H**ave you ever lost a really good friend, but didn't know why, and felt really bad about it?" asks Laura, 14. "I have, and so have many people I know."

Fragile friendship ties characterize junior high relationships.

At this delicate age, junior highers seek friends for many reasons: companionship, safety and familiarity, affirmation . . .

But the bonds are often severed for many reasons: gossip about a friend, betrayal, mood swings that forget a friend's feelings, jealousy . . .

Use this meeting to help your junior highers identify the valuable qualities of friendship. By learning how to improve as friends, young people can strengthen their friendship ties.

OBJECTIVES

Participants will:

● discuss and list qualities of friendship by considering their own friendships, media friendships and Bible friendships;

● evaluate themselves on seven qualities of friendship they consider most important;

● each choose one quality of friendship to develop or improve in themselves and agree to support each other in these at-

tempts; and
- show appreciation for friends in the youth group.

SUPPLIES

Gather friendship songs or upbeat Christian songs on cassette tapes or records; a cassette player or turntable; stick-on name tags, decorated with three to six (depending on the size of your group) orange suns (●), three to six blue half-moons (☾), three to six yellow stars (★), three to six purple rain clouds (☁), three to six red rainbows (⌒) (repeat shapes in different colors until you have enough decorated name tags for each group member to have one); markers; a stack of magazines; scissors; glue; construction paper; newsprint; a container such as a collection plate; masking tape; string; crayons; the song "Friends" on cassette tape or record by Michael W. Smith (or "Candle on the Water" by Helen Reddy or "Bridge Over Troubled Water" by Simon and Garfunkel); for each small group of three to six, a TV Guide, People Magazine or other media magazine, a Bible, a strip of paper with Philemon verses 4-7, Ruth 1:15-18 or 2 Samuel 23:13-17 written on it; gingerbread-man cookies or people-crackers; and, for each person, a "7 Important Friendship Qualities" handout, a slip of paper and a deflated balloon.

BEFORE THE MEETING

Read the meeting and collect supplies.

Decorate the walls of the meeting area with colored posterboard shapes of a sun with "bright, happy times" written on it, a half-moon with "quiet, thoughtful times," a star with "times to share dreams and goals," a rain cloud with "stormy, hard times" and a rainbow with "times of promise and hope."

Set up a collage-making table with magazines, scissors, glue and construction paper or newsprint.

NOTES TO THE LEADER

During the meeting, realize that while some junior highers in the group may have many friends both at church and school, others may have only a few. The young people will bring a variety of feelings about friendship. Be sensitive to those who haven't experienced many good friendships.

100

Listing qualities of friendship may be difficult for some kids; qualities of friendship are intangible. By encouraging junior highers to compare friendship to elements of weather as well as look at media and Bible friends, you'll help them develop a tangible framework in which to identify friendship qualities. Junior highers think more easily about the abstract when they can compare it to something concrete.

During the body-painting affirmation exercise, have designated sponsors and group members watch for any body figure that doesn't get many colors and notes; the watchers can quietly alert others to fill them in so no one feels hurt.

You may hear giggles or sense uneasiness during the closing friendship celebration because it is an unusual posture. But keep it—it's a good way to provide kids with non-threatening touch and also to help them concentrate on friendship qualities.

THE MEETING

1. *A friendly welcome*—Play friendship songs as kids arrive.

Have each group member use a marker to write his or her name on a stick-on name tag (with a colored sun, half-moon, star, rain cloud or rainbow on it) and wear it.

Then direct each person to a table to work on a friendship collage. Group members are to glue pictures and words from magazines on construction paper or newsprint to illustrate what a friend is like. For example, a collage might have a car to show that a friend is dependable or a band instrument to show how well a friend fits in. Group members could also include items that indicate places friends go: a bowling ball to show they spend time together bowling, or a movie ad to show they often go to movies.

Group members may work individually on the collages or they may join others who are already working.

2. *Qualities of friendship*—When the collages are finished, tape them onto a wall. Tell members to break into small groups of three to six persons according to the colored symbols on their name tags: all orange suns form a group; all purple rain clouds; and so on. Make sure you have one adult in each small group.

Tell the groups to each think of ways their particular symbol represents an aspect of friendship. Say: "You can compare relationships to the weather: Often there are bright, happy times (point to the sun on the wall); quiet, thoughtful times (the half-moon); times to share dreams and goals (the star); stormy, hard times (the rain cloud); and times of promise and hope (the rainbow). Think about the time of friendship your group's symbol represents, and talk about the qualities of a friend that are meaningful to you during a time like that.''

Make sure the adult in each group understands the task. For example, the "rain cloud" group might think of qualities such as listens to me, doesn't judge, sticks around even when things don't go well, etc.

After a few minutes, give scissors and 15 sheets of construction paper to each small group. Ask each group to cut out 15 construction-paper shapes of the symbol on its members' name tags. (A group would cut circles for suns, half-circles for half-moons, stars for stars, blobs for clouds *or* arcs for rainbows.) Then have each group's members write on five of the symbol-shapes important friendship qualities they thought of while working on the collages and discussing the friendship-time represented by their particular symbol. They should write one quality per symbol-shape.

Collect the five qualities from each group.

Now instruct the groups to each think about "media friends" they know—TV characters who are friends, for example. Give each group a recent TV Guide, People Magazine or some other media publication to help members get started. Ask members of each group to discuss and then choose five more friendship qualities they think of with media friends in mind. Have them write these qualities on five of their symbol-shapes.

Collect these five qualities from each group.

Finally, give each group a Bible and a slip of paper with one of these Bible friendship passages written on it: Philemon verses 4-7; Ruth 1:15-18; 2 Samuel 23:13-17.

Have the small groups read their Bible passages and discuss what's happening in them. Have them think together about friendship qualities of the people in the passages as well as some people in your church. Once again have them choose five qualities and list them on their symbol-shapes.

Collect the last five qualities from each group. Place all the symbol-shapes in a container such as a collection plate, and set the container in the middle of the room.

3. *A look at yourself*—Change the atmosphere by playing upbeat music in the background. Supply masking tape, scissors and string. Tell everyone to tape the symbol-shapes onto string and, if possible, tape the string onto the ceiling—if not, then onto walls, furniture or anything else. The bright-colored qualities of friendship should hang at eye level all around the room.

Give everyone a "7 Important Friendship Qualities" sheet. Have markers available. Tell group members to wander around the room and look at all the friendship qualities listed on the hanging symbol-shapes; have each person choose seven qualities he or she considers most important and list them on the sheet. Tell group members they have three minutes.

---

7 Important Friendship Qualities

1._____ ○

2._____ ○

3._____ ○

4._____ ○

5._____ ○

6._____ ○

7._____ ○

After the three minutes, have group members get back into the same small groups.

Ask group members to each rate themselves on the seven qualities they listed. They should put a happy face (☺) in the circle next to a quality they personally feel good about; a sad face (☹) in the circle next to a quality they don't feel good about; and an I-don't-know face (😕) in the circle next to a quality they're not sure how to rate themselves on. For example, next to "fun-loving," a member may put a happy face to show he or she always enjoys a fun time; next to "a good listener," he or she may put a sad face to show a need to work on better listening skills; next to "likes to spend a lot of time together," he or she may put an I-don't-know face while thinking of how much time is also spent alone.

Have group members each tell their small group the qualities they ranked with happy faces and with sad faces—and why. Remind everyone to be a good listener—*no disagreeing or negative comments*—during this serious time.

Provide slips of paper and deflated balloons. Say: "Now, each of you choose one sad-face quality you want to improve. Write your name and that quality on your slip of paper. Fold the paper so it's small, put it into a balloon, blow up and tie the balloon."

Have group members each tell their small groups which quality they decided to work on. Have the small group members discuss ways to develop those qualities. Have the adults lead their groups in a brief time of prayer supporting each person's desire to improve in friendship.

When the small groups are finished praying, have everyone throw the balloons into the center of the meeting area. Tell group members to be careful not to break any.

4. *Body painting—an affirmation exercise*—Provide newsprint and crayons. Have group members create for each person a life-size body tracing on a roll of newsprint, or a cutout gingerbread-man-shaped figure from a sheet of newsprint. Have each group member write his or her name on the head of the figure. Tape the figures onto the walls.

Say: "It's time to show appreciation for friends here in the group. Think about the positive 'colors' of friendship. For example, hot pink could mean a friend is 'off the wall'; red could mean a friend is full of energy; yellow could mean a friend always sees the bright side of things."

Play music and allow time for kids to go around the room and add colors of friendship to everyone's body figures. Also tell them to write the reason for the color they add. For example, a person might color someone's body figure red on the foot and then write over it in black "full of energy."

5. *Friendship celebration*—Have all group members (and adults) lie on the floor on their backs, hold hands and form a circle with their heads in the center like spokes of a wagon wheel. Place the balloons on the floor in the center of the circle.

104

Tell everyone to look up at all the different qualities of friendship hanging from the ceiling or around the room. Say: "Just as Jesus is a special friend, God gives a special gift of friendship to people who love him. Listen to the words of this song as you think about the friendships you have with people in this room."

Play "Friends" by Michael W. Smith. (Two other suggestions: "Candle on the Water" by Helen Reddy and "Bridge Over Troubled Water" by Simon and Garfunkel.)

When the song is over, tell group members to each take a moment to pray silently for help in improving the friendship quality they decided to work on.

Challenge them to show appreciation for friends more often. Say: "When the music begins again, stand up and get a balloon from the center of the room. Get a balloon that's a different color from the one you had earlier. Pray for God's help for the person in improving the quality listed on the slip of paper inside. Wait until you get home to pop the balloon."

Play music, beginning with "Friends" again (or another of the suggestions). Serve gingerbread-man cookies or people-crackers for snacks to represent friends. For fun, ask group members to create a special friendship handshake or greeting. ∎

17 *Talk to Me*

By Kristine Tomasik

Most people might think junior highers have no trouble carrying on a conversation. Not so. Many junior highers experience a period of painful shyness as they grow up. Plus many kids find themselves starting over again as the "new kid" due to family splits or moves.

Use this meeting to offer junior highers basic skills in simply talking to people. It will also let them know that God is always waiting for them to talk to him.

OBJECTIVES

Participants will:
- learn and practice basic conversational skills;
- identify and hear how to avoid comments that kill conversation; and
- discover that God is eager and waiting to carry on a conversation with them.

SUPPLIES

Gather a basketball, soccer ball or other bouncy midsized sports ball for every four to six group members; newsprint; markers; masking tape; two giant posterboard keys, one printed with "Be genuinely interested in the other person," and the other, "Ask questions"; four smaller posterboard keys to attach to the "Ask questions" key, labeled "Opinion question," "Information question," "Wild-card question" and "Follow-up question"; and, for each person, a pencil, a piece of paper and the "Conversation Keys" handout.

BEFORE THE MEETING

Read the meeting and collect supplies.

Place the six posterboard keys out of sight until the "Conversation Keys" section.

Think about conversation skills you've learned; add your own ideas to those given here. Then practice having a conversation with God. What did God say to you?

THE MEETING

1. *Hot-potato conversation*—Divide the group into smaller groups of four to six. Give each group a ball. Explain how to play: One person begins the game and the conversation by making a comment or asking a question. He or she bounces the ball to someone else, who must carry on the conversation by making a related statement or by asking a question. This second person then bounces the ball to a third person, who must also make a statement or ask a question that continues the conversation. If a player can't think of anything to say after five seconds, he or she is out. Continue until there's a winner in each group.

When the game is over, get the kids together and ask:

● How is talking to another person like our hot-potato game?

● Have you ever felt like you "dropped the ball" in talking with someone? What was that like?

● Why is it important to be able to talk to other people comfortably and naturally?

2. *Conversation killers*—Divide the group into pairs and have them present skits on the following conversation killers: whines, knives, mumbles, grunts, filibusters and any other conversation killers you want to portray. A sample skit might go like this: One person says, "Hey, hi, great day, isn't it?" to which the *mumbler* might reply, "Uhhhhh, ummmmm, yeah, like, well, aahh . . ." To a similar greeting the *whiner* might say, "Aww, it's not so great! Who knows, it'll probably rain soon." The grunter grunts, the knife thrower makes nasty comments and the filibusterer goes on and on and on until the other player tries to choke him or her. You get the idea.

3. *Conversation keys*—Get everyone together. Discuss briefly:

● Why do comments like the ones we just heard cut off conversation?

● What can you do to start a conversation and keep it rolling?

Let junior highers brainstorm conversation helps. Record their comments on newsprint, then incorporate them into the following talk. Print the main ideas on the newsprint as you speak.

Say: "There are some keys to good conversation I'd like to share with you. The first conversation key is to *be genuinely interested in the other person.* (Tape the first key onto the wall.) Really care. Nobody likes to talk to someone who doesn't pay attention or show a sincere interest.

"The second conversation key is to *ask questions.* (Tape the second key onto the wall.) Conversation can fall flat if you make a comment and the other person has no response except 'Oh' or 'Uh' or 'That's interesting.' Asking questions gets the other person involved, and before you know it you're both really talking to each other.

"Some questions work better than others to start a conversation and keep it rolling. Stay away from questions that can be answered with 'yes' or 'no' because the conversation will dead-end. Then you have to start again.

"So, instead, ask *opinion* questions. (Tape the third key onto the wall.) You might ask: 'What do you think of (name a popular musician)?' or 'How do you like Pizza Hut?'

"Ask *information* questions. (Tape the fourth key onto the wall.) Ask: 'What's your favorite thing to do on Saturday afternoon?'; 'Tell me about the school you just moved from'; or 'What are your brothers and sisters like?'

"You could even ask *wild-card* questions. (Tape the fifth key onto the wall.) Say: 'If someone gave you a free plane ticket to anywhere in the world, where would you go?' "

Give each person a "Conversation Keys" handout and a pencil. Ask kids to rewrite the yes or no questions to one of the other kinds of questions.

After kids have completed the handouts, talk about a few of their rewrites. Of course, there aren't right or wrong ways to reword these questions—they could be rephrased any number of ways.

108

Conversation Keys

Reword these questions to help keep a conversation rolling. Change these yes or no questions to an opinion, information or wild-card question. The first one is done for you.

Opinion—"What do you think of," "How do you feel about," "How do you like?"

Information—"Tell me about," or any questions beginning with "Who," "What," "Where," "When" or "How."

Wild card—"If _____ then _____?"

1. Do you like (name a popular TV show)? You could reword this to: What do you think of (name a popular TV show)?

2. Are you going to the basketball game Friday night?

3. Do you like going fishing on your summer vacation?

4. Do you get along with your brothers and sisters?

5. Did you just move here?

6. Don't you wish you had a million dollars?

4. *Talk to me, Round 1*—Have kids each pair off with someone they don't know well and practice conversing. They should remember to be genuinely interested in each other, and to use questions to keep the conversation rolling.

Let kids talk for about five minutes, then discuss:
● How did your conversation go?
● What did you learn about carrying on a conversation?
● What did you learn about each other?

5. *Talk to me, Round 2*—Point out that kids can use *follow-up* questions to continue drawing out a person once a conversation-starter question has been asked. (Tape the sixth key onto the wall.) Follow-up questions include: "Why do you say that?"; "Will you tell me more?"; "What do you mean?"; "Can you give me an example?"

Have kids choose new partners and practice talking to each other using conversation-starter questions and follow-up questions.

After five minutes, discuss the three questions from Round 1 again.

6. *Talking to God*—Say: "God is always ready and willing to talk with us. But sometimes we don't know how to start the conversation or carry it on. Yet talking with God isn't much different than talking with a friend. We can ask God questions about things we wonder about or things that bother us. And, we have to be interested enough to really *listen* so we can hear what he says."

Give kids paper and invite them to each write or doodle a conversation between themselves and God. Point out that putting the conversation on paper will help them realize that God really is talking with them.

Suggest they begin the conversation by asking a question. Then they should listen carefully to hear what God says in return. If they don't understand something God says, they should ask him to explain further.

Participants can write their conversation in two-part dialogue, cartoon bubbles or any other way they want.

Close by inviting anyone who wants to, to share his or her conversation. ▪

18 When Friends Clique

By Katie Abercrombie

Close friendships are good for junior highers. A circle of friends offers acceptance, people to do things with and people to identify with—at a time when fitting in is crucial.

But circles of friends become cliques when they leave out others. And cliques aren't good for youth groups.

Use this meeting to help junior highers learn how to have close friendships while also reaching out to new friends.

OBJECTIVES

Participants will:

● experience and discuss how it feels to be included and excluded;

● look at positive and negative characteristics of cliques, and different kinds of cliques;

● explore what the Bible teaches about cliques;

● evaluate how they relate to other people; and

● think of ways to reach out and include others in their circles of friends.

SUPPLIES

Gather 6-inch-diameter construction-paper circles in different colors, four of each color, enough for all group members except three; three 6-inch-diameter construction-paper circles of colors different from the others; markers; masking tape; five large sheets of newsprint cut into circles with one of these incomplete sentences written on each: I tried to get into a circle of friends by . . ., We tried to keep someone out of our circle by . . ., When I was excluded from a circle or circles, I felt . . ., Leaving someone out of our circle made me feel . . ., When I realized I couldn't get into a circle, I . . .; paper; five Bibles; five 3×5 cards, each with one of these Bible references written on it: Mark 2:13-17, Luke 7:36-50, Luke 19:1-10, John 4:4-10, John 8:2-11; a large stack of magazines; five pairs of scissors; five containers of glue; 10 deflated balloons; string; smiling-face cookies; and, for each person, an "Open and Closed Circles—A Self-Evaluation" handout and a pencil.

BEFORE THE MEETING

Read the meeting and collect supplies.

Choose three group members with high self-esteem to be the ones who are left out in the first activity. Warn them ahead of time so they won't feel humiliated and will understand what's happening.

Tape the five circles of newsprint with the incomplete sentences onto the wall.

Brainstorm characteristics of groups, what makes them open to others or closed and harmful. Also think about different types of closed circles so you can help the junior highers think about them.

THE MEETING

1. Closed circles—As junior highers arrive, give them each a construction-paper circle as a name tag. Give your pre-chosen group members the odd-colored construction-paper circles. Ask junior highers to write their names on their name tags with the markers and then tape the name tags onto their shirts.

Begin the meeting by having the kids form groups according to the color of their name tags—blue with blue, green with green, and so on. When groups are formed, the three pre-chosen junior highers will be left out.

Tell the group that this meeting deals with cliques—circles of friends that actively exclude some people. Ask them to pretend that their small groups are cliques or closed circles. Tell the left-out group members to each try to get into a group. Tell the groups to actively exclude them by forming tight circles, turning their backs on them, walking away from them, ignoring them or doing anything else that isn't physically or verbally harmful. Let the left-out kids try to get into the circles until you call time, after three minutes.

2. *Feelings discussion*—Have group members sit in a circle. Ask them to look at the newsprint circles on the wall and think about how they'd complete the sentences. Say that not all of the sentences apply for everyone. Read the sentence beginnings aloud one at a time and discuss them. Write several endings for each sentence in the appropriate circle.

Summarize what the group discussed. Focus especially on how a left-out person feels and how he or she responds to being left out.

3. *Clique characteristics*—Have junior highers form small groups of three by each joining two other kids with different-colored name tags. (Each small group has three colors.) Hand out paper and a pencil to each group. Explain that although cliques can be harmful, particularly for people who aren't included, circles of friends also have good characteristics. Give the small groups three minutes to brainstorm and list six traits of cliques. Tell them some of the traits should be positive and some should be negative.

After the three minutes, have small groups take turns reading their characteristics, one per turn. Junior highers should applaud when they hear a characteristic they think is positive, and they should boo when they hear one they think is negative. Some may be both! Discuss: "What did you learn about circles of friends? What can you be careful of in your circle of friends? Do you feel mostly good or bad about cliques? Explain."

4. *Kinds of cliques*—A typical junior high school has a number of cliques: athletes, surfers, intellectuals, student-government types. Ask group members to each think of the cliques at their schools and think of a way to mime (act out without words) one of them. Have each person take a turn and act out a type of clique while the other group members guess what the person is miming. The first person to guess correctly becomes the next mime. If that person already has had a turn, let him or her choose who goes next.

5. *A look in the Bible*—There are many instances in the Bible where Jesus befriends or shows compassion for someone who isn't generally accepted. Divide the group into five groups. (If you have a small group, use only two or three of the Bible passages and divide kids into two or three groups.) Give each group a Bible and a scripture reference written on a 3×5 card. Have each group read its passage and then prepare a short skit to present the passage's meaning in terms of cliques. Allow about 10 minutes for groups to create the skits.

Have the groups present their skits. Read John 13:34 aloud. Discuss what Jesus might say about cliques and how cliques include some people but exclude others.

6. *Balloon collages*—Have junior highers stay in their skit groups. Hand out magazines, scissors, glue and two deflated balloons to each group. Instruct each group to make two balloon collages by blowing up the balloons, cutting out pictures, words and phrases from the magazines and gluing them onto the balloons. Tell groups that one balloon should represent cliques that don't reach out to other people. For example, it might show people who all look alike doing things while others are left out; or some of the things that help people belong to a clique; or the feelings of people who are "out" of a clique; or ways people are excluded. Tell groups to make their other balloon show circles of friends that include other people. For example, it might show ways circles of friends reach out to others; the feelings of people who are welcomed into a circle; or the feelings of people who reach out.

After the small groups have finished their balloons, give them each a few minutes to tell the large group about their balloons. Then use string and tape to hang all the balloons from the ceiling.

7. *A look at myself*—Give everyone an "Open and Closed Circles—A Self-Evaluation" handout and a pencil. Explain you'd like group members to take a little time to think about how they relate to other people and whether they encourage open or closed circles. Ask junior highers to answer all the questions on their handouts and score themselves according to the directions at the bottom. Say they won't have to tell all the results of their questionnaires. But do ask group members to each choose an area where they do well at encouraging openness among circles of friends, and an area where they'd like to improve. Ask group

Open and Closed Circles—A Self-Evaluation

This questionnaire will help you think about whether you and your friends tend to form open or closed circles. Answer the questions as honestly as possible. Check "yes," "maybe" or "no" for each. Then score yourself according to the instructions at the bottom.

	YES	MAYBE	NO
1. All my friends and I spend time together doing the same things.	___	___	___
2. I have many different friends.	___	___	___
3. My friends and I all dress alike.	___	___	___
4. When I'm with a group of people, I look for people who might be feeling lonely or left out and try to make friends with them.	___	___	___
5. When I see a new person being included in my circle of friends, I feel jealous.	___	___	___
6. I tend to do different activities with different people.	___	___	___
7. I'm embarrassed if my friends see me with someone they don't like.	___	___	___
8. I appreciate the different interests and hobbies my friends have, even when they aren't what I like.	___	___	___
9. I'm most comfortable doing things with the same people all the time.	___	___	___
10. I like to get to know new people.	___	___	___
11. I'm careful about who I introduce to my friends.	___	___	___
12. When I go to a party, I don't always know who I'll hang around with.	___	___	___
13. When I'm in a group of people, I stick mostly with my friends.	___	___	___
14. I go out of my way to make a new person feel welcome in my circle of friends.	___	___	___
15. My group of friends keeps me from having to meet and get to know new people.	___	___	___
16. When I meet someone who acts, dresses or talks differently from me and my friends, that just makes me want to get to know him or her even more.	___	___	___
17. I depend on my friends to give me something to do; I just sit around at home if we aren't doing anything together.	___	___	___
18. When I see someone whom everyone else doesn't like, I try to be nice to him or her and include that person in the conversation.	___	___	___
19. Certain behavior, clothing, and activities are acceptable to my circle of friends; not conforming to them could cause me to be left out.	___	___	___
20. If I brought a new person to a party with my friends, he or she would be welcome.	___	___	___

SCORING: For each question you answered "maybe," give yourself one point. For each odd-numbered question you answered "no," give yourself two points (no points for "yes"). For each even-numbered question you answered "yes," give yourself two points (no points for "no").

27-40 points: You tend to include others in your circle of friends. Keep it up!

14-26 points: You are in the "middle of the road." Although you can reach out, you may sometimes exclude others—perhaps without knowing it. Work on including new friends.

0-13 points: You tend to belong to a closed circle of friends. Concentrate on reaching out to new people and developing friendships outside of your group.

members to each write these two items on their name tag.

Divide the group into small groups of three. Have the small group members each tell why they chose the two areas on their name tag. Also have them discuss ways they can help each other as they try to improve.

8. *Open circles*—To symbolize that everyone is included in your youth group's open circle, have all group members sign each other's name tags. Then have them all put their arms around each other for a circle hug. Encourage junior highers to contact new or inactive group members and invite them to be part of your group.

9. *Friendly snacks*—Offer smiling-face cookies to represent "circles of friends" as junior highers head home. ■

Section Three:

FAMILY

19 Brothers and Sisters

By Kristine Tomasik

" "**M**y brother—what a creep!" "My sister—
she thinks she's 'Ms. Cool'!" Brothers
and sisters may seem to junior highers like the
bane of their existence. But since siblings are here
to stay, junior highers need to make peace with
their brothers and sisters.

Use this meeting to help junior highers see siblings as God's unique gifts—and that there's no
"better" or "worse" in the world of brothers and
sisters; only "different" and "special."

OBJECTIVES

Participants will:

● gain a new perspective on their brothers and sisters as
God's gifts;

● minimize sibling rivalry by seeing their own uniqueness
as well as their siblings' uniqueness; and

● begin to discover their larger family of Christian brothers
and sisters.

SUPPLIES

Gather toothpicks; construction paper; scissors; "doodads"
such as buttons, pins, nails, paper clips, rubber bands and bits of
yarn (just empty a junk drawer in your kitchen, office or work-
shop and you should have all you need); a sheet of newsprint
with the "My Favorite Gift," questions from activity #3 written
on it; paper; markers; a whistle, trumpet or other noisemaker;

three sheets of newsprint, each with "First group," "Second group" or "Third group" instructions from activity #4 written on it; blank newsprint; and, for each group member, a potato and a "Scriptural Brothers and Sisters" worksheet.

BEFORE THE MEETING

Read the meeting and collect supplies.

Think about your relationship with your own siblings. What were your biggest areas of conflict while growing up? How do any of those conflicts still exist today? How can you be at peace with your brother? your sister?

Call or visit any group members who don't have siblings. Tell them about the meeting, and encourage them to attend. Say they can think about a cousin or close friend as their brother or sister during the meeting.

THE MEETING

1. *Hello*—Welcome kids to the meeting and introduce the theme: brothers and sisters. Ask all those who have one brother or sister to raise their hand. Those who have two, three, and so on. Find out who has the most siblings, and give that person a big group cheer.

2. *Build a sibling*—Give each group member a potato. Make toothpicks, construction paper, scissors and doodads available. Say: "Every one of you has probably wished you could build your own brother or sister from scratch. Well, here's your chance! Create your ideal brother or sister. Give him or her all the qualities you wish he or she had." Turn kids loose and let them create their ideal siblings 'a la "Mr. Potato Head."

When kids are finished, let everyone explain his or her ideal brother or sister.

3. *The gift of brothers and sisters*—Say: "It might be nice if we got to pick our brothers and sisters. But then, we might end up making a bunch of 'Mr. Potato Heads.' So maybe it's just as well we don't get to choose our brothers and sisters. Instead, our brothers and sisters come to us as *gifts*—gifts from God."

Divide the group into small groups of four to six. Have an adult sponsor in each group. Ask small group members to each think of a favorite gift they got recently—perhaps for a birthday or at Christmas. Display the ''My Favorite Gift'' sheet of newsprint and have small group members answer the questions.

My Favorite Gift

- What's your favorite gift?
- How did you feel when you received it?
- Why do you like it so much?

Make the point that gifts are generally good—exciting—wonderful—something you look forward to and like.

Hand out paper and markers. Ask kids to each draw a gift their brother or sister reminds them of. Suggest that kids with more than one sibling draw a gift to represent the brother or sister they have the most trouble with right now. Have small group members each show their drawing and describe how their sibling is like that gift.

4. *I'm a gift, you're a gift*—For this activity, get the kids into groups of three or four. You'll switch them to new groups of three or four every six minutes or so. In each group, junior highers will discuss a different question. When time is up, blow a whistle, sound a trumpet (or use some other noisemaker) and yell ''Switch!'' Kids must regroup with completely new groups.

Get kids into their first groups of three or four and display these instructions on newsprint:

First group—Each show your gift drawings and complete this sentence: ''My brother/sister, (name), is a gift to me because . . .''

After six minutes or so, sound your noisemaker and yell ''Switch!'' Get kids into their second groups of three or four and display these instructions on newsprint:

Second group—Pass your gift drawings one person to the right. Using someone else's drawing, each of you now tell how your own brother or sister is like this gift. ''My brother/sister, (name), is like this gift because . . .'' Get your own drawings back.

Scriptural Brothers and Sisters

1. Read these Bible verses:

● "Be devoted to one another in brotherly [and sisterly] love" (Romans 12:10, NIV).

● "For God himself is teaching you to love one another. Indeed, your love is already strong toward all the Christian brothers [and sisters] throughout your whole nation. Even so, dear friends, we beg you to love them more and more" (1 Thessalonians 4:9-10, LB).

● "Make every effort to add to your . . . godliness, brotherly [and sisterly] kindness; and to brotherly [and sisterly] kindness, love" (2 Peter 1:5-7, NIV).

2. Answer these questions based on the above Bible verses—by drawing pictures. You don't have to be a great artist. Just draw them like cartoons.

● What's God saying about brothers and sisters in these verses?

● What difference would it make if you thought of other kids as your brothers and sisters in Christ? How would you treat them?

● What difference would it make if you thought of your flesh-and-blood brothers and sisters as brothers and sisters in Christ? How would you treat them?

Again, after six minutes or so, sound your noisemaker and yell "Switch!" Get kids into their third groups of three or four, provide markers and display these instructions on newsprint:

Third group—Each turn over your drawing and make another gift drawing on the back to complete this sentence: "I am a gift to my brother or sister because . . ." Tell your group about your new drawing.

Conclude this activity by saying: "As you can see, brother-and-sister gifts come in all shapes and sizes. Each brother or sister—including you!—isn't better or worse than any other—only different. We're each special and unique, carefully packaged by God as a gift to the world. So we don't have to compare ourselves with our brothers and sisters or compete with them. We can just be ourselves."

5. *A larger family*—Point out that we all have more brothers and sisters than we think—a whole world full! In Christ, we're spiritual brothers and sisters. Have group members return to the small groups of four to six from activity #3. Hand out markers and the "Scriptural Brothers and Sisters" worksheets. Let kids complete their worksheets.

When kids have finished drawing the worksheet pictures, ask small groups to brainstorm ways to improve their relationships with their flesh-and-blood brothers and sisters. For example, "Don't do stuff you know will make them mad." Then ask all groups for their ideas and list them on newsprint. Have the whole group discuss which ideas will work best and why. Challenge group members to use some of these to improve their relationships with their brothers and sisters.

6. *Heading home*—Close by having group members each share one thing they learned about brothers and sisters. ■

20 Dealing With Anger

By Kurt Bickel

Uncontrolled anger can destroy family relationships. Marriage counselors David and Vera Mace say "you can't be loving when you're angry and you can't be angry when you're loving." It's important for young teenagers to learn to handle anger in healthy ways.

Use this meeting to help junior highers identify and choose positive responses to anger.

OBJECTIVES

Participants will:
- discuss ways they handle anger at home;
- identify three ways people handle anger;
- practice a positive approach to anger; and
- see how God deals with anger.

SUPPLIES

Gather lots of small deflated balloons; several large trash bags; two sets of large clothing (a shirt, pair of pants, hat and wig for each set); a sheet of newsprint with the three responses to anger written on it; a straight pin; refreshments such as nuts, fruit or fresh juice; four chairs for the skit; and, for each person, three 3×5 cards, a pencil, a "Dealing With Anger" handout and a "Rocky Concert" handout. Optional: video camera, videocassette recorder and TV-screen monitor.

BEFORE THE MEETING

Read the meeting and collect supplies.

Ask two adult sponsors and two group members to prepare to perform the "Forgiveness Skit" at the end of the meeting. Give them copies of it.

THE MEETING

1. *A fun welcome*—As kids arrive, invite them to help you blow up the small balloons and put them in large trash bags. Hold informal "blow-up" races.

2. *"You Can't Fool Me"*—Divide the group into two teams for this game. Give each team a set of large clothing and say to create a team mascot by stuffing balloons into the clothes. Encourage team members to use as many balloons as possible.

Give each group member three 3×5 cards and a pencil. Ask kids to remember times when they've gotten angry with family members, and each choose three particular incidents. For each incident, they should write on one side of a 3×5 card what happened to make them angry and, on the other side, how the story ended or what they did about their anger.

Display the newsprint with the three responses to anger written on it.

Three Responses to Anger

1. BLOW UP: Shout and argue in rage.

2. BOTTLE UP: Give in, walk away or silently try to get over it.

3. STEP UP: Say you're angry but you won't take it out on that person, and ask for a chance to talk.

Have the two teams line up on opposite sides of the room and face each other. You get a straight pin and stand in the middle of the room with the two team mascots next to you.

Begin the game: Have a member from the first team read an incident from a 3×5 card. Let members of the second team consult and guess how they think the person responded—by blowing up, bottling up or stepping up. Then have the person turn over the card and tell the story's actual ending. Determine whether it was a blow-up, bottle-up or step-up response. If the second team guessed wrong, pop a balloon from its mascot.

124

Rocky Concert

Bobby (guy or girl) comes home with two or three friends (guys or girls). The family is all gathered watching television—Mom and Dad and one or two brothers and (or) sisters. Bobby wants to go to a rock concert with his friends. He has to ask his parents for permission and for $15 to buy the ticket.

The parents are concerned: Mom talks about the cost being too high. Dad says things about the concert being a bad place to be. Drugs, crowds, strange people. He isn't fond of rock music.

The friends try to help. They tell about their parents taking them. One says he has gone many times before, and nothing happened.

The parents still won't change their minds. They repeat their concerns.

Now little brother and sister make the situation worse: One says Bobby asked them to get the $15 out of their piggy banks. "If Bobby gets to go, we want to go too."

Mom and Dad agree that it's unfair for one to get to go to a concert while the other children stay home.

Bobby says it's unfair to treat him like a little kid. Just then the little brother/sister says, "I'll bet Mom and Dad didn't know you already went to a rock concert. You went the time you were supposed to be at the campout with your friends . . . "

Dealing With Anger

Anger is a normal, healthy emotion. If you don't get angry, you're not alive. There's no need to feel guilty or embarrassed about anger; you can't decide whether or not to be angry.

But once the anger is there, you can decide what to do about it. The Bible says, "Do not let the sun go down on your anger" (Ephesians 4:26, RSV). Anger can be controlled.

Some people think that venting anger gets rid of it. But "blowing up"—angrily ranting and raving—only produces more anger.

Another way some people handle anger is to "bottle it up." They train themselves to hide anger. But the anger just simmers inside of them and makes them sad and depressed.

A positive way to deal with anger is to "step up to it":

● **Step 1**—Announce that you're angry, but don't try to explain your anger. That only makes things worse.

● **Step 2**—Tell the person you're angry with that you won't take out your anger on him or her.

● **Step 3**—Ask to talk with that person. Make sure you cool down first so you'll be able to talk about the problem.

Forgiveness Skit

Characters: Mother; Father; Karen, an older sister with a drivers license; and Ron, a junior higher.
Setting: the breakfast table.

Mother: Good morning, honey. Would you like some coffee?

Father: Yes, and make it black!

Mother: You didn't sleep last night either, did you?

Father: No, I didn't. I was up all night tossing and turning, worrying about Karen and her car accident.

Mother: How could she be so stupid?

Father: I'm sure it doesn't come from my side of the family. Well, it's time to get the kids up. Let's discuss it over breakfast.

Mother and Father: Kids, wake up. Come on, it's time to eat! Hurry on down here. Karen, come down here at once.

Ron: Hi, Mom. Hi, Dad. Let's hurry up and eat. I don't want to miss Sunday school.

Mother: Well, it's all ready. As soon as Karen comes, we can eat.

(Karen comes in, walking slowly, looking dejected. She slumps into her chair.)

Father: Let's pray.

(Father begins leading a unison prayer and others join in, saying it quickly.)

Father: Karen, I'm really angry with you. It's bad enough to have a car accident, but what in the world possessed you to leave the scene of the accident? What was in that head of yours? Can't you understand that you got yourself and the whole family in a pile of trouble? The insurance rates are going to go up. You may never be able to drive again. Karen, I just can't believe it. Don't you know that when an accident happens, you have a legal responsibility to stay at the scene?

Mother: *(chiming in with anger)* I thought they taught you that stuff in drivers ed. Karen, we just have to think of some punishment for you to make you realize the seriousness of this situation.

Father: Karen, don't just sit there! Don't you have anything to say for yourself? You owe us an explanation.

Karen: I'm sorry, Mom and Dad. I didn't mean to wreck the car. But when it happened I became so afraid. I was afraid of you. I was afraid of the police. I just wanted to run and hide. I feel terrible. I'm sorry I let you down.

Father: Karen, in this situation "sorry" is just not good enough. Not only do I have to pay for our car, I have to pay for the Joneses' car too. We'll also be paying for insurance. Plus, you might even lose your license.

Mother: Karen, we have to punish you for what you've done wrong.

Ron: Mom, what's seven times 70?

Mom: 490.

Father: I thought you were doing your Sunday school lesson, not your math lesson. Let me see that.

(Father reads silently at first, then begins reading aloud.)

Father: Then Peter came to Jesus and asked, "Lord, if my brother keeps on sinning against me, how many times do I have to forgive him? Seven times?" "No, not seven times," answered Jesus, "but 70 times seven."

(Everyone pauses and looks at each other.)

Father: Karen, we know that you feel bad and we're glad that you're sorry. We forgive you.

(Dad hugs Karen. Mother comes over behind Karen and Dad.)

Ron: Hey, what's going on here? Come on, you guys. Aren't you all going to Sunday school?

Father: Yes, let's go together as a family.

(All exit.)

126

Next have a member from the second team read an incident, and so on. Continue play until one mascot is totally deflated, all the cards are used or a time limit has been reached.

3. *Snack time*—Enjoy a healthy snack of nuts, fruit or fresh juice.

4. *Talking about anger*—Have group members form groups of six or less, each with an adult sponsor. Distribute the "Dealing With Anger" handouts. Have small group members read and discuss the information, paraphrased from David and Vera Mace's system of dealing with anger.

5. *Role plays*—Divide the group into three groups, each with an adult sponsor. Say you're going to role play the three different anger responses for the same situation. Designate the "blow-up group," the "bottle-up group" and the "step-up group."

Give each person a "Rocky Concert" handout. Let groups each cast their own characters, practice the beginning of the situation and create their own appropriate endings.

Have the groups, one by one, perform their role plays. To add to the excitement, videotape them. Then play the videotapes back and have group members return to their small groups of six or less from activity #4 to discuss the different outcomes. Encourage kids to choose the step-up approach to anger in their lives.

6. *Forgiveness skit*—Close by having the four pre-chosen people perform the "Forgiveness Skit." ■

21 Good Things Come in Family Packages

By Kristine Tomasik

When they reach junior high, most kids probably wonder why anyone tries to live in a family. The teenage years create special stress for both the young people and parents.

Despite this, the family remains the "home base" for a young person's sense of identity and well-being.

Use this meeting to help kids find and focus on the good in their own families.

OBJECTIVES

Participants will:
- hear positive features of families;
- discuss ways to honor their families;
- tell good things about their families; and
- have an opportunity to give thanks for their families.

SUPPLIES

Gather Twister boards (or make them—see "Before the Meeting" notes), one for every four group members; special Family Twister cards (see "Before the Meeting" notes); newsprint; masking tape; markers; on newsprint, outlines of these kinds of trees: oak, willow, beech; brown construction paper cut in the shape of a branch or a strip of newsprint with a branch drawn on it; and, for each person, an 8½ × 11 piece of paper, a crayon and a green construction-paper leaf.

BEFORE THE MEETING

Read the meeting and collect supplies.

If you don't have Twister boards, make them: Use markers to color in red, blue, yellow and green squares on old white sheets or dropcloths. Draw the squares in this pattern:

Prepare the Family Twister cards: On separate 3 × 5 cards, write "Move right hand to red—families give love and care"; "Move right hand to blue—families are a place to come home to"; "Move right hand to yellow— families are friends"; and "Move right hand to green—families feed you." Repeat the four colors and family statements for left hand, right foot and

Twister Board Pattern

R	R	R	R	R	R
B	B	B	B	B	B
Y	Y	Y	Y	Y	Y
G	G	G	G	G	G

left foot. You should have 16 cards in all. (Feel free to think up additional positive statements about families for the cards.)

Think about how you'll explain the meaning of the "Honor your father and your mother" commandment's promise (Exodus 20:12, RSV).

Tape the three tree outlines onto the wall.

Tape the construction-paper branch or branch drawn on a strip of newsprint onto the wall.

NOTES TO THE LEADER

As you plan the meeting, think about your junior highers' family situations. Be sensitive to those whose families are having more than their share of problems.

During the meeting, emphasize that everything doesn't have to be rosy for kids to see some good about their families. Your goal is to break down "My family is *awful*" thinking and replace it with "There *are* some good things about my family, after all!"

THE MEETING

1. *Family Twister*—Kids love the game Twister. Play this version, Family Twister, to introduce the theme of the meeting.

Have junior highers begin by standing on any color squares. Fit four kids onto each board. Randomly choose your cards. When you call out the cards, kids have to change positions—until they're all tangled up! With each card, you'll be reading a positive function of families, so kids will begin to think about families in a good way.

After the game, say: "Sometimes we have to stretch to see what's good about families—just like we did in this game." Discuss: "What are some other good things families do for their members?"

2. *Honor your family*—Ask how many group members know the Ten Commandments. Ask if anyone knows which one has a promise attached to it: "Honor your father and your mother, that your days may be long in the land which the Lord your God gives you" (Exodus 20:12, RSV). Explain how the promise is meaningful for kids now. Suggest that this commandment is saying to honor families.

Briefly talk about what it means to honor someone. Have kids name things they can do to honor someone. List ideas on newsprint. Then have the group define what it means to honor someone. Write the definition on newsprint also. Point out that among other things it means finding and saying the best about someone. Ask: "Is it a lie to say good things about someone you're not always happy with? Why or why not?" Point out that every family member has some good traits, and it's good to focus on those.

Say: "The promise attached to the commandment—longer life—isn't magic. It's simply a natural result. If you find the best about your family, you'll feel more at peace. Not that anyone's family is perfect! But it's better for your health, and everyone else's, if you focus on the positive."

3. *Family storytelling*—Divide the group into small groups of three or four. Have small group members share stories of good things about their families. Tell them to keep their stories short—about one minute long. Tell them the first topic: the most fun you recently had with your family. Every four to seven minutes, create new small groups to cover these other story topics:

● the thing you're proudest of about your family;

● the most ridiculous or embarrassing thing that ever happened to your family; and

● one thing that's special about each member of your family, including the pet(s).

4. *Family trees*—Say: "Just as there are many kinds of trees, there are many kinds of families. And each family is unique." Briefly describe the qualities of some trees: oaks are strong and mighty; willows are graceful and sometimes sad-looking; beech trees are peaceful and spreading.

Ask kids to each choose a tree to represent their family. Hand out the 8½ × 11 paper and crayons. Have kids copy the outline of their kind of tree to make their own "family tree." They should each write or draw symbols on their tree to show what makes them proud of their family. They should also represent family members in words or symbols, perhaps as leaves, flowers, branches, roots, stems—maybe even a nut or two!

Tape the family trees onto the walls, and let everyone admire this gallery of families.

5. *Closing*—Give group members each a green construction-paper leaf. Have them each write on the leaf one sentence of thanks for their family. For example, "I'm thankful my family has a sense of humor." Gather everyone in a circle. Have kids, one by one, read their sentences as a closing prayer, then tape their leaves onto the branch on the wall.

Encourage kids to go home and enjoy their families! ■

22 Measuring Up

By Joani Schultz

‘‘**M**y mom thinks I never get good enough grades!’’

‘‘Why do my parents treat me like a baby when it comes to Saturday night curfew, then turn around and expect me to act like an adult all the time?’’

‘‘My parents say I gotta go to youth group, but they don’t do anything extra at church.’’

‘‘My dad wants me to be a basketball star—that’s what he was.’’

Parental expectations play a subtle, yet powerful role in junior highers’ lives. Striving to meet expectations—real or imagined—affects young people’s attitudes. In an extensive study of young teenagers and their parents, Search Institute found that nearly half of all young people want to talk more with their parents about how they get along together (49 percent) and what parents expect of them (47 percent).

Since junior highers need ways to open the doors of communication at home, use this meeting to help them explore parental expectations.

OBJECTIVES

Participants will:

● experience activities that show how parental expectations affect their lives;

● tell about times when their parents were pleased with them; and

● write letters explaining how they and their parents can better understand each other concerning expectations.

SUPPLIES

Gather six 6×9-inch Manila envelopes, each labeled with one of the following categories: friends, grades, church, family, opposite sex, me; 1-inch square sheets of white, blue and black construction paper, about six of each color per person; a sheet of newsprint with "White—too little, Black—too much, Blue—just right" written on it; masking tape; a Bible; and, for each person, a "Letter to My Parents" handout, a pencil and a stamped envelope.

BEFORE THE MEETING

Read the meeting and collect supplies.

Tape the six Manila envelopes in various places around the room.

NOTES TO THE LEADER

When discussing parental expectations, be prepared for a variety of feelings to surface: pressure, satisfaction, frustration, joy, disappointment. Remind young people that feelings aren't good or bad; it's how they act out feelings that's important. Challenge junior highers to express feelings, look deep within themselves and move toward positive action and communication at home.

Throughout the meeting, keep a positive attitude even if kids vent hostility or impatience. Remind them that no one is perfect. Not Mom. Not Dad. Not themselves. God placed families together for support and love—and *everybody* needs to work at that.

If some young people don't want the letters sent to their parents, let them say no. Remember that some kids may be experiencing conflict with one or both parents, and some may live in other than family settings.

THE MEETING

1. *Crazy expectations game*—Begin by asking each person to find a partner. Have the partners whose birthdays are closest to your meeting day stand on one side of the room; have the other partners stand across the room.

Say: "We're going to play a game. I'll say what I expect the teams to do. Then you must do what I expect as quickly as you can. Ready? Walk across the room."

Both teams will head toward each other, pass with some confusion in the center and end up at opposite sides of the room.

Continue giving expectations. Each time make the expectation a bit more demanding. For example, tell team members to hop on one leg or walk backward across the room. For variation, have kids choose partners from the members of their teams. Ask partners to link left arms and walk across the room while each uses only one foot; or walk with both arms interlocked; or walk back to back; or crawl piggyback-style. Be zany and make up some of your own crazy expectations!

2. *Getting into the theme*—Have the group members sit down. Say: "I expected you to do things that needed different levels of activity. Which do you prefer? Something simple or something challenging? Why?" Discuss answers.

Say: "We're going to look at expectations during our meeting—specifically, parents' expectations for kids. Sometimes we feel parents expect too little, neglect us or treat us like little children. Other times we feel they expect too much and we could never possibly meet those high expectations. Then there are times when what parents expect is just right! We're going to do an activity to see what you feel your parents expect from you."

3. *Expectation envelopes*—Point out the Manila envelopes labeled friends, grades, church, family, opposite sex, me, displayed around the room. Supply the sheets of colored construction-paper "ballots." Explain that each color will represent a feeling about expectations: White means parents expect too little. For example, it might seem that parents set no boundaries or rules and leave their kids to fend for themselves. Black means parents expect too much. For example, parents expect straight A's on a kid's report card because the older sister got straight A's. Blue means parents' expectations are just right. For example, parents expect Sunday afternoons to be "family" times—and the kids like that time together. Tape the sheet of newsprint with colors and meanings onto the wall.

Instruct the junior highers to walk around the room, look at the envelopes and place their ballots inside. They should each put one ballot into each envelope. After everyone's finished, divide the group into six groups. Give each group an envelope of ballots to tally according to color. After the group members have counted the ballots, they should decide which expectation is most common for each category.

Instruct each group to create a brief skit that shows an example of that expectation happening. For example, if grades got mostly black ballots, that small group might show a person coming home from school with an unsatisfactory report card. Have each group perform its skit. After each skit, ask the whole group: "Why do parents expect that? What makes you glad or sad about that expectation?"

4. *"This is my son; this is my daughter"*—For this activity, divide the group into small groups no larger than five, with an adult sponsor in each. Say: "We're going to talk about times when our parents were really happy with us. Even though expectations can be hard to deal with, there are times when expectations have positive effects. Here's a passage from the Bible about a father and a son." Read Matthew 3:16-17.

Say: "God said, 'This is my son, in whom I am well pleased.' Think of a time when one of your parents said to or about you, 'This is my daughter or son; I'm pleased with her or him because . . . ' Tell what made your parent happy and why. Also tell how that made you feel."

5. *Letter-writing*—After all members of the small groups have talked, distribute the "Letter to My Parents" handouts and pencils. Have each junior higher complete the letter. Remind group members that these letters will be read by their parents, so it's important to be serious and say the things they really feel and really want to talk about. Tell them these letters will provide a special chance to talk about expectations with parents.

Have each person, in the same small group of five or less, tell about an item from the letter for which he or she especially needs prayer support. Give kids permission to pass.

Hand out the stamped envelopes for junior highers to write

Letter to My Parents

Dear _____,

Letting you know my feelings isn't always easy. But there are some things I'd like to tell you.

First, I want you to know you're important to me because _____
_____.

I'm thankful for your _____.

At church, we talked about parents' expectations and how the first step to understanding is talking about them. Lately, I've felt your expectations of me have been _____.

Because of that, I often feel _____.

I want life at home to be _____.

So I need you to be _____.

And I want to be more _____.

If we work together, we can understand each other better. Let's talk about this letter (when and where) _____.

Then let's make a list of four practical things I can expect from you, and four practical things you can expect from me.

Love,

_____

their parents' name and address on. Have them place their letters in the envelopes and seal them. Collect them.

6. *Going home*—Have group members form a circle and join hands. Say: "Dealing with your parents' expectations isn't always easy. But the first step is talking with them. Take a risk. Make the first move. Take time to talk with your parents. In a day or two, they'll receive the letter you wrote. Use it to help you understand each other and communicate about expectations.

"As a youth group, it's important that we support each other. One way to do that is through prayer. Pray for the person on your right during our closing prayer. Be sure you know that person's name. We'll go around the circle and you can say 'Help Stan and his parents.' You can say more in your prayer if you feel comfortable." You begin the prayer.

When the circle prayer is completed, have one giant group hug.

Mail the letters as soon as possible. ■

23 Putting the Pieces Back Together

By Joani Schultz

Brokenness surrounds us. And junior highers aren't immune. Statistics prove you probably have group members who've experienced the pain of shattered home lives.

Use this meeting to reach out to kids in your group from broken homes.

OBJECTIVES

Participants will:
- identify feelings about their home situations;
- support each other through personal sharing and problem-solving;
- realize God's presence in their situations; and
- set personal goals for improvement.

SUPPLIES

Gather a paper bag; a metal container or coffee can; matches; a large newspaper cross; masking tape; and, for each person, a sheet of newspaper, three pieces of paper, a pencil and a Bible.

BEFORE THE MEETING

Read the meeting and collect supplies.

Decide the best way to use this meeting with the kids in your group who come from broken homes. Three options:

1. Meet at a special time, different from the regular junior high meeting. Have kids come by invitation only.

2. Use this meeting while the rest of the group meets on a different family emphasis.

3. Plan this meeting as a special-interest session during a junior high retreat.

NOTES TO THE LEADER

This special meeting has been designed for a group of eight or fewer. If your group is larger, divide it into smaller groups with an adult leader for each group.

Be prepared for all kinds of home situations: single-parent, stepparent, no parent, a parent living with a boyfriend or girlfriend, both natural parents who are fighting. As kids open up about their homes, listen with care. Don't judge, criticize or act shocked. Each situation is unique. Some kids feel frightened, confused or frustrated. Whatever their feelings, offer your support.

Realize kids are reluctant to talk about their broken homes. Frequently junior highers carry guilt, embarrassment or hurt. They don't want others to know they struggle. Encourage kids to discuss, but don't force them. Give each person the option to pass.

Be ready to refer kids to professional help if necessary. Acquaint yourself with family resources in your community such as Alcoholics Anonymous, Alateen, school support groups and professional counselors.

THE MEETING

1. *Knots*—Have everyone stand in a circle. Say: "Put your hands in the center of the circle. Grab and hold two different persons' hands—who aren't next to you. Now, without letting go, untangle yourselves." If group members quickly accomplish the task, have them do it again. Point out: "This activity is like family problems we experience sometimes. We get tangled up in frustrations; we need time and cooperation to work things out. During our meeting, we're going to work together and support each other."

2. *Newspaper symbols*—Give kids each a sheet of newspaper. Tell them to tear or shape their newspaper into a symbol that represents how they feel about their family. For example, someone might tear the newspaper into strips to show everyone's torn apart or crush it into a ball to show anger.

Go around the circle and have kids, one by one, explain their symbol to the group. Not only should they say what it is, but why they made it that way. Save the symbols for later.

3. *Dear Abby*—Give each person two pieces of paper and a pencil. Say: "We're going to support each other in a fun, anonymous way. Are you familiar with 'Dear Abby' in the newspaper? People write to her about their problems and she gives them suggestions. We're going to write to 'Dear Abby,' only the group members will give suggestions. Write two different problems or struggles you face with your family. Write one on each paper, and don't sign your name. After you've written your problems, fold them once and put them into this bag."

After the "Dear Abby" notes are in the bag, pass the bag around and have one person draw a problem and read it aloud. Then have group members respond. They can offer help, ideas, solutions and understanding. Continue this for all the problems in the bag. (If you're afraid kids will be embarrassed by someone recognizing handwriting, read the notes to the group yourself.) Kids will probably "claim" their problems if they trust the group.

Use this exercise as prime time for support and creative problem-solving. Be prepared to offer referrals or follow-up to any special problems.

4. *Scripture hope*—Place the large newspaper cross in the center of the group. Hand out Bibles and assign each person one of these Bible passages: Matthew 5:14-16; 11:28-30; Romans 8:31-32; 8:38-39; 12:17-21; 1 Corinthians 10:13; Ephesians 3:16-18; Hebrews 13:5b.

Give kids time to find and read their Bible passages. Have kids, one by one, each read their passage aloud and complete "The good news here for me is . . . " As kids finish sharing, have them tape their newspaper symbols onto the newspaper cross. Remind them that Jesus gives hope and new life in family situations.

5. *Personal goals*—Give each person a piece of paper. Make sure everyone still has a pencil. Have kids divide the pieces of paper into two columns: On one half they should write "One thing I want to get rid of . . . "; on the other half, "One thing I want to make new . . . " Have them each complete the sentences. Give suggestions such as "I want to get rid of my temper or bad attitude" or "I want to make new my relationship with my dad."

Ask kids to first tell what they want to get rid of. (Remember they have the option to pass.) After they've shared, have them each tear off that half of the page and "get rid of it," by throwing it into a metal container or coffee can and burning it.

Next, have kids tell what they want to make new. Have them place that paper around the cross as a symbol that Christ helps make things new.

6. *Thanksgiving*—Invite everyone to stand in a circle and join hands. Encourage kids to each offer a prayer of thanks for their family. Close with a group hug.

Ask junior highers to take their "new" commitment papers home as reminders of their desire and Christ's help to make things new. ∎

24 *Talking With Parents*

By Barry Gaeddert

" "**M**y parents don't listen to a word I say."
"I'm tired of asking my folks for permission; they always say no!"

"I couldn't tell my parents about that; they'd be furious."

Universally, teenagers and parents are a difficult combination. There seems to be a communication gap between young people and parents.

How can we encourage junior highers to open up—to talk more, share more, feel more—with their parents? The key is helping them learn to initiate communication.

Use this meeting to help your group members experience barriers in communication and find ways to overcome them.

OBJECTIVES

Participants will:

● experience communicating by building a project with or without barriers;

● understand that communication barriers exist and must be overcome;

● learn that parents and teenagers have equal responsibility to communicate with each other;

● see what the Bible says about communicating with parents; and

● plan practical ways to talk more freely with parents.

SUPPLIES

Gather paper; markers; straight pins; a variety of "building materials" such as macaroni, coat hangers, string, marshmallows, toothpicks, paper cups, yarn, chewing gum, Popsicle sticks, construction paper, glue, scissors and tape; several 3×5 cards, each with one of the barriers listed in activity #2 written on it; 10 to 15 large newsprint or construction-paper "bugs" (large ovals, each with a head and six legs); masking tape; three Bibles; and, for each person, a "Talking-With-Parents Evaluation Sheet," a "Talking-With-Parents Worksheet" and a pencil.

BEFORE THE MEETING

Read the meeting and collect supplies.

Tape the bugs onto the walls of your room at a height comfortable for junior highers to write on.

NOTES TO THE LEADER

Be aware that your group members probably come from a variety of home backgrounds. Some may live with one parent, some with two, some with stepparents, some with foster parents, maybe even some with grandparents or other relatives.

Encourage group members to relate the meeting to their own home situations. And avoid referring to a two-parent home as the norm; be sensitive to your young people.

THE MEETING

1. *Name tags*—As group members arrive, give them pieces of paper and markers. Have them each make a name tag by drawing a picture that represents their family. Suggest animals, birds, trees, places—anything. Have them pin on the name tags.

2. *A building project*—Divide the group into family units by putting them in pairs or threes. Assign roles of parent(s) and teenager within each group. Give family units a variety of building materials. Tell them they may construct anything they want to such as houses or animals, but they must fulfill their roles of parents and teenagers. Encourage them to "play it up" if they want; for example, teenagers could insist on building different things from what the parents want, or parents could assume the teenagers will do what the parents want.

Give several family units 3×5 cards, each with one of the following barriers written on it. Tell the family units they must still build their projects but they will need to overcome one of these problems:

● You must work without speaking to one another.

● You have only one builder; the other(s) give directions.

● You must separately construct parts of the whole, then put them together at the end.

● One family unit member must pretend to not hear anything said to him or her.

The idea is to get young people working as parents and teenagers, and to realize the importance of clear communication.

When the projects are built, have each family unit show its creation. Ask group members to tell about any frustrations they had while building.

Talking-With-Parents Evaluation Sheet

For each statement, circle the diagram that best represents your answer.

1. My parents and I really listen to each other.

2. My parents and I regularly tell each other what happened to us during the day.

3. My parents and I say good things about each other.

4. My parents and I ask questions to find out how each other is feeling.

Say: "You worked as parents and teenagers and had fun with some problems in communicating. Now let's discuss ways to talk more effectively with parents."

3. ***Evaluating how I talk with my parents***—Have group members sit together in a circle. Hand out the "Talking-With-Parents Evaluation Sheets" and pencils. Ask kids to be honest as they fill them out. When they've finished, discuss some answers to the questions. Tell group members their ideas are important and you're interested in what they have to say. Give everyone the chance to talk. Ask whether group members found anything surprising.

4. ***What bugs me***—Say: "You've evaluated how you communicate with your parents, but sometimes things happen so that you can't talk to Mom or Dad. Now it's time to say what 'bugs' you about situations like that. For example, it might bug you when you can't talk to your mom because she's worried about something, or when you can't talk to your dad because he has to work late."

Distribute markers and have group members move around the room and write what bugs them about communicating with parents on the bugs posted on the walls.

5. ***Reflecting***—This may be the longest part of your meeting. Gather group members back together in the circle. Get the bugs and read them. Let group members express any feelings that may come from the statements. Your goal here is not to have a gripe session, but to reflect on the fact that often it's difficult to open up to Mom or Dad.

Briefly discuss the role of responsibility in communicating; your goal here is to show that both teenagers and parents have a part in opening the lines of communication.

In your discussion, ask kids to reflect on some of these questions:

● What pressures are your parents under that may affect their communication with you?

● What can you do to help your parents through the pressures?

● Does Dad feel overworked? Does Mom? Explain.

● Is it difficult for your parents to work and be parents at the same time? Why or why not?

● Do you help the situation or make it worse? Explain.

144

Reverse Questions

Do your parents respect your rights? . . .
    Do you respect your parents' rights?
Do your parents listen to you? . . .
    Do you listen to your parents?
Do your parents trust you? . . .
    Do you trust your parents?
Are your parents friendly to you? . . .
    Are you friendly to your parents?

You may also want to ask "reverse questions" to show that teenagers can play important roles in talking with Mom and Dad. See the examples.

Again, your discussion should move toward the goal of letting kids see they *can* do many things to improve relationships with their parents.

6. *What does the Bible say?*—Ask group members if they know of any Bible verses that tell how to talk with parents. (You will probably hear the fifth commandment, "Honor your father and mother.") Say: "We're going to look at some verses. We'll see what the Bible does say."

Divide the group into three groups, each with an adult sponsor. Give each group a Bible.

Assign each group one of these passages: Ephesians 6:1-3; Colossians 3:17, 20; and Luke 2:41-52. Ask each group to read its passage and decide what it says about talking with parents. Does it give any rules? Does it set any examples?

Tell groups they must each present their verses' message to the other two groups. Allow several minutes for groups to create skits, commercials, songs or whatever to demonstrate the scripture messages.

When the groups are ready, have them "give their lessons" to the other groups. Make sure that the real messages come across. For example, in the Luke 2 passage, the emphasis should be on Jesus' decision to be obedient to his parents—not on the fact that he forgot to tell his parents where he was going.

To reinforce the learning, have each group do a superfast "instant replay" of its presentation while you paraphrase the message.

7. *What will I do?*—Praise the junior highers for their presentations. Have them remain in their groups.

Say: "I hope you've gained some insight about talking with your parents. You know, many barriers do exist, and we all have responsibility to work through them. Being honest with Mom and Dad about your feelings is the best place to start."

Hand out the "Talking-With-Parents Worksheet." Ask group members to fill in their answers privately and to take the sheets home. Encourage them to look at the sheets once or twice during the week and try to do what they say.

Talking-With-Parents Worksheet

Complete each sentence.

1. One barrier that stops me from having the best conversations with my parents is:

2. One thing I can do to help overcome that barrier is:

3. An area where I need to be more understanding of my parents is:

4. Three ways I could be more helpful or spend more time with my parents are:

5. To help improve communication with my parents, this week I will:

Close the meeting with prayer. Invite junior highers to share in the prayer time by thanking God for their parents or asking for help to be able to talk with them more effectively. ■

25 *Walk a Mile in Parent Shoes*

By Kristine Tomasik

Parents and junior highers live in different worlds. And, unfortunately, few kids are inclined to think about their parents' world and try to understand it.

Use this meeting to help your group members develop empathy for their parents' point of view. Give junior highers a chance to "walk a mile in parent shoes."

OBJECTIVES

Participants will:
- describe differences between their world and their parents' world;
- discover that God has already "walked a mile" in their shoes and understands them;
- put themselves in their parents' shoes through role playing; and
- brainstorm five rules for parents and five rules for themselves in parent-teenager relationships.

SUPPLIES

Gather teenage magazines such as Seventeen and TIGER BEAT; scissors; glue; record or cassette tape of the sound track from *E.T.* or *STARMAN* (or another more current movie about someone from outer space); turntable or cassette player; magazines adults read such as LIFE, TIME, Good Housekeeping, and Better Homes and Gardens; a Bible; newsprint; markers; for every four to six group members, two large sheets of posterboard; and, for every four or five group members, a "Role-Play Situations" handout.

BEFORE THE MEETING

Read the meeting and collect supplies.

Think back on your own relationship with your parents during your junior high years. What "cultural" barriers did you face in communicating with them? Think of ways you can help today's kids gain empathy for their parents.

THE MEETING

1. The extraterrestrials are coming—Say: "Imagine you meet an extraterrestrial—a creature from outer space. You have to try to explain your life and customs to him. What differences could you name between his life and yours?"

Have kids get into small groups of four to six. Give each group one large sheet of posterboard. Make the teenage magazines, scissors and glue available. Tell the groups to make posters of the aspects of their lives they'd have to explain to the star-person. For example, junior high earthlings would have different food, language, houses, clothes, music and hobbies from an extraterrestrial.

Play the *E.T.* or *STARMAN* (or other) music while kids create their posters. When they're finished, turn off the music and say: "Trying to get through to an extraterrestrial could be tough! You'd have so little in common!"

2. The extraterrestrials are here—Have kids, still in their small groups, now try to explain their *parents'* lives to the extraterrestrial.

Give each group another large sheet of posterboard. Make the magazines adults read available. Tell the groups to make second posters to portray their parents' music, language, food, fashions and so on. Turn on the music again while kids work.

When they're finished, turn off the music and display the two sets of posters side by side. Have volunteers explain the posters. Say: "Parents and kids can seem like extraterrestrials to each other! No wonder they have trouble communicating sometimes. They live in different worlds."

Briefly discuss particular differences between teenage culture and parent culture. For example, parents like "elevator music," while teenagers like hard rock. Don't let the discussion become a lengthy rehearsal of stereotypes, however. Not all parents hate rock music. And not all junior highers like it. The idea is to help the kids recognize differences between youth and adult cultures, not to create differences where none exist.

3. *Walk a mile in my shoes*—Get everyone together in a circle. Say: "You can't really understand someone else till you've walked a mile in his or her shoes. Jesus, the greatest 'extraterrestrial' of all time, came to Earth and walked in our shoes and understood us." Read aloud John 1:14 and 3:16-17.

Elaborate on what it must have been like for Jesus to become human, get thirsty and hungry and tired. Suggest that one way to be Christlike is to put ourselves in someone else's shoes. Say kids can better understand parents by walking a mile in their shoes.

4. *Role plays*—Use role plays to help kids put themselves in their parents' place.

Have junior highers get in groups of four or five, with an adult sponsor in each. Give each group a "Role-Play Situations" handout. Explain that for each situation, one kid should play the

---

Role-Play Situations

- A junior higher comes home later than curfew and the parent is furious.
- A parent has had a rough day at work and comes home to a house full of loud rock music.
- A junior higher has a disgustingly messy room and refuses to clean it when the parent asks him or her to.
- A parent has just been loudly bickering with his or her spouse and walks into the room where the junior higher is reading.
- A junior higher comes home with grades that are unacceptable to the parent.

parent role and another should play the junior higher role. The two should try to realistically work things out.

Let the groups begin, with kids taking turns so each group member plays the role of a parent at least once. Have the adult sponsor in each group call time when a role play reaches a conclusion or when players run out of steam.

When groups finish, let them watch the others until all the role plays are finished. Then get everyone together in a circle and briefly discuss the role plays by asking these questions:

● What did you learn from the role plays about being a parent?

● How did the junior highers in the role plays make their parents' job harder? easier?

5. *Golden Rules*—Ask kids to think about what they've observed in the role plays and in their own relationships. Have a group member or adult sponsor read aloud Ephesians 6:4 and Hebrews 12:7. Challenge kids to brainstorm "Five Golden Rules for Parents" in relating to junior highers; for example, "Listen to your son or daughter before making up your mind about something." Note ideas on newsprint. Have kids rank the top five rules.

Have a group member or adult sponsor read aloud Proverbs 23:22 and Ephesians 6:2. Challenge kids to also brainstorm "Five Golden Rules for Junior Highers" in relating to parents; for example, "Listen to your parents' reasons when they say no to something." Take notes on newsprint, and have kids rank the top five.

6. *Closing*—Wrap up the meeting with group members standing in a circle. Encourage kids to speak sentence prayers telling God why they're thankful for their parents.

Compile the two "Five Golden Rules" lists, refine them with some group members' help, and circulate them to parents and all the junior highers. ■

Section Four:

FAITH

26 I Have Questions About My Faith

By Kevin Miller

Junior highers are reaching a stage Swiss psychologist Jean Piaget termed "formal reasoning." They can increasingly think abstractly, wrestle with paradox—and doubt. And though it sounds strange, questioning their faith now helps junior highers hold a stronger faith later on, for then the faith will be truly their own.

But now, doubt is scary. Kids' doubts are tied up with who they are and who they're becoming; kids hurt when they doubt.

What junior highers need from you when they doubt isn't a well-articulated theological proposition; they need a good, strong hug and the assurance that they—and their questions—are okay. Use this meeting for a good start.

OBJECTIVES

Participants will:

- play a game and respond to statements, to realize that every Christian has doubts about faith;
- see how Jesus responded to a friend who doubted him;
- present newscasts on good and bad ways to handle questions about faith;

● identify faith questions they currently struggle with and get help in answering them; and

● realize their doubts won't separate them from God's love.

SUPPLIES

Gather 24 2×4-inch paper name tags, each with a doubt from the "Doubt Bingo" card written on the back (if you have more than 24 group members, repeat some doubts on name tags); "doubtful snacks" such as a dark blue drink, purple cookies, green bread or similar refreshments; markers; straight pins; a tennis ball for every 15 group members; a sheet of newsprint with the "Toss and Talk" instructions from activity #4 written on it; a "Newscast Stories" handout for every three group members; paper; newsprint; a cassette tape or record of the song "Do I Trust You" by Twila Paris; a cassette player or turntable; and, for each group member, a "Doubt Bingo" card, a pencil, a Bible and a 3×5 card.

BEFORE THE MEETING

Read the meeting and collect supplies.

NOTES TO THE LEADER

You don't need to have answers for all of the kids' questions. This meeting's goal is to assure junior highers they're still okay when they doubt, and to encourage them to get help with their doubts.

THE MEETING

1. Name tags—As group members arrive, give each a name tag with a doubt printed on the back. Make markers available and have kids sign their names on the tags and pin them on. If you have fewer than 24 people, distribute 24 name tags anyway; some kids will simply wear more than one.

2. Doubt bingo—Give each junior higher a "Doubt Bingo" card and a pencil. Announce you're going to play "Doubt Bingo." The winner is the first to mark five squares in a row—up, down or diagonally. Say: "Here's how you mark off a

Doubt Bingo

How can I be sure God cares about me?	Why do all the churches teach different things?	Why do so many Christians act no better—even worse—than non-Christians?	Why is there only one way to God?	How can I know there's a devil?
If God created the world, why do so many scientists and teachers believe in evolution?	If God forgives me, why do I still feel guilty?	How can I know there's a God?	Why does God let people starve?	How can I be sure Christianity, not some other religion, is right?
How can I know God hears me when I pray?	If someone's more popular than I am, does God love him or her more?	**FREE**	Why doesn't God just send everyone to heaven?	If God is in my life, why can't I feel him?
If God loves everyone, why would he send people to hell?	Why are there so many different versions of the Bible?	How can I know the Bible is true?	If Adam had never sinned, would Jesus still have died on the cross?	Can demons possess me if I'm a Christian?
Why is Christianity so hard to understand?	If God loves me, why can't I get good grades?	My friend isn't a Christian. Does God hear his prayers?	Why do some sick people pray and pray but never get better?	Will God let the world be blown up by a nuclear war?

square: Run to another person and find out which doubt he or she has printed underneath his or her name tag. Find the square on your card that matches that doubt, and have the person mark it with his or her full name. The game ends when someone yells 'Bingo!' ''

Give the starting signal: ''I doubt it! Go!''

After the game, have kids sit in a circle. Say: ''Look at your 'Doubt Bingo' card. Of all the questions listed, which most bugs you or interests you?'' Say you're going to look at doubts and faith questions and how to handle them.

3. *The people meter*—Tell junior highers to spread out so each person has lots of room. Say you'll read a statement, and

they should:
- shake their *hands* in the air if they agree; or
- shake their *feet* in the air if they disagree.

Tell them to choose the response they're closer to if they're not sure. And the more they agree or disagree, the harder they should shake their hands or feet.

Start with these fun statements:
- Eighth-graders are the greatest people alive.
- People with blond hair have more fun.
- Country music is wonderful.

Then choose some of these:
- Our pastor sometimes has doubts about his or her faith.
- If you doubt, you don't have faith.
- It's okay to question God.
- Bible heroes had lots of doubts.

Pause after each statement. If there are both "agrees" and "disagrees," have some kids explain their responses. Move to the next activity by saying: "Just about every Christian will have questions about his or her faith sometime. Let's see how Jesus treated a friend who doubted him."

4. Toss and talk—Have junior highers sit in a circle. If you have more than 15 kids, form more than one circle. Pass out a Bible to each person. Toss a tennis ball to someone in each circle.

Explain: "Each circle will toss the ball around to decide who reads the Bible verses and who answers some opinion questions. The receiver reads one verse or answers one question, depending on where you are in the instructions. Make sure everyone in your circle gets the ball at least once."

Display the "Toss and Talk" instructions on newsprint. Tell kids to refer to it to know what to do next. Say "Go."

When all the circles finish, summarize: Believers as great as John the Baptist had doubts; Jesus didn't yell at John, but helped him remove his doubt; the important thing is not that we have doubts, but what we do with them.

5. Doubtful snacks—Serve the strange-colored snacks. After kids eat the snacks, ask whether they had doubts about eating them and why they ate them anyway.

Ask how many understand how a car engine works. Ask those who don't know how, why they ride in cars anyway. Discuss this faith analogy.

Toss and Talk

1. Read Matthew 11:1-7, 11, one verse at a time.

2. Give your opinion on:
● John sent other people to Jesus to try to help him with his doubts. What can we learn from this?

● Why didn't Jesus give John a simple yes or no?

● Even though John doubted, Jesus called him "the greatest person who ever lived." What does this say about doubting?

Newscast Stories

Your newscast should cover these three stories:
● a junior higher who had a doubt about his or her faith (tell viewers what), handled it in a good way (tell viewers how; for example, talked to a youth pastor), and what happened as a result.

● another person who had a doubt and handled it in a bad way (for example, never said or did anything about it), and what happened to him or her.

● a person who handled his or her doubt in a crazy way (for example, wrote it on pieces of Gravy Train and fed it to his dog).

6. *The good, the bad and the crazy*—Have kids form groups of three. Each group will plan and present a short newscast. Give each group a "Newscast Stories" handout. Provide paper and pencils.

Give groups five or 10 minutes to plan. Have them present their newscasts. List on newsprint the various good, bad and crazy ways the people handled their doubts.

After the skits, read the list and discuss other ideas. Some "good ways": ask other Christians; pray and admit to God you doubt him; study the Bible and other books that might help; be patient. Some "bad ways": ignore your doubts and hope they go away; feel guilty; never tell anyone; give up your faith because you don't understand part of it.

7. *Who you gonna call?*—Say that one of the best ways to handle doubts is to talk about them with more mature Christians, and you'll be glad to talk to anyone in the group about questions. Pass out 3×5 cards and pencils. Tell kids to write any questions they'd like to talk with you about. Tell kids who don't currently have questions to write "No questions for now." Have kids sign their names. Collect the cards.

Tell kids how you'll respond. You could:
- call each person during the week;
- write each person a short note; or
- spend the next meeting talking about some of the doubts listed (without identifying the askers).

Whichever you choose, listen well; assure kids they're okay; suggest tentative answers, helpful scriptures and books; and tell them that not having all the answers is normal.

8. *Closing*—Wrap up the meeting on a strong, assuring note that nothing—not our worst doubts, fears or questions—can cut us off from God's love. Have kids form a circle and lock arms. Read Romans 8:38-39. Close in prayer. Play the song "Do I Trust You." ∎

27 Light in the Darkness

By Larry Keefauver

Junior highers experience many forms of "darkness" in their lives: loneliness, discouragement, fear of the future...

Use this meeting to explore with your young people how God's gift of Jesus brings light to the world...to their personal worlds. And help them see how, with Christ's light, they can also brighten other people's lives.

OBJECTIVES

Participants will:
- pantomine Bible passages about darkness and light;
- listen to a song about one form of darkness and identify darkness in their own lives;
- experience a vivid candle illustration of Jesus' light in their lives; and
- discover how they can light up others' lives.

SUPPLIES

Gather yellow and white construction paper; scissors; glue; markers; masking tape; cassette tape or CD of upbeat contemporary Christian music; cassette or CD player; large candle (to be the Christ-candle) and holder; matches; flashlights; a large sheet of newsprint; for each small group of three or four, a Bible; for every two group members, a "Stuff Discussion" handout and a "Stuff Lyrics" handout; and, for each person, a cupcake with a special candle that won't blow out stuck in it.

BEFORE THE MEETING

Read the meeting and collect supplies.

Cut out pieces for a large construction-paper candle (yellow for the flame and white for the candle), and glue the two shapes together.

Pull down any shades in the meeting room, or cover the windows.

THE MEETING

1. *A lighthearted welcome*—Have upbeat Christian music playing as kids arrive. Direct kids to a table with the yellow and white construction paper, scissors, glue, markers, masking tape and example construction-paper on it. Instruct group members to each create a construction-paper candle, write their name on it and tape it onto the wall.

2. *Introducing the theme*—Hold the large candle (in its holder) and matches. Turn out the lights.

Say: "We're going to talk about darkness and light in our lives, and how Jesus brings light into our world. Jesus says, 'I am the light of the world.' (Pause and light the Christ-candle. Set it in a safe place were it can burn visibly.)

"In the Bible, in the book of John, it says Christ's light will overcome the darkness. Let's see what else the Bible says about light and darkness."

3. *Checking it out*—Turn on the lights. Divide the group into small groups of three or four. Assign each group one of these scripture passages: John 1:4; 1:5; 1:6-7; or 1:8-9. Give each group a Bible. Tell groups they have five minutes to create short pantomines to illustrate the passages.

Randomly hand out all the flashlights to group members. Tell the flashlight-bearers to flash light back and forth on the performers as small groups present their Bible passages. This will make your "show" seem like an old-time movie. Turn off the lights.

Let each small group do its Bible presentation for the whole group; have the small groups go in order according to their Bible verses (for example, all the John 1:4 small groups would go before those performing John 1:5). Turn on the lights; collect the flashlights.

4. *Darkness in our lives*—Divide the group into pairs. Say: "Darkness takes many forms. Darkness is war, hunger, poverty, sickness, loneliness, depression. For different people, darkness is different things. It may be anything that 'gets in the way' in your life.

"Several years ago a contemporary Christian musician named Tom Franzak sang a song titled "Stuff" about a different kind of darkness. In your pairs, read the lyrics to this song and think about what darkness is for the person who wrote it."

Give each pair a "Stuff Discussion" handout and a "Stuff Lyrics" handout. Tell the partners to do what the handout says.

Tape a large sheet of newsprint onto the wall. Write "Darkness Stuff" at the top. Set markers nearby.

5. *Seeing the light*—With the whole group in a cirle, briefly discuss the darkness stuff listed, and how Jesus helps us overcome the dark areas of our lives. Say in your own words: "If we hand to keep our lives free from darkness stuff, we couldn't do it. But Jesus can light up our lives in a special way. Even when we struggle with darkness, Jesus is a light in our lives that won't go out. (Point to the still-burning Christ-candle.) Just as he is the light of the whole world, he can be a light in our personal lives too."

Give everyone a cupcake with a special candle that won't blow out stuck in it. Have kids each light their candle from the Christ-candle and quickly return to the circle. Turn off the lights and say, "Blow out your candles at the count of three—one, two, three!"

When the candles don't blow out, sing "This Little (Gospel) Light of Mine." The candle will soon burn out; turn on the lights and let kids each their cupcakes.

6. *Being the light*—Say: "The candles represent Jesus' light in each of our lives. We can be the light in others' lives too. Think of ways people here are 'lights' or encouragers in your life, and write those good things on their candles taped to the wall. For example, you might write on someone's candle, 'helps me with homework' or 'laughs with me.' " Make markers available.

160

Stuff Lyrics

It's hanging out of my house
And it's jam-packed in the garage
If it's computerized mechanical junk—
    I've got it
I'm into every kind of fad and hobby
    and sport
More than most people could name
I got a bad case of "Gimme, I want"
    as a kid
And things have never been the same

(Chorus)
If you want it, you should have it
When you're tired of it, just trash it
Take it back if what you've got ain't
    fun
There's more where it came from
Stuff, stuff, gimme some stuff
Stuff, stuff, gimme some

I was bitten by Madison Avenue's
    latest disease
Wrap up that time-saving, money-
    saving, entertaining thing,
    if you please
I know that modern technology's great
It's my mind that I can't trust
Because when someone says to me,
    "You need this!"
Sensibility bites the dust

(Repeat Chorus)
I want you to know I'm not insensitive
When I die I leave my stuff to you
But for now I'm here
So please don't touch my stuff
Can't I have all this and heaven too?

I'm gonna get me a wife
The best-looking you've ever seen
We'll have the best-looking kids
    around
If you know what I mean
I'll get a great job and we'll buy a nice
    house
Big enough to entertain
You'll see us Sunday mornings at
    church
To be sure just the same

But if it doesn't work, don't make it
If she can't relate don't fake it
Just return her to the point of
    purchase, son
There's more where she came from
Stuff, stuff, gimme some stuff
Stuff, stuff, gimme some

Stuff Discussion

1. Think about the lyrics you just read. What do you think the writer is saying?

2. Discuss: The writer claims he has to have all that stuff. How is that bad?

3. Stuff becomes darkness in our lives when it gets in the way of our relationships with God and other people. Think about and discuss some "darkness stuff" in your own lives. (For example, feeling sorry for yourself or being jealous.)

4. Go to the "Darkness Stuff" newsprint on the wall, and each list one "darkness thing" in your life. Then go sit and form a circle as other pairs join you.

When kids finish, tell them to each remove their candle from the wall, return to the circle and silently read how they already shine for others. Discuss more ways they can brighten other people's lives.

7. *Closing*—Close with a prayer thanking Jesus for being the light in our world and helping us be light for others. Send junior highers off to light up more people's lives! ∎

28 Lost and Found

By Margaret Rickers

" **S** ometimes I feel like I just wander around without any purpose or reason for being," Mike confessed to his counselor. "My dad always says: 'It's a jungle out there! Be careful!' He's right, and I'm just one of the animals running around, but I don't know where I'm going."

Many junior highers find Mike's comments similar to their own feelings. In a recent survey of one seventh-grade class, 60 percent of the students couldn't give one good reason why they existed on Earth. All of the 32 students could identify with the feeling of being lost and helpless.

Use this meeting to help your young people realize they're not alone in the battle "against the world."

OBJECTIVES

Participants will:
- recall times they've been lost and tell about those times;
- read and act out Bible stories about Moses and the children of Israel in the wilderness;
- experience the feeling of being lost and then found through a gaming activity; and
- make new friends.

SUPPLIES

Gather masking tape; a sheet of newsprint or posterboard; an instant-print camera and enough film to take a snapshot of all group members either individually or in pairs; scissors; about six markers of different colors; a horizontal banner made from three sheets of newsprint or posterboard, with the words "To know God is to know that when you're alone, you're not!" written on it; a bus, van or cars and drivers to transport the group to and from the site of the final part of the meeting; and, for each person, a Bible and an "I'm Glad I Found You!" handout.

BEFORE THE MEETING

Read the meeting and collect supplies.

Several weeks before the meeting, find another junior high youth group about the same size as yours to meet with for "The wandering" section. If possible, choose a group your own group doesn't know. Meet with the leader to give him or her a copy of the meeting and discuss its logistics. Decide whether kids will join together for a snack or for dinner at the end.

Plan to start this meeting at about 4 p.m. on a Saturday or Sunday. Agree with the other group's leader to rendezvous at a specific time at the mall (or airport or Main Street), about an hour and 30 minutes after the start of your meeting. This allows for one hour of meeting time and 30 minutes to get the group to the location.

Recruit some adult sponsors to help in the meeting and provide transportation.

Recruit a group member who has an interest in photography to be at the meeting early and take photos of group members as they arrive.

Inform kids whether to bring enough money for a snack or for dinner.

Tape the sheet of newsprint or posterboard onto the meeting room wall.

NOTES TO THE LEADER

This meeting may bring out some strong feelings in young people who feel rejected by their family and friends. Try to keep the atmosphere of the meeting light but serious. Be sensitive to group members' feelings. If someone expresses feelings of hopelessness that need to be further addressed, be prepared to do so or to seek help from a professional counselor.

THE MEETING

1. *Instant photos*—As young people arrive, have your amateur photographer take a snapshot of each group member. (If the kids are wearing coats, ask them to keep their coats on while you take the pictures.) Or to save expenses, have two young people photographed at a time, then cut the photos in half vertically. Spread the photos on a table to develop.

2. *Opening prayer*—Have group members sit in a circle. Begin the meeting with a prayer asking God to guide you.

3. *The day I got lost*—Say: "Today we'll learn more about the Israelites' wilderness wanderings. To help get in touch with what it's like to wander, think back to a time when you were really lost such as when you were given wrong directions to get somewhere or when you got separated from your parents."

Give each kid a chance to tell his or her story. If your group is larger than 10, break into smaller groups with an adult sponsor in each group.

When everyone's finished, get group members back together in the circle. Ask the young people to say words that describe how they felt when they were lost. Write the adjectives on the newsprint or posterboard on the wall. Discuss why group members chose those words and what feelings lie behind them.

Allow about 15 minutes for this portion of the meeting.

4. *Lost in the Bible*—Tell the kids: "A familiar story in the Bible talks about a large group of God's people wandering around for many years—40 to be exact!" Divide the group into four groups, each with an adult. Hand out Bibles. The groups should each focus on one of these four scripture passages: Exodus 15:22-27; 16:1-12; 16:13-21; and 16:22-35. Have each group choose someone to read its scripture aloud.

Have each group develop a role play based on its scripture passage. Allow about 10 minutes; the total time for this part of the meeting shouldn't exceed 15 minutes.

5. *Drama time*—Gather group members together to present your youth group's original drama. Beginning with Exodus 15:22-27, link the four episodes into one complete play while the four readers provide the narrative. Approximate time: 15 minutes.

6. *All is not lost*—This part of the meeting should also take about 15 minutes. Divide the group into the four groups again. Ask the group members to discuss how many words on the list on the wall might describe the children of Israel in their wanderings.

Have each group choose someone other than its reader to be a "circler." Each circler gets a marker, each of a different color, and circles the words his or her group said might describe how the Israelites felt. When circlers from different groups circle some of the same words, the strongest feelings of being lost will be emphasized.

Say: "Not only haven't people changed in their feelings of helplessness and futility when they feel lost, God hasn't changed either. Just as he provided for the children of Israel during their 40 years of wandering, he also provides for us each day of our lives."

Now hang the banner on the wall. Have kids read it aloud in unison. Ask: "What does this mean to you? How does it make you feel? What does it mean for the rest of your lives?" Kids should discuss answers in their groups.

After a few moments, say: "Now discuss special ways God has already provided for you. For example, a difficult situation God helped you out of, or people God brought to you to help you."

7. *The wandering*—Up to now, your meeting should have lasted about one hour. You should have kept the upcoming trip a secret, by having just said you're going out for a snack or dinner, with no further details.

Now say: "We're going to take a trip to a shopping center (or airport or Main Street). There, we're going to meet the kids from _____ Church. But they won't be together and neither will we. We're going to have to *find* each other. Each of you will get a snapshot of a member of this other youth group—and they will get the pictures of you. The first one to find his or her 'missing person' will win a free Coke (or hamburger meal)."

At the location, you and the other group's leader meet privately to exchange the pictures. Then each return to your own group and pass out the exchanged pictures. Tell group members the central point to finally return to in the mall. They should return when they find their person or are found, and again in 20 minutes. A few at a time, let the young people into the mall opposite where the other group is entering. Limit young people to the *halls* of the mall!

Remember the idea is for everyone to *wander* around the mall to find the "missing person" on his or her snapshot. When one person finds another, that couple should report in at the central meeting place, and then go back to look for the missing person in the other partner's photograph. And so on.

The group leaders and adult sponsors for both groups should stay at the central point in the mall where the young people will all finally meet.

8. Refreshments—After all the "lost" have been "found," go with the other group to a soda shop or restaurant. Treat the first couple that returned to the central point to free Cokes or hamburger meals.

As the young people munch on their food, hand out the "I'm Glad I Found You!" sheets for them to discuss.

I'm Glad I Found You!

1. What's your full name?

2. How old are you?

3. Which school do you go to?

4. How did you feel when you were looking for someone? frustrated? excited? nervous?

5. Knowing someone was looking for you, how did you feel?

6. How would you compare this to your relationship with God?

---

9. Goin' home—Back at the vans or cars, have kids gather together in a circle for a closing prayer. Thank God for the guidance and direction he gives for our daily living. ■

29 Making It All Brand New

By Joani Schultz

It's not easy.

Many junior highers wonder how God fits them personally. "To have God the center of my life" was one of the top 10 cries voiced in Search Institute's study of young adolescents and their parents.

At a time when kids are trying out new behaviors and beliefs, it's essential for the church to equip kids with a realistic, practical faith for living. And healing forgiveness when they fail.

Use this meeting to help junior highers tackle tough, sticky issues with biblical guidelines.

OBJECTIVES

Participants will:

● discover what the Bible says about Christian living in Ephesians 4:22-32;

● focus on the difference between the "old self" and the "new self" through situation role plays and discussions;

● evaluate their own personal decisions in various situations; and

● have an opportunity to confess their shortcomings and celebrate the goodness of forgiveness.

SUPPLIES

Gather the five station role-play cards in activity #2; newsprint; crayons; masking tape; seven Bible verse posters (see "Before the Meeting" notes); cassette tapes or records of upbeat Christian music; a cassette player or turntable; a stack of newspapers; markers; two or three Bibles; two to four garbage bags; an "Adults' Instructions" handout for each adult sponsor; and, for each person, an "Old Self/New Self" handout and a pencil. Optional: an instant-print camera and film, and a large sheet of newsprint or posterboard.

BEFORE THE MEETING

Read the meeting and collect supplies.

Prepare the meeting room with five "stations." Place the role-play cards at the appropriate stations.

Ask a few artistic junior highers to arrive early and make seven Bible verse posters for the meeting. Each poster should have one of these Bible passages on it: Ephesians 4:23-24, 25, 26-27, 28, 29, 30 and 32. Use an easy-to-understand translation such as Today's English Version or the New International Version. Give the kids newsprint and crayons. Encourage them to brightly decorate the posters so the Bible verses can hang around the meeting room for a few weeks. Tape the posters at the appropriate stations or around the room.

NOTES TO THE LEADER

Early adolescence is a time for testing new behavior and making decisions. It's important for young people to connect God with those decisions. The station role plays in this meeting aren't easy to solve. Remind junior highers that making the "God" decisions doesn't always bring *immediate* good feelings. Don't hesitate to share God's deep love and concern for them and that he doesn't want anyone to get hurt—that's why God's given biblical guidelines for living.

THE MEETING

1. *Getting rid of the old*—Play upbeat Christian music as group members arrive. Get everyone together in a circle. Give each person a few sheets of newspaper. Ask the group members

Adults' Instructions

When your group arrives at a station, point out the Bible verse poster. Have participants each write key words from the Bible passage on their handout.

Read the role plays found at that station. Have the group members choose one of the situations to role play, decide how many actors are needed and act out the scene described. But they must act it out twice: The first time reflects the "old self" point of view; the second time, the "new self."

Then ask the group: "Why is this situation difficult? Which way is easier to live? Why? How would you be different if you always followed the 'new self' way? What advice can you give your friends who struggle with this?"

Have kids each mark their "Old Self/New Self" handout for that station. Explain that the continuums on the handout represent what they *generally* do in similiar situations. If for one they usually follow "old self" instincts, they should mark it closer to "old self." And vice versa. Say: "This is a way for you to see areas that need improvement. It will also show areas to celebrate."

Old Self/New Self

Key words from scripture   **In these situations, I'm usually . . .**

1.   old self |_____,_____| new self

2.   old self |_____,_____| new self

3.   old self |_____,_____| new self

4.   old self |_____,_____| new self

5.   old self |_____,_____| new self

to each use markers to write on the newspaper something they want to change or something they don't like about themselves. For example, "I eat too much" or "When I'm with my friends, I can't say no" or "I wish I had more self-discipline."

When everyone finishes, say: "Our 'old self' represents the part of us God doesn't control. All the things you've written could be considered parts of your 'old self.' "

Have a young person read Ephesians 4:22. Remind the group members once again that the things they wrote are parts of the "old self."

Have another young person read Ephesians 4:23-24. Direct the group's attention to that Bible verse poster. Then say: "As a way of getting rid of the 'old self' and putting on the 'new self' that God desires, read aloud what you wrote on one or more of your newspaper pages. If you don't want to say anything, simply crumple your newspaper into a ball and throw it into the garbage bag. If you're willing to share what you wrote, tell the group, crumple the newspaper into a ball, and stuff it into the garbage bag. We'll continue around the circle until everyone has gotten rid of the 'old self.' " Place a garbage bag in the center of the circle and do this activity.

Say: "A lot of people wonder how God can really make a difference in their lives. Sometimes it's hard to tell because we act one way when we're around church and act another way when we're with someone else. Having a relationship with God is meant to make a difference in *every* part of our lives. Being friends with God helps us with the decisions we make and the actions we take. Sometimes it's hard to understand where and how God fits into all of this. The Bible does give practical, down-to-earth suggestions that can make life a bit easier. By following those guidelines, our lives become a reflection of God. Remember: God loves us and wants the best for us. Following our 'old self'—human desires and bad influences—only leads us to unhappiness, frustration and hurt. Taking God's advice really helps us in the long run. During this meeting we're going to see the practical kinds of things the Bible says that help us be Christians—not only when we're at church, but wherever we are."

2. Situation stations—If your group is larger than 20, split into smaller groups, each with an adult sponsor. Give each sponsor an "Adults' Instructions" handout. Have each small group visit different stations at different times. If your group is 20 or less, begin with station one and continue to all the sta-

Station Role-Play Cards

Station 1—*Ephesians 4:25*
● Situation A—Your friend's parents are out of town. You tell your parents you are staying overnight at that friend's house. Instead you and your friend stay out late, party and do some things you don't feel right about. The next day your parents ask you where you were and what you did last night. What do you tell them?

● Situation B—Your youth group talks a lot about caring for each other. At youth group you tell certain group members you care about them, but in school you ignore them. One of the ignored youth group members confronts you and asks what you really feel. What do you say?

Station 2—*Ephesians 4:26-27*
● Situation A—You find out some of your friends are talking about you behind your back, spreading lies and making it look as though you have a bad reputation. What do you do?

● Situation B—Your parents set a curfew you feel is unrealistic. For weeks you've been arguing about it and they don't seem to understand you. What do you do?

Station 3—*Ephesians 4:28*
● Situation A—Two of your friends dare you to shoplift. It sounds like a challenge and kind of fun to see what you can get away with. Your friends dare you to steal a record album you've wanted for a long time. What do you do?

● Situation B—You've got to make a good grade on this test. You thought you'd studied enough, but the answers aren't coming to you. You know one of your friends is a lot smarter than you and probably knows the answers. You could see his paper if you tried. What do you do?

Station 4—*Ephesians 4:29*
● Situation A—You know it's not right to "take God's name in vain," but that's how everybody talks. Swearing has become a habit. You don't even think about it, so you feel swearing really doesn't matter that much. What do you do?

● Situation B—Someone in your family made you mad. You feel you're always the one to get the blame. No one really tries to understand your point of view. What do you do?

Station 5—*Ephesians 4:30*
● Situation A—Your friends don't go to church. They tease you and make fun of you because you worship and go to youth group meetings. What do you tell them?

● Situation B—You've heard that your body is the temple of the Holy Spirit. You've been going out with someone for a few months. Now that person is pressuring you to "go all the way." You don't want to lose that person and, besides, you're curious to know what it is like. What do you do?

● Situation C—You've heard that your body is the temple of the Holy Spirit. Lots of your friends have been experimenting with drugs and drinking. Now they're pressuring you to join them. You don't want to lose their friendship and, besides, you're wondering what it feels like to get high. What do you do?

tions. Make sure each person has an "Old Self/New Self" handout and a pencil.

3. *Confession*—After all the members finish the stations, have the small groups (or your whole group of 20 or less) sit together in circles. Read aloud Ephesians 4:31.

Ask the group members to each share one struggle they still have. Have them write the struggles on newspaper sheets. For example: "I still get upset with my parents, they don't understand me and we always fight. It seems whatever I try never works." When each person finishes sharing, he or she crumples the newspaper and throws it into the garbage bag. When all have finished, say: "Christians always have struggles. The filled garbage bag is a symbol of the struggles we share. The best things Christians have going for them are God's love and the strength of sharing our problems as a group."

4. *Forgiveness*—Gather the group members in one circle. Have the young people read Ephesians 4:32 in unison (from the poster on the wall). Have one young person close the garbage bag. Point out that it is *possible* to be new, that God can help us get rid of the old. Join hands and pause for a brief silent prayer. Suggest that each person pray silently for the power to live like a Christian both in and away from church.

For the optional closing, do the following.

After the silent prayer, ask the group members to again read together the final Bible verse poster (Ephesians 4:32). Say: "As a reminder of our newness in Christ—and our commitment to grow—let's pose for a photo. After we have it we'll add words such as 'All new and improved!' like an advertisement for our faith."

Take an instant-print photo. Tape it onto a large sheet of newsprint or posterboard. Create a colorful advertisement with the words "All new and improved!" Then write Ephesians 4:22-24 beside it.

Hang the photo and caption on the church bulletin board for the congregation to see. ∎

30 Turning the Other Cheek

By Kurt Bickel

A*father told his eighth-grade son: "I don't want you to fight. But if they hit you first, hit them back." The father repeated this to me as we sat outside the junior high principal's office. His son had been fighting in school. We were waiting to hear what disciplinary action would be taken.*

The biblical concept of "turning the other cheek" isn't easy. It's especially tough for junior highers. According to recent research by Search Institute, 47 percent of fifth- through ninth-graders admit to hitting or beating up another kid within the past year.

Use this meeting to challenge junior highers to see how God's perspective on kindness can fit in their own lives.

OBJECTIVES

Participants will:

● play a game demonstrating that being forceful doesn't always mean winning;

● be contestants in a "TV game show" to see that they can choose to be kind and loving in difficult situations;

● compare the world's views on revenge to Jesus' views;

● take an active part in a Bible reading on love by doing a rhythmic response; and

● be challenged to consider how God's perspective on being kind and loving fits in their own lives.

SUPPLIES

Gather contemporary Christian music cassette tapes; a cassette player; contestant name cards—8½×11 sheets of construction paper numbered at the top (in sequence), with two feet of yarn attached in a loop—as many as you have group members; markers; if possible, two podiums; a large poster that says "Get tough and aggressive"; a large poster that says "Be kind and loving"; three, five or seven (depending on how many judges you'll use) sets of "Get tough and aggressive" and "Be kind and loving" cards, 8½×11, cut from posterboard; a large supply of "tokens" (buttons, chips or tickets); a watch that shows seconds; a list of numbers written out—as many as you have group members; a pencil; a prize such as a jawbreaker candy for each group member; for every four or five group members, a Bible and a "Reflections" handout; and a prerecorded cassette tape of various group members each reciting portions of the prayer of St. Francis.

BEFORE THE MEETING

Read the meeting and collect supplies.

Set up the meeting area in the style of a TV game show (see the "TV Game Show Setup"). Put the two posters on opposite sides of the room. Add as much "atmosphere" as you wish: lights, decorations, microphones.

Ask a bright kid or an adult sponsor to keep score during the TV game show. Explain his or her responsibilities, described in activity #3.

If you wish, add some situations to the list for the game show. But avoid calling attention to any specific problem behaviors in your group. This isn't the time to confront problems.

Find someone to bring refreshments such as brownies or popcorn, and punch.

Meet with several group members and tape the prayer of St. Francis (in activity #7), with different kids reciting it phrase by phrase.

TV Game Show Setup

Ready-go area

"Get tough
and aggressive"
poster

"Be kind and
loving" poster

◯

Scorekeeper

◯

Host

▢

Speaker's podium

▢

Speaker's podium

■ ■ ■ ■ ■

Judges' seats

NOTES TO THE LEADER

The typical junior higher's moral development is usually described as "what's fair is fair," according to Thomas A. Droege in *Faith Passages and Patterns* (Fortress Press). The concept of "turning the other cheek" in Christian love is at the highest level of moral development—even beyond many adult Christians.

Realize that this meeting will probably not raise kids to the higher level. But it will introduce them to God's perspective and prepare them for future development. Don't push or belittle kids' choices in this meeting. They will tend to go with fairness rather than mercy. That's okay. You're planting seeds for future growth.

THE MEETING

1. *Welcome*—Play contemporary Christian music as kids arrive. Greet kids and give them each a numbered contestant

Contestant Name Card

name card (see diagram) with yarn attached. Provide markers. Have each group member print his or her name in the middle of the card, and his or her favorite TV game show at the bottom. Tell kids to wear their name cards around their necks.

2. *Warming up*—Have kids get into pairs. Tell partners to stand toe to toe and put their hands together palm to palm. Explain that the partners are competing against each other. They should push against the other person's palms to make him or her lose balance. When a partner loses balance, the other partner wins.

Let kids do this. Have them change partners and do it again. And perhaps again. When the play-value is running out, stop the game. Say that in this game, as in life, the most forceful or aggressive person isn't always the winner.

3. *The choice is yours*—Tell kids it's time to play "The Choice Is Yours"—a new TV game show.

Choose three, five or seven kids to be judges (depending on the size of your group). Have the judges sit in their seats. Give them each a set of "Get tough and aggressive" and "Be kind and loving" cards.

Give your pre-chosen scorekeeper the tokens.

Gather the rest of the group in the Ready-go area (refer to

the diagram).

Explain to kids the rules of the game:

● The host (you) will read a situation. The kids have 10 seconds to each go stand by either the "Get tough and aggressive" poster or the "Be kind and loving" poster to indicate a response. (Call time after 10 seconds.)

● The host (you) will choose a speaker from each group. (Checkmark on your list of numbers which two kids you choose so you don't keep calling on the same ones.) Each speaker has 30 seconds to convince the judges to vote for his or her side—either "Get tough and aggressive" or "Be kind and loving." (Call time after 30 seconds.)

● The judges vote by each holding up a "Get tough and aggressive" or "Be kind and loving" card. The scorekeeper gives each speaker a token for each judge who votes for that side. And since majority vote wins, the scorekeeper gives each contestant on the winning side a token.

● All players return to the Ready-go area for the next situation.

When kids understand, begin the game. Here are the situations:

1. You're walking with your brother, age 8, to school. Two boys who look like they're 16 or 17 pass by and trip your younger brother. He spills his books and lunch and begins to cry. What will you do?

2. The physical education teacher keeps hounding you. He says you never hustle. You try to do your best, but he keeps calling you lazy and fat. What will you do?

3. Kay likes John, but nothing is happening yet. Kay told her best friend, Bev. Bev likes John too, so she went to John and said: "Do you know what Kay said about you? She said she doesn't think you're her type." What would you do if you were Kay?

4. Pete, Steve and Ray are best friends, but Ray called up Steve and said: "Let's go to the show, and could we go without Pete? He's getting on my nerves." Steve told Pete what happened. What would you do if you were Pete?

5. You find $5 missing from your locker. The last time you lost $3, you found out your locker partner took it. She said she'd pay you back. She hasn't in three weeks. What will you do?

6. The only place you can play ball after school is in Bill's back yard. His neighbor has a chain link fence. When a ball goes

over the fence, the neighbor comes out and yells at you and keeps the ball. What will you do?

7. You have a paper route. When you go collecting, one family keeps putting you off. They gave you one check that bounced. What will you do?

8. You ride a crowded bus to school. The last kid to board the bus is a big guy who always makes kids give up their seats. If they refuse, he slugs them. Today he wants your seat. What will you do?

9. David sits next to you in school. He's a poor student. He's always looking at your paper to copy. You ask him to stop. He says, "What's it to you?" What will you do?

10. Jim is always getting into trouble of some kind. Today he sits next to you at lunch. When you aren't looking, he pours milk into your Coke and then laughs about it. What will you do?

11. Yes, your friend Sheryl is overweight, but it makes you angry when Jed calls her names. He says to you, "Hey, who was the hippo I saw you with today?" You say she's not that fat and he says, "How would you know, pimple nose?" What will you do?

After the last situation, have kids count their tokens. Declare the winners.

4. Refreshments—Give all the kids prizes for their performance in the game—how about jawbreakers?

Serve the refreshments.

5. Reflections—Get kids into small groups of four or five with an adult sponsor in each. Give each group a Bible and a "Reflections" handout. Have small groups do what the handout says.

6. God's point of view—Say that it's not always easy to choose to do good to people we don't like, but that's God's way.

Have kids get into seven groups, and give each group one of the following letters or words. (If your group is seven or less, assign each person one or more letters or words.)

- Group #1: L
- Group #2: O
- Group #3: V
- Group #4: E
- Group #5: God
- Group #6: Is
- Group #7: Love

Reflections

1. Discuss these questions:
- What did you think about the game we played? Why?
- There is a saying, "Revenge is sweet." What does it mean?
- Is doing what's fair always the Christian thing to do?
- What situation from the game was the hardest for you to decide what to do in? Why?
- What would Rambo (or current tough character) have done in that situation?
- What would Jesus say to do in that situation? Read Matthew 5:38-48.
- What would the world be like if Jesus had behaved like a Rambo? Read Matthew 26:47-56.

2. Read Romans 12:18-21. What does this mean in your life?

Have the groups practice saying their letters or words in order, in rhythm: "L-O-V-E, God Is Love." After they've practiced "the wave" a couple of times, tell them to repeat it every time they hear the word "love" in the following Bible reading.

Read 1 John 4:7-16. Pause after each "love," then continue after the group response.

7. *Closing* —Have everyone sit in a circle. Play your pre-recorded tape of the prayer of St. Francis: "Lord, make me an instrument of Your peace: Where there is hatred, let me sow love; where there is injury, pardon; where there is doubt, faith; where there is despair, hope; where there is darkness, light; and where there is sadness, joy. O divine Master, grant that I may not so much seek to be consoled as to console; to be understood as to understand; to be loved as to love; for it is in giving that we receive; it is in pardoning that we are pardoned; and it is in dying that we are born to eternal life."

Challenge group members to consider God's perspective in situations this coming week. ■

31 *Who Is This Guy Called Jesus?*

By Kurt Bickel

How would your junior highers describe Jesus? Use this meeting to help kids encounter Christ and find in him a God of compassion and mercy, a God as close to them as their own beating hearts.

OBJECTIVES

Participants will:

● explore Jesus' characteristics by experiencing several activities; and

● discover that their relationship with Christ is based on *his* love for them and their faith in him, rather than their knowledge of who he is.

SUPPLIES

Gather a variety of posters and pictures of Jesus, each with a number taped to it; masking tape; markers; a Today's English Version Bible; a roll of newspaper, thin but in a large circle; a cassette tape or record of a song that talks about Jesus such as "The Outlaw" by Larry Norman or another contemporary Christian song; a cassette player or turntable; and, for each person, a pencil, a 3×5 card, a Bible, a piece of paper, and a special name tag made from a 5×7 card folded in half and taped around (to conceal) a cross, a sticker that symbolizes Christ *or* a folded dollar bill (if possible, use the dollar bill), with a yarn necklace attached through a paper-punched hole.

BEFORE THE MEETING

Read the meeting and collect supplies.

Tape the numbered posters and pictures of Jesus around the room.

Privately select a young person who'll agree to play the role of Jesus in one of the learning games. This person will receive the punishment other players deserve. Assure him or her that it won't hurt. Ask this person to keep the role secret from the rest of the group. Explain the learning experience in detail. Suggest that this person respond as Jesus would.

THE MEETING

1. Arrival activities—As kids arrive, invite them to use markers to write their names on name tags. Have them wear the name tags around their necks. Explain that the name tags will help with a game they'll play later.

After group members have their name tags, give them each a pencil and 3×5 card. Encourage them to walk around the "Jesus Gallery" and write a word that describes each of the paintings in the room.

Continue this process as everyone arrives. Tell group members to keep their 3×5 cards for activities throughout the meeting.

2. The rhythm game—This game follows a simple four-beat rhythm. On the first beat, slap both hands on knees; second beat, slap both hands on knees again; third beat, snap fingers; and fourth beat, snap fingers again. Begin that rhythm and have all group members do it together. Then explain that you'll say your own name on the third beat while snapping, then say someone else's name on the fourth beat while snapping. Then the other person named repeats the process, saying his or her own name first and then passing it on to another person. The goal is to play without missing a beat and without repeating the same name twice. Decide how to designate different people with the same name. Play the rhythm game until the junior highers no longer seem interested. Tell them they'll play this game later as a way to learn who Jesus is.

3. A stormy Bible story—Explain that even the disciples wondered at times who Jesus could be. Ask the group to help tell the story of Jesus calming a storm.

Divide the group into seven groups. (A group may be one or more persons. If your group is smaller than seven, assign some group members more than one part.)

Assign each of the groups a word and an action. Whenever they hear their word, they should do their action. Use the "Group, Word, Action" diagram.

Group	Word	Action
One	"disciples"	say "What?"
Two	"boat"	sing "Row, Row, Row Your Boat"
Three	"wind"	sound like the wind
Four	"wave"	say "Splash!"
Five	"sleep" or "sleeping"	snore
Six	"die"	fall over and say "Ugh!"
Seven	"frightened" or "afraid"	say "Eeek, oh, eeek!"

Read the story from Mark 4:35-41 from a Good News Bible (Today's English Version). (If you're unable to get that translation, adapt the words to fit the translation you're using.) Allow time for the groups to react when you read the "trigger" words.

After the story, have kids each write another descriptive word or phrase about Jesus on their 3×5 cards. The description may be something learned from the Bible story.

4. The "hidden" treasure—Announce to group members that there's a special treasure waiting for each of them as they seek to find out who Jesus is. Say: "Like the disciples who wondered how Jesus could calm wind and waves, we wonder many things about our Savior too. Perhaps the greatest mystery of all is how Jesus comes into our lives. A clue for solving the mystery and finding the treasure Jesus offers can be found in Romans 10:5-10." Hand out Bibles. Allow time for junior highers to find and read the passage.

Have someone read verse 8 aloud. Explain that you'll demonstrate that verse by having a treasure hunt with clues. Tell group members you'll help by giving more clues during the search, and they can ask you questions about where the treasure is hidden. Announce clearly that there's a treasure hidden for each one of them in this room; they don't need to leave the room. Say "Go!"

Here are other clues to give while they're searching for the treasure:

● You're all close to finding it.

● What's the most precious thing in life?

● How close is Jesus to us according to Romans 10:8 ("God's message is near you, on your lips and in your heart")?

● Sometimes Jesus surprises us by being with us all the time, even when we think he's far away.

The junior highers may not find their treasures on their own. Don't extend the search to the point of frustration. When the young people become disinterested, bring them all together and say: "Jesus is close to you at all times. Like the scripture says, 'He knows you by name.' He's as close to you as your heart."

If they still haven't discovered the treasure, hold up your name tag and repeat the last statement. Finally, open your name tag to reveal its contents. After all group members have opened their name tags and found their treasures, ask: "How does this experience remind you of your faith? What can we learn from this exercise? How does it help explain the scripture passage we read?"

5. Taking the punishment—Tell the group you're going to use another activity to better understand Jesus.

Invite the group members to once again play the rhythm game. Explain, however, that this time the group represents all the people in the world and you, the leader, will represent God. Announce that, as God, you're holy and just and you can't tolerate sin. No mistakes may go unpunished; otherwise you wouldn't be righteous. Explain that anyone who makes a mistake in this game by breaking the rhythm will receive punishment.

Begin the rhythm game, with you first. When someone breaks the rhythm, go to that person with the rolled-up newspaper and say: "You made a mistake! You deserve punishment. Do you want the swat?" Whether he or she says yes or no, go to your pre-assigned young person and administer the swat. The roll of newspaper should be thin but in a large circle so it makes a loud sound but won't hurt. There should be no chance of hurting the young person.

This game produces many kinds of responses from the junior highers. Observe these responses to recall them during the discussion; they often symbolize the various responses and reactions to Christ's suffering. Play the game until the experience is adequately established (about four or five rounds).

Ask players to share what they feel the game was trying to teach. Ask: "How did the person who received the punishment represent Jesus? Did any of the players want to take the swats themselves? Why or why not? Are there people in our world who feel the same way about their sins? Explain. Is it possible to play the game of life without making mistakes? Why or why not? How do you think the person who was punished felt? Have you ever been punished for something you didn't do? How did it feel? What did Jesus say when he was being punished?"

Have your junior highers each write another description of Jesus on their 3×5 cards.

6. *Collect your thoughts*—Have young people each take a piece of paper and write three short sentences about three things they learned from this meeting. Have them form groups of three and share their learnings with each other. When the small groups are finished, have junior highers tell some of their learnings to the whole group.

7. *Closing meditation*—Have junior highers close their eyes and listen to a song that talks about Jesus.

After the song, have kids write one more descriptive word for Jesus on their 3×5 cards.

Have everyone join hands. Close with a circle prayer using the descriptive words collected throughout the meeting. Have kids each choose one of the words or phrases they've written. It can describe Jesus or their feelings about him. Begin by saying, "Lord Jesus Christ, we praise you, for you are . . ." Have members each add a word or phrase to complete the prayer sentence. End with a special prayer thanking God for the discoveries about Jesus. ∎

32 Who's Your Hero?

By Ann Carr

Junior highers continually look for role models and heroes.

Use this meeting to help kids see that Jesus is the best role model for how we should act toward one another.

OBJECTIVES

Participants will:
- think about people they admire;
- learn how Jesus set an example for us; and
- discuss how we should act toward others.

SUPPLIES

Gather scissors; glue; newsprint; a marker; masking tape; colored pencils or crayons or markers; a 15- or 20-foot clothesline; two push pins; snacks such as fruit, nuts or veggies and fruit juice; for every two group members, a Bible, a cross-shaped piece of paper with a "Jesus Did" scripture reference from the "Jesus Did" Example in activity #3 written on it; an 8½ ×11 sheet of construction paper; a snap clothespin; and, for each person, at least one of a variety of magazines (for example, sports, fashion, news), a pencil and a 3×5 card.

BEFORE THE MEETING

Read the meeting and collect supplies.

186

THE MEETING

1. *Welcome*—Greet junior highers at the door and offer to do something for them such as take their coats or help them find seats.

2. *Admiration collage*—Have junior highers look through the magazines and rip or cut out pictures of people who represent what they'd like to be. Let them glue the pictures onto a large sheet of newsprint to form a collage. With a marker, label the collage "People We Admire." Tape the collage onto the wall.

Say: "We admire people because of what they represent to us—fame, fortune, good bodies, intelligence, concern for others. Today we're going to look at Jesus as a role model. We'll look at how he acted around and with others. And we'll think about how we should act as examples of his love."

3. *Looking at Jesus*—Give each person a pencil and a 3×5 card. Have group members each write how they'd finish the following sentence: "One thing I admire about Jesus is . . ." While they're completing their answers, write "One thing I admire about Jesus" on the top of a sheet of newsprint. Have the kids one at a time glue their 3×5 cards onto the newsprint. Make sure the cards don't overlap, so all the answers are visible.

Divide the group into pairs. Give each pair a Bible and a cross-shaped piece of paper with a "Jesus Did" scripture reference written on it. Ask partners to look up the scripture verse, then discuss: "What's a time you were in a situation similar to that? How did you, or would you, act if faced with that same situation?"

4. *Greeting cards*—Give each pair an 8½×11 sheet of construction paper and colored pencils or crayons or markers. Ask the partners to fold their sheets of construction paper in half to make greeting cards based on the Bible verses they just looked up. Explain that each pair should make a greeting card that illustrates something Jesus did such as an act of kindness, how he reacted to a situation, or words of wisdom or encouragement he gave (see the "Jesus Did" Example).

Get everyone together in a large group. Ask each pair, one at a time, to show its greeting card and tell its message about how Jesus acted and how we should act.

After group members share their greeting cards, have them clip the cards to the clothesline with clothespins. Use the push pins to hang the clothesline where other congregation members will enjoy it during the week.

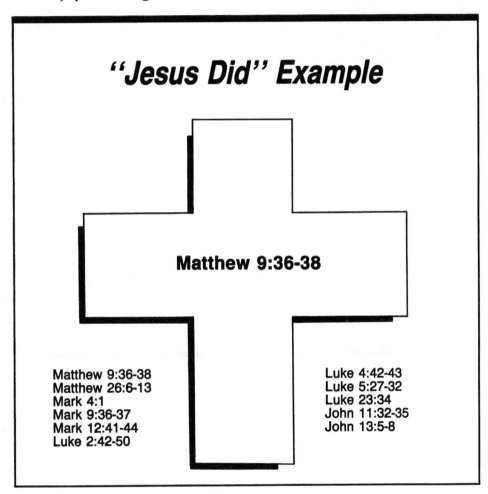

"Jesus Did" Example

Matthew 9:36-38

Matthew 9:36-38
Matthew 26:6-13
Mark 4:1
Mark 9:36-37
Mark 12:41-44
Luke 2:42-50

Luke 4:42-43
Luke 5:27-32
Luke 23:34
John 11:32-35
John 13:5-8

5. *Helping one another*—Have a volunteer read Matthew 25:40. Divide the group into two groups. Have one group, the Helpers, serve snacks and juice to the other group, the Brothers. Remind the Helpers they're doing a kindness as unto the Lord. After the Helpers serve the others, they may also enjoy the refreshments.

6. *Closing*—Ask group members to form two lines and intersect to form a cross, then repeat: "Help us, Jesus, to be more like you. Help us to be loving, kind, compassionate, understanding, helpful and firm in what we believe. Amen." ■

Section Five:

ISSUES

33 *At All Costs*

By Ben Sharpton

Competition is part of life. We can't escape it. Its impact can be positive or negative depending on how we react.

Junior highers learn patterns of dealing with competition that carry over into their adult lives. Some kids respond to competition with a fierce aggressiveness that ignores others' needs or feelings. Some flash jealousy or anger. Some give up. Many can't enjoy a competitive event without feeling frustration over winning or losing.

Competition creates losers. And losing can damage self-esteem and lead to compromising personal beliefs and values in order to win.

Use this meeting to help young people examine positive and negative aspects of competition and the purpose of competition.

OBJECTIVES

Participants will:
- identify positive and negative aspects of competition;
- examine what the Bible and important people say about competition; and
- list possible ways to keep competition from becoming too negative.

SUPPLIES

Gather a list of items (for activity #1) that girls are more likely to have with them than guys, for example, blush, a mirror, lip gloss, a hairbrush, a photo of a friend, perfume, sunglasses, a note from a friend; a pencil; newsprint; markers; for the "Cotton balls" relay: one teaspoon, 10 cotton balls and a water glass for each team of three to eight; for the "Do it on paper" relay: two sheets of newspaper for each team of three to eight; for the "Great tissue blow" relay: one facial tissue for each team of three to eight; for the "Waddle to the bottle" relay: a coin and water glass for each team of three to eight; and, for each person, a Bible.

BEFORE THE MEETING

Read the meeting and collect supplies.

NOTES TO THE LEADER

Competition brings out strong emotions. Avoid embarrassing individuals during the game(s). If feelings are hurt or emotions flare, remind the group that these emotions are a product of the game(s).

THE MEETING

1. *Indoor scavenger hunt*—Divide group members into teams of three to eight. Stack the deck by sending almost everyone with a purse to one team, or pit the girls against the guys. Be subtle.

Place each team in a different section of the room and stand in the center, the same distance from each team. Ask one person from each team to serve as a runner. Call out, one by one, the items on your list. Only the runners may bring the items to you. The first team to get an item to you receives a point. Keep track of points on your list.

Build excitement by emphasizing scores, encouraging cheers, praising the winning team, offering two points for a special item, and so on. After a few minutes, gather group members together and discuss:

● Was the game fun? Why or why not?
● How did it feel to win?

● How did it feel to lose?
● What did you do to avoid losing?
● Was the game fair? Why or why not? (Tell how and why you chose teams.)
● Are games ever fair? Explain.

2. *Quotable quotes*—Get everyone in a circle. Read the following quotes. Ask kids to listen carefully to each one and vote on whether they agree with it (thumbs up), disagree with it (thumbs down), don't care (arms crossed) or don't understand what it means (both hands up in the air while shrugging shoulders). Have kids practice the response actions. Discuss the meaning of each quote after kids respond.

"We compete with God any time we try to put something else at the center of our lives"—John Shaw, former high school football star.

"The Christian concept of competition that comes through from Jesus is that the Christian is basically qualified to compete against himself—not against other people"—Anthony Campolo, sociologist.

"I don't think that playing to win is a conflict with Christianity"—Tom Landry, head coach, Dallas Cowboys.

"In athletics, to a large degree, what we do generates feelings. If you go out and violently attack somebody on the field, it won't be long before you'll hate that person"—Anthony Campolo, sociologist.

"A competitor is one who has been given potential and talent by God to give his or her all. Competition brings the best out of both of you, so that God may be glorified by the event"—Madeline Manning Mims, Olympic champion.

"It is not what the game does to us but what we do to the game. It is not what the game brings to us but what we bring to the game. Bring Jesus. Or maybe you'd better stay away"—Gary Warner, author of *Competition* (David C. Cook Publishing Company).

3. *Situations*—Ask your group to name situations where people compete. List these on newsprint. *Don't discuss them until the list is complete.* Possible situations: among friends, on the job, in the family, classroom, sports, in church.

4. *Scripture*—Divide the group into the same small groups of three to eight. Assign each group one of the following scripture passages. Hand out Bibles. Ask group members to study the passage and decide what it says about competition. After five minutes, have each group report findings to the large group. The passages: 1 Corinthians 9:24-27; Philippians 2:3-5; 3:12-14; Romans 5:1-7.

5. *Good and bad*—Bring the group members back together in a circle. With everyone's input, list on newsprint:
  ● good things about competition,
  ● bad things about competition, and
  ● different purposes for competition.
Have kids discuss positive and negative aspects of competition by reviewing each item on the list and thinking about the scriptures they studied.

6. *Solutions*—Ask your group to think of specific suggestions for keeping competition from becoming too negative. List these on newsprint.

7. *Additional suggestions*—Do one or more of the following relays.

Divide the group members into the same groups of three to eight. Each small group is a team. If the teams aren't equal, have some players on teams with fewer members repeat turns to equalize competition.

Clearly establish a starting line, a spot across the room to go around or perform a specific activity at, and a starting signal for each relay. Team members must stay behind the starting line, start only on the signal, proceed to the designated place across the room, perform the task described by the leader, return to the starting line and tap the next team member who then repeats the process. The first team to have all its members finish wins.

Remind the kids that relays are good examples of competition which can be either positive or negative. This is a good time for them to practice positive aspects of competition. Tell them to play hard, play fair, be good losers and good winners.

Cotton balls—At the signal, one member from each team crosses the room to the designated place where (for each team) 10 cotton balls, an (empty) water glass and a teaspoon are placed. The player is to use the teaspoon to put the 10 cotton balls into the glass. When the task is completed, he or she dumps out the balls, runs back to the starting line and tags the next person to repeat the process, and so on.

Do it on paper—Give each team two sheets of newspaper. At the signal, team members are to go around the designated point at the other end of the room and return to the starting line. The catch: They must do this by stepping only on the two sheets of newspaper. A player steps on one sheet, turns around and picks up the sheet behind him or her, places it in front, steps on it, and so on. When a player returns to the starting line, he or she tags the next person to repeat the process.

Great tissue blow—Give each team one facial tissue. At the signal, the first member from each team blows it along the floor, around the designated point and back across the starting line without touching the tissue. The player tags the next member in line to repeat the process.

Waddle to the bottle—Place the glass for each team on the floor at the designated spot across the room. Give each team a coin. At the signal, the first team members must begin at the starting line, hold the coin between their knees, waddle across the floor and drop the coin into the glass. If a player drops the coin along the way, he or she must start over. Back at the starting line, a player tags the next person.

Two sources for more relays are *Fun-N-Games* by Rice, Rydberg and Yaconelli (Zondervan) and *Guide for Recreation Leaders* by Bannerman and Fakkema (John Knox Press).

8. A spiral prayer—Have everyone get in a circle and hold hands. Tell the person at your left to remain standing exactly where he or she is. Drop that person's hand.

Lead the person at your right and everyone else, connected by their held hands, in a spiral around the stationary person. End with a tight, close spiral of people.

Ask group members to bow their heads and close their eyes. End with a prayer thanking God for the gift of positive competition and asking for help for group members to use what they've discovered about it as they return to the world. ■

34 *Dealing With Death*

By Joani Schultz

Death. Not a likely topic to explore with exuberant, energetic junior highers. Yet the mystery of death, the unknown, and just the fear that someone close might die can haunt young teenagers.

Use this meeting to unravel fears and focus on Jesus' victory over death.

OBJECTIVES

Participants will:
- play a game that evokes fear;
- tell about experiences they've had with death;
- discuss scripture that explains death; and
- create "life vests" to express Jesus' victory over death.

SUPPLIES

Gather a sheet of newsprint with the Bible passages from activity #3 written on it; masking tape; paper; pencils; a sheet of newsprint with the Bible passages from activity #4 written on it; and, for each person, a 3-foot piece of string, a Bible, a sheet of newsprint, scissors and one or more markers. Optional: Life Savers Popsicles or Life Savers candy.

BEFORE THE MEETING

Read the meeting and collect supplies.

Get in touch with your own feelings about death. Recall experiences you've had with people dying and how you handled them.

THE MEETING

1. *Scare tactics*—Begin by turning out the lights and having group members close their eyes. Say: "Everybody keep your eyes closed and mingle around the room. Adults will be the referees to make sure everyone abides by the eyes-closed rule. I'll select one person to use 'scare tactics.' This person can open his or her eyes and find a victim in the group—someone to scare. The scare tactics can include a tap on the shoulder or a grabbed arm with a 'boo!' If you're captured by the scare-tactics person, you can open your eyes, join hands with him or her and help find another victim. The game is finished after everyone becomes a part of the scare-tactics team." Expect lots of screams.

2. *Fearful feelings*—Say: "Death, like this game, manages to scare us. There's so much we don't know; death is something most of us fear. During this meeting, we're going to talk about our fears of death and how Jesus conquered it."

If your group is larger than eight, form smaller groups. Then give each person a 3-foot piece of string. Tell kids to each shape their string in a form that reminds them of an experience they've had with death. For example, a horror movie, a funeral, the death of a pet.

Have kids each explain their string picture, tell about their experience with death and tell how they felt about it.

3. *What's the Bible say?*—Form small groups of three or four by having every three or four people tie their pieces of string together. Have them use their string to form a string circle and sit around it. Hand out Bibles. Tape onto the wall the sheet of newsprint with these Bible passages: Genesis 3:19; Ecclesiastes 12:7; Matthew 10:28; Romans 5:12; Philippians 1:20-25; 1 Thessalonians 4:13-18; Revelation 14:13.

Have each group look up and read the verses. Give each group paper and a pencil. Tell groups to each select a recorder to write their answers to "What did you learn about death from these verses?" Then have everyone get together in a circle and share discoveries with the large group. Ask: "What surprised you most about death? What questions do you still have?" (Any unanswered questions could be brought to the pastor for discussion at another meeting.)

4. *Life vests*—Give each group member a sheet of newsprint, scissors and one or more markers to make a "life vest." Show how (see the life-vest pattern), and let kids make their vests. Tell them to put their names on their vests.

Display the sheet of newsprint with the following Bible passages: John 3:16, 36; John 11:25-26; 1 Corinthians 15:24, 51-57. Have kids each look up each passage. Tell them to find their favorite, most meaningful "life" words from each passage—words that take away the fear of death. Then have them each write the words on their vest and decorate it with other "life" symbols. Have kids wear their vests and tell why they chose the words they did.

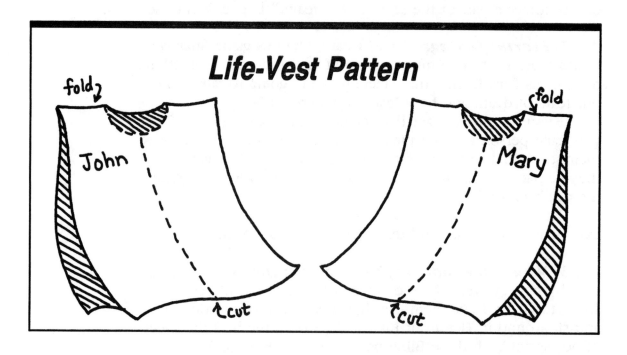

5. *Jesus is our lifesaver*—Have group members, still wearing their vests, form a "lifeline" by joining hands and making the shape of a lifesaver (a circle). Have kids each choose one word from their vest to say as a prayer of hope. Begin the prayer with the person who wore a life jacket in the water most recently. Go around the circle to the right, with each person adding his or her "life" word to the prayer.

6. *Life Savers to savor*—Why not give kids Life Savers Popsicles or Life Savers candy as they head home? Encourage them to take along their vests. ■

35 Facing Fears

By Debra Farst

Everyone has fears.
     But for junior highers, fears can be especially scary. These young people haven't yet developed the wisdom and maturity to know how to face fears.

     Use this meeting to help your group members see that they're not alone in their fears—and that they can look to each other and God for help.

OBJECTIVES

Participants will:
- identify common fears of teenagers, including themselves;
- discover how they respond to fear and hear new ways to face fear;
- choose a personal plan for facing fear; and
- be encouraged to seek help from God and others in fearful situations.

SUPPLIES

     Gather a gorilla mask; 20 3×5 cards, each with one of the "Top Fears" written on it; markers; string; masking tape; sheets of newsprint with the discussion questions in activity #2 written on them; a sheet of newsprint with the incomplete sentences in activity #5 written on it; three Bibles; and, for each person, a file folder, a pencil, a "Top Fears" handout, a "Fear Test," a slip of paper and a deflated balloon the same color as everyone else's.

198

BEFORE THE MEETING

Read the meeting and collect supplies.

Find an adult sponsor who'll agree to be the scary gorilla as kids arrive.

Choose a room other than the meeting room to be the "fear room." Use string and masking tape to hang the 20 "top fears" cards from the ceiling at different spots around the room.

Invite someone who recently faced a fearful situation to come and tell your group how he or she handled it.

NOTES TO THE LEADER

This meeting will help you discover some deep fears your group members have. Be sensitive to your kids. Treat all of their fears seriously.

THE MEETING

1. *The arrival*—As kids enter the room, have an adult sponsor wearing a gorilla mask jump out from a hiding place and roar at each person.

When everyone's arrived, get kids together in a circle. Ask whether anyone was frightened by the gorilla. Announce the meeting's topic: being afraid.

2. *Identifying fears*—Have kids remember and tell about times they were really afraid; for example, at a Halloween haunted house or a scary movie. Give each person a file folder and a pencil. Have group members title the folders "Facing Fears." Then have them open the folders and write on the right side what they think are their friends' greatest fears. For example, that their parents might divorce or that they might lose a best friend. Then have group members each write three of their own greatest fears at the bottom of that same side.

Take the group into the "fear room," where cards with teenagers' fears from the national survey are hanging from the ceiling. Tell group members that these are kids' worst fears, according to a survey. Challenge kids to each find the #1 worst fear and stand by it. When they've made their choices, tell them the #1 worst fear is school performance. Ask: "Are you surprised? Why or why not? Why is this the worst fear?"

Have everyone return to your meeting room and get in

small groups of four or five. Give everyone a "Top Fears" handout.

Display these questions on sheets of newsprint for groups to discuss: "How do your fears compare to the fears on the survey? If your fears are low on the list or not on the list, does that mean they're less important? Why or why not? Why do we fear things? Think about one of your top three fears and try to decide why you're afraid. For example, if you worry about grades, are you afraid your parents will yell, afraid of being called stupid, or afraid of your chances for a good job someday? How can fear be good? How can fear be bad? How can God help you handle fear?"

Have the kids put their "Top Fears" handouts in their folders.

Top Fears

In a national survey, teenagers named their most serious fears, in this order:

School performance	(57%)	That I might not get a good job	(30%)
About my looks	(53%)	Physical development	(26%)
How well other kids like me	(48%)	Nuclear destruction of the United States	(25%)
That a parent might die	(47%)	That my parents might divorce	(22%)
How my friends treat me	(45%)	That I may die soon	(21%)
Hunger and poverty in the United States	(38%)	Sexual abuse	(19%)
Violence in the United States	(36%)	That my friends will get me into trouble	(18%)
That I might lose a best friend	(36%)	Drinking by a parent	(15%)
Drugs and drinking	(35%)	That I will get beat up at school	(12%)
		Physical abuse by a parent	(12%)
		That I might kill myself	(12%)

Abridged from Table 3 (p. 82) "The Worries of Young Adolescents" in *Five Cries of Parents: New Help for Families on The Issues That Trouble Them Most* by Merton P. Strommen and A. Irene Strommen. Copyright © 1985 by the Authors. Reprinted by permission of Harper & Row, Publishers, Inc. Any copying to be done by youth group leaders must be re-cleared by Harper & Row, Publishers, Inc., San Francisco, 1-800-638-3030.

3. *How I respond*—Give everyone a "Fear Test." Make sure kids still have their pencils. Tell them this test will let them see how they usually act when they're afraid. Ask them to answer the questions honestly.

Discuss the test results with the whole group in a circle. Ask: "How do you feel about having 'a,' 'b' or 'c' answers?

200

Fear Test

For each situation, check your most likely response.

1. You are beginning at a new school. The night before, you:
   (a) carefully choose your clothes so you'll make the right impression. _____
   (b) go to bed in a cold sweat and have nightmares all night. _____
   (c) don't think about it at all. _____

2. A group of high-school kids asks you to ride in their new car. You:
   (a) think for a moment, then say no because you don't know the driver. _____
   (b) feel nervous around high-school kids and stammer "n-n-n-o." _____
   (c) immediately hop in. _____

3. Your parents don't usually argue, but you hear them yelling at each other. You:
   (a) worry, but figure they'll make up soon. _____
   (b) break out in a rash from worrying that they'll divorce. _____
   (c) shrug it off. _____

4. You're asked to give a special closing prayer at a youth group meeting. You:
   (a) select a Psalm you know well, but read it from the Bible anyway. _____
   (b) say no to the request, and pretend you don't feel well. _____
   (c) offer a prayer from your heart without planning it beforehand. _____

Do you have more "a," "b" or "c" answers? If you have mostly "a" answers, you're cautious in scary situations. If you have mostly "b" answers, you tend to stay afraid and let the situation get the best of you. If you have mostly "c" answers, you don't let many things frighten you for long.

What does this tell you about yourself? Are you surprised? Why or why not?"

Have the kids put their "Fear Tests" in their folders.

4. Facing fears—Tell group members that now they'll hear a number of possible responses to their fears. So if they're unhappy with their own way of responding, they'll have new ideas.

Give everyone a slip of paper and a balloon. Make sure kids still have their pencils. Have everyone write his or her #1 fear on the slip of paper, without writing his or her name. Kids should then fold the slips of paper, stuff them into their balloons and blow up and tie the balloons.

Let kids have a few minutes to play with the balloons. Challenge them to keep the balloons from falling to the floor.

Gather kids back in a circle, with the balloons in the middle. One at a time, let a junior higher choose a balloon, pop it, and read the fear aloud. That junior higher should then pretend he or she is a "group doctor" or "fear expert" and suggest a way to handle it. Then let all other group members brainstorm ways to handle the fear. Have the junior higher to the right of the balloon-popper go next.

Continue this problem-solving process for all of the balloons. At the end, tell junior highers to hold onto the slips of paper they chose; they'll use them later.

5. Choosing a plan—Have group members sit in pairs. Make sure they have their folders and pencils. Display the newsprint with these incomplete sentences:

- I've had this fear for (how long) . . .
- I'm afraid because . . .
- I'm most afraid when . . .
- Someone who could help me overcome this fear is . . .
- I will overcome my fear by . . .

Tell the kids to think about how they'd finish the sentences and write their answers on the inside left section of their folders. Also tell group members to each think of a symbol for their fear and draw it under their answers. For example, a junior higher may draw a book to represent the fear of getting bad grades.

Let partners discuss their answers and symbols.

6. Help from God—Have everyone sit in a circle. Let your visitor briefly tell about when he or she faced a scary situation, how he or she handled it and how God helped. If you don't have a visitor, give similar information from your own life or summarize the Bible story of God bringing the Israelites out of slavery in Egypt.

7. Closing—Have group members put the slips of paper with the fears on them in the center of the circle. Remind group members that God wants to help them overcome their fears. But they must ask for his help.

Have volunteers read aloud Isaiah 41:10; Matthew 7:7-8; and Mark 11:24. Close with a prayer that junior highers will seek help in handling fears and will overcome them. ∎

36 *Fair's Fair*

By Phil Baker

Sometimes life just isn't fair. The star of the football team breaks his leg; parents divorce; fathers are transferred. How do you help junior highers deal with situations that happen unexpectedly and there's little they can do about them?

Such situations are tough for adults. They're even tougher for junior highers. Young teenagers have little experience with unavoidable disasters.

Use this meeting to help junior highers see that unfair situations aren't the end of the world.

OBJECTIVES

Participants will:
- experience activities that break down barriers, encourage openness and build community;
- focus on a familiar Bible story about a life situation that's not fair;
- role play helping friends face unavoidable life problems; and
- be exposed to the wisdom and faith that help Christians deal with unavoidable problems.

SUPPLIES

Gather masking tape; markers; a list of possible "people machines" for activity #2, for example, a washing machine, a lawn mower, an electric mixer; a sheet of newsprint with the Serenity Prayer in activity #5 written on it; for every four to eight group members, a "Scripture Search Questions" handout and a "Role Plays" handout; and, for each person, a piece of paper for a name tag, a straight pin and a 40-inch piece of string.

BEFORE THE MEETING

Read the meeting and collect supplies.

Tape the Serenity Prayer onto the wall near the place where you'll have the closing worship.

THE MEETING

1. *As they arrive*—Have each person make a name tag with a piece of paper and markers, and pin it on.

Have an adult sponsor tie the ends of a piece of string to the wrists of one person. The string must be carefully tied around each wrist with the loops snug. Have the adult tie one end of another string to a wrist of a second person, bring the loose end through the inside of the loop made by the string and arms of the first person, and tie the second end to the other wrist of the second person. The string will loop the two group members together. Do this for all group members.

The object is for the partners to escape without breaking or untying their strings. Allow enough time for successful escapees to share the secret with those who are still tied together.

2. *People machines*—Divide the group into small groups of four to eight, with one adult in each group. Whisper the name of a machine to each group. Tell the group members to use *every* person and make the machine with their bodies. Allow time for each group to decide how to make its machine and practice the movements.

Have all group members sit while you call on one group at a time to demonstrate its machine. See if the other groups can guess the machine. Applaud when each group is finished.

3. *Scripture search*—Have the same small group members sit in circles with their knees touching. Give a "Scripture Search Questions" handout to each group's adult sponsor. Read "The Older Brother's Story" and stop at the indicated places for groups to discuss the "Scripture Search Questions."

4. *Role play*—Role plays present situations with conflicts or potential conflicts. The players supply the dialogue and try to

204

Scripture Search Questions

Lead your group in these discussion questions after each break in the reader's story.

● **Luke 15:11-13**—An inheritance is usually received after the death of a person. Imagine you're the father. How would this make you feel? What would you say to your son? What advice would you give your son as you give him the money?

● **Luke 15:14-24**—When a junior higher is away from home, gets in trouble and returns, what's the reaction of most parents? If you were the father, what would you do differently? Why?

● **Luke 15:25-32**—Answer the older brother's request for group members to tell about a time when they felt the way he did. (It helps the discussion if the leader begins with a brief unfair experience from his or her own life.)

find solutions. This activity's aim is to *practice* helping friends with unavoidable problems.

Continue with the same small groups. Give the "Role Plays" handout to each group's adult sponsor. Have the adult in each group select the two role players and set the scene for each role play. After about one minute, have the leader ask the two role players to switch roles or stop the action. After each role play, have the leader discuss with group members ways to deal with the particular problem.

5. *Closing worship*—Have group members get in a circle near the newsprint with the Serenity Prayer on it. Say: "In this meeting we dealt with situations that weren't fair. Nothing could be done to avoid them. They just happened.

"Life is like that too. From time to time bad things happen to good people. Jesus uses the story of the older brother to help us understand this.

"There are things we *can't* change. To survive, we must learn to stop worrying about things beyond our control and concentrate our efforts on things we *can* change.

"A man once wrote the poem you see on the newsprint. He asked God to give him serenity, or calmness, in the midst of difficult times. Read it silently . . . Now think of an incident in

The Older Brother's Story

"My story is told by Jesus in Luke 15:11-32. I have no name. Just call me Older Brother. There are two other characters in my story: my younger brother and my father.

"We're a typical farm family. We work hard and honor our father as our scriptures teach. One day, my younger brother asks our father for his part of the farm. Our religious law says that's one-third of all we have. My father agrees.

"My younger brother quickly sells the land and leaves this country. Can you believe it? He leaves me with all the work, takes his money and goes. Now I ask you, is what my brother did fair?"

● ● ●

"Okay, let's continue the story. My brother travels to a country a long way from our home. He lives well. So well that he quickly spends all of *our* money in wild living. After a while he's dirty, hungry and takes a job caring for a farmer's pigs. Imagine, a good Jewish boy tending pigs! I just can't believe it.

"My brother is completely broke now and the pig farmer won't advance him any money. He envies the pigs' food and begins to think about home. He remembers our father's servants eat well and are treated fairly.

"It isn't long until he starts home. When he sees Dad he asks him to treat him like a servant rather than a son. Dad hugs him, calls the servants and orders a welcome-home party for him. I can't believe it. I ask you, why did my dad treat him this way?"

● ● ●

"Let's end this story. I've worked hard all day in the fields. I'm tired, hot and sweaty, I want to relax, bathe, have supper and then talk with my father about the day's work.

"I hear the sounds of a party, find out from a servant what's going on and I get mad—madder than I've ever been in my life. I find my father and remind him what a faithful son *I've* always been. I didn't ask for my inheritance. Instead I worked harder than I've ever worked before.

"Furthermore, I honor him, stay at home and I'm a good son. What does he say? 'Son, you're always with me and we thought your brother was dead. It's right that we give this party to show how happy we are.'

"Now I ask you. Fair's fair! What's fair about this? Have you ever felt this way before? Tell your group about it."

206

Role Plays

● **Role Play A**—John's the star quarterback on his school's football team. It's the day before the first game. He passes by the park where his friends are playing a rough game of touch football. He joins the fun. Five minutes later he feels something snap; he falls to the ground in pain; his leg is broken. The doctor tells him: "No football for the rest of the season." He can only watch the games from the sidelines.

His friend Bob comes by the house and finds John depressed. John says: "It just isn't fair, Bob. Why? Why did it happen?" What does Bob say?

● **Role Play B**—Sue's a cheerleader. She's excited when she returns from cheerleading camp. It's going to be a good year and she's ready for it.

Suddenly everything changes. Her parents break the news: Dad has a new job and they're moving to another state right away.

Bev, a good friend, enters Sue's room and finds Sue on her bed crying. Sue finally tells Bev the story and ends with: "It just isn't fair, Bev. Why? Why do we have to move?" What does Bev say?

● **Role Play C**—Sandi's parents divorced in May. The summer was miserable. Sandi and her mom had to move into a small apartment. But at least Sandi will be in the same junior high school this fall.

To fill the time, Sandi and her best friend Lisa spent hours prowling the malls. Sandi had her school wardrobe all planned.

Now her mom tells her there just isn't enough money to dress the way she planned. They can afford only two of the nice outfits, or Sandi can get more at the discount stores.

Sandi calls Lisa on the phone: "Lisa, it isn't fair. How can I ever go to school again?" What does Lisa say?

● **Role Play D**—(The characters in this story could be male or female; it doesn't matter.) You just had the most fabulous summer of your life. Your dad's a computer programmer. He took the family to Hawaii on an all-expense-paid trip while he worked. For three months you had the vacation everyone dreams of.

Now you're home, two weeks after school started. It's your first day back and you're late. You rush into your class and discover you're now the shortest boy or the tallest girl. After the first class you meet your best friend in the restroom and say: "It isn't fair. I can't stand it! Why?" What does your best friend say?

your life that was unfair and unavoidable . . . Remember how hard you tried to change it . . . The more you tried, the more miserable you became. Remember . . . But you survived.

"Now think of a crisis in your life that you changed . . . Think of everything you did to make things better . . . Think of how you felt when you knew they were better.

"Now, what's the difference? One circumstance could be changed, one couldn't. . . . One thing that helps is finding someone who cares, really cares, about your problem. For a Christian, that's often God. Remember, in the story God loved and understood the older brother and he loves and understands us too. We can use God's love to help us through the terrible and unchangeable things. And we also need God's help with the things we can control. But, to survive, we need to know the difference."

Have group members pray the Serenity Prayer in unison:
"God grant me the serenity
To accept the things I cannot change,
The courage to change the things I can,
And the wisdom to know the difference. Amen." ∎

37 Forgiving Myself and Others

By Mary Blake

''That's okay!'' Those words are important to kids when they mean ''You're forgiven!'' When forgiveness is given and received, a healing occurs in both the giver and the receiver. Forgiveness removes guilt that can eat away at young lives.

Use this meeting to show junior highers how forgiveness can wash away guilt.

OBJECTIVES

Participants will:
- identify sin in their own lives and community;
- read about sin and forgiveness from God's Word;
- experience God's forgiveness and love; and
- be challenged to practice forgiveness in their own lives.

SUPPLIES

Gather masking tape; three 3×5 cards, each with one of the three role plays on it; for every four to six group members, a pile of newspapers, scissors, an 18×24-inch sheet of construction paper, several small plastic garbage bags, two balls of modeling clay; for every two group members, a towel, a washcloth, a bowl of soapy water; and, for each person, a 3×5 construction-paper name tag, a marker, a straight pin, a Bible, a ''Together, Apart, Together'' handout, a pencil, a 2×4-inch slip of paper, a "Talking to God" handout (without the parenthetical instructions), and a 7×9-inch construction-paper heart, cut in half jigsaw puzzle style, with one side marked "#1—Jesus Loves You" and the other "#2—and Forgives You" and the pieces paper-clipped together.

BEFORE THE MEETING
Read the meeting and collect supplies.

THE MEETING

1. *Name-tag mixer*—As kids arrive, give each junior higher a name tag, marker and straight pin. Tell group members each to write their name and one good thing that happened to them this week. Have kids pin on their name tags.

Divide the group into small groups of four to six, each with an adult sponsor. Within the small groups, have group members each give their name and tell the good thing that happened in their life.

2. *What is sin?*—While the kids remain in their small groups, relate an incident in your life that shows how you sinned against someone. Tell how you felt about it, and what you did because of it.

Explain: "Sins are thoughts, words or actions that go against God's will and hurt another person and (or) ourselves. Sin has been present since Adam and Eve ate the forbidden fruit in the Garden of Eden."

3. *Sin in our communities*—Say: "Everyone sins. I sin, you sin, your parents sin, and your friends and neighbors sin. We hear about it on the news and we read about it in newspapers. I'd like each of you to find a newspaper article that tells about someone who sinned."

Hand out newspapers and scissors to each group. Say: "Find some articles that represent sin. Discuss each article within your group. Explain what the sin is, who did it and to whom it was done."

Have individual groups cut out and tape their newspaper articles onto an 18×24-inch sheet of construction paper when they finish discussing.

4. *Sin, guilt and forgiveness: A game with news-*

papers—This game helps kids discover what guilt is and how Jesus forgives. Divide the remaining newspapers into equal piles. Give a pile of newspapers and several small plastic garbage bags to each group. Have the kids tightly wad up individual sheets of newspaper and stuff them into the plastic bags, one bag at a time. The winning group stuffs the paper into the least number of garbage bags. (The object is for kids to get ink all over their hands.)

Have all group members get on their knees in a circle. Ask: "If the newspaper represents sin in our lives, what could the black all over your hands be? Yes, just as black ink is all over us, so sin leaves us with a yucky feeling called guilt. Wouldn't it be terrific to get this black stuff off?"

Divide the group into pairs and hand out towels, washcloths and bowls of soapy water. Have group members wash the black ink off their partners' hands.

After everyone is clean, have group members get back into one circle. Ask: "If the newspaper is a symbol for sin and the black is a symbol for guilt, what's the water? the soap? the washcloth?"

Next, have someone read Ephesians 1:7. Ask: "How does this verse tie in to what we've just done and talked about?" Allow time for discussion. Explain the parallel between the hand-washing to remove the ink and Jesus Christ's blood cleansing us from sin through forgiveness.

5. *Sin happens to our friends and families*—Select six young people to role play the following three scenarios. Give each pair a 3×5 card with a role play on it.

After the role plays, discuss: "Is it easy to forgive? Is it easier to forgive or to receive forgiveness? Do you have to forgive?"

6. *Jacob and Esau*—Say: "Forgiveness is the 'glue' that mends our broken relationships with Christ and with one another. Let's look at an example from scripture to see how forgiveness kept some people together, and how the lack of forgiveness kept some apart."

Divide the group into groups of three. Hand out Bibles. Have kids read these passages: Genesis 27:1-46; Genesis 32:1-31; and Genesis 33:1-11. Then give a "Together, Apart, Together" handout and a pencil to each person.

7. *Forgiveness comes from the heart*—Tell the kids to

Forgiving
Myself and Others

211

Three Role Plays

● Your parents' car and another car just collided head-on. The other driver was drunk and at fault. You and the other driver suffered minor bruises and scrapes, but your parents have been rushed to the hospital in serious condition. As you are giving your statement to the police, the other driver comes over and says: "I'm sorry. I didn't mean to hit you, but I was blinded by your bright lights!"
Have someone read Matthew 6:14.

● Your best friend was murdered in her home by a robber. The person accused is convicted and sentenced to life imprisonment. As you leave the courtroom after his sentencing, you meet the murderer. Have someone read Colossians 3:13.

● You're taking a final exam in a classroom. Your grade on this test determines whether you pass or fail. A bright student sitting next to you is checking his or her answers; you copy some of them. Your teacher sees you and rips up your test. You try to defend yourself by saying: "I was just changing some of my answers. I just have to pass this test!"
Have someone read 1 John 1:8-10.

Together, Apart, Together

1. In the story of Jacob and Esau, who was sinning? Jacob? Esau? both? What sin was committed?
2. What happened to their relationship as brothers as a result of sin?
3. Who helped them to forgive? Who offered forgiveness?
4. What happened to their relationship as brothers as a result of forgiveness?
5. Sin makes me feel . . .
6. Forgiveness makes me feel . . .

Talking to God

I TALK TO GOD ABOUT MY SINS . . .

(Have group members read this aloud together.)

Dear Lord,
    I did some wrong things, and I'm sorry.
    I forgot about loving and became hateful instead.
    I forgot about understanding and became angry instead.
    I forgot about helping and became selfish instead.
    I forgot about you, Lord, and thought too much about myself.
Right now, Lord, I'm thinking about the time I . . .

(Have each person write on a 2×4-inch slip of paper a sin he or she has committed.)

and I broke my relationship with you. I am sorry, Lord. Please forgive me and grant me a new start.

(Have group members add their slips of paper to the newspaper articles and clay symbols in the area designated "Sin.")

Forgive me, Lord.
Hug me with your love.
Make me feel happy again!

. . . AND GOD FORGIVES.

(Have each group bring its forgiveness symbol to an area designated "Forgiveness.")

God says this:
    I have forgotten all about your wrongs
    and I will never hold them against you.
    I will love you, no matter who you are
    or how you act.

    Go and be happy again! Rejoice! You are forgiven! Amen!

(Lead the group in the following chorus, sung to the tune of "I've Got Peace Like a River.")

Yes, my sins are forgiven. Yes, my sins are forgiven! Yes, my sins are forgiven every day!

Yes, my sins are forgiven. Yes, my sins are forgiven! Jesus Christ takes my sins all away!

return to their original small groups of four to six. Give each person a two-part heart puzzle. Say: "On the #1 piece, write a sin someone committed against you. How did you feel? What did you do? On the #2 piece, write a sin you committed against someone. How did you feel? How do you think the other person felt? What did you do? When you finish writing, share answers with each other."

Give each small group two balls of clay. Ask each group to create a symbol of sin and a symbol of forgiveness. Have groups put their symbols of sin and their posters of newspaper articles in a spot designated "Sin." Tell them to keep their symbols of forgiveness for the closing worship.

8. *Closing worship*—Lead the group in singing "They'll Know We Are Christians by Our Love." Give each person a 2×4-inch slip of paper and a "Talking to God" handout. (Be sure you haven't included the parenthetical instructions on their copies. They're for your reference only.)

Go through the handout together.

After the group sings the chorus, say: "It's great knowing that Jesus forgives our sins, but we should also remember that Jesus forgives the sins of others as well. So the next time you fail to forgive someone for something wrong done to you, remember that person is forgivable too. Treat him or her as Jesus would. Remember what the Lord's Prayer says: "Forgive our trespasses, even as we forgive those who trespass against us."

Close by having the group recite the Lord's Prayer. ∎

38 Rules, Rules, Rules

By Linda Snyder

Young adolescents need rules. But they often view rules as a barrier to freedom.
Use this meeting to help junior highers experience rules as a positive part of life.

OBJECTIVES

Participants will:
- play two games—one with no rules and one with unreasonable rules—in order to experience the need for rules;
- discuss the positive and negative aspects of rules;
- write 10 commandments that apply to their lives; and
- take part in a "freedom" worship experience.

SUPPLIES

Gather a 1-inch-diameter paper star; masking tape; markers; two small prizes such as McDonald's coupons; for every four to six group members, a "Discussion Questions for Unreasonable Rules" handout, a Bible, two sheets of newsprint; and, for each person, a chair, a color 3×5 construction-paper name tag (use different colors for groups of four to six), a straight pin, a piece of paper and a pencil.

BEFORE THE MEETING

Read the meeting and collect supplies.

Arrange enough chairs for your group in a circle. Place one chair in the center and tape the paper star underneath the seat.

NOTES TO THE LEADER

In activity #1, there may be a point at which behavior becomes too aggressive. If your junior highers forget about being careful to not hurt each other and instead play only to win, simply stop the game and move on.

THE MEETING

1. *The everything-goes game*—As kids enter, ask them to sit in the chairs. Say: "We're going to play a new game. When time is called, the winner is the person sitting in the chair with the star taped on it." Say nothing about where the star is located; if the kids find it, ignore them.

Give *no* rules. Allow the game to continue for three to five minutes. Call time and award the prize. Allow *no* comments.

Send the young people and adult sponsors out of the room while you set up for the next game. Quickly place the chair with the star back in the circle of other chairs.

2. *Name tags*—Outside the meeting room, have adult sponsors hand out the name tags, markers and straight pins and ask each person to write his or her first name on the tag, pin it on, then return to the room for the second game, find a chair and sit down.

3. *The unreasonable-rules game*—Explain Simon Says: You'll give a series of commands. Players follow the directions only if the phrase "Simon says" is included. For instance: If you say "Simon says everyone with blue eyes move one chair to the right," everyone with blue eyes must follow the instructions. However, if you say only "Everyone with blue eyes move one chair to the right," then anyone who moves is out.

When a person is forced out of his or her chair by another person's move, he or she must find a new, empty chair. The last person seated after a move is also out of the game.

Insert or leave out the phrase "Simon says" as you wish, and use your imagination to create commands. Some ideas: move four chairs to the left, all guys move two chairs to the right, everyone with blue eyes move one chair to the left, everyone wearing glasses move three chairs to the right, everyone wearing white socks move four chairs to the right.

Expect anger and confusion. Unless your junior highers are

extremely calm, after a few minutes many will be out of the game and will be grumpy about the unrealistic rules.

Now give group members new rules that you "forgot" to tell them at the beginning. As you give them Simon Says instructions, add new ones such as anyone wearing green is out, anyone who was born in another state is out, anyone who is wearing braces is out. Use your imagination; mix these with the regular commands.

When you've inserted several new rules or when 10 minutes is over, award a prize to the person sitting in the star seat. If no one is sitting there, don't give a prize.

4. *Huddle*—Have group members get into small groups according to the color of their name tags and form huddles by sitting cross-legged on the floor in circles. Be sure there's one adult sponsor for each huddle.

Say: "We're going to talk about the two games we played. Your leader will ask questions about how the games made you feel."

Give each small group leader a "Discussion Questions for Unreasonable Rules" handout. Allow about 10 minutes for discussion.

Discussion Questions for Unreasonable Rules

Have your small group discuss:
- What was the most frustrating part of the two games?
- The rules for Simon Says were changed on purpose as you played. How did that make you feel? Why do game rules need to be clear? consistent (the same for everyone)? Why does everyone need to follow the rules?
- In real life, some people don't follow the rules. How does it feel if you have to follow the rules when others don't?
- What would school be like if there were no rules? home? Does school ever change the rules? If so, how? How does that make you feel? Does your family ever change the rules? If so, how? How does that make you feel?
- What makes a good rule?

par据

5. *10 commandments according to junior highers*—
Give each small group a Bible, two sheets of newsprint and markers.

Say: "God showed his love by giving us rules to live by. He didn't want us to be hurt, and he knew that rules were the best way to avoid this.

"Remember what happened in the game with no rules, and then in the game when the rules were changed. Think about what you said about rules in your huddles.

"Your small group leader will first read the Ten Commandments from Exodus 20:1-17. Then your job is to write your own 10 commandments—rules that touch your life. Use positive statements such as 'You shall always remember to . . .' and so on. Write them on newsprint.

"You have 15 minutes to make your own rules that cover any part of your life. I'll remind you how much time remains every now and then. Begin."

6. *Mime a charade*—When time is up, have each group select two of its 10 commandments and pantomime them (act out using only motions) for the other groups to guess. (If you have a small junior high group, have the kids write each commandment on a slip of paper. Then have each person draw a commandment and act it out as other group members guess.)

Give each person a piece of paper and a pencil. Have the kids each copy their group's 10 commandments onto their paper.

7. *Freedom worship*—Get kids together in a circle. Have each group member place the 10 commandments paper on the floor in front of him or her, cross his or her arms in the front (left over right) and hold the hands of the people on either side.

Read John 13:34: "And now I give you a new commandment: love one another. As I have loved you, so you must love one another."

Say: "Think for a moment about the difference in this commandment of Jesus and the Ten Commandments from Exodus. Jesus' commandment doesn't give a list of dos and don'ts. It simply tells us to love each other.

"This kind of commandment gives us freedom—freedom from the don'ts. What kind of school would you have if everyone lived by Jesus' commandment? What kind of church? What kind of family?

''Now look at the 10 commandments on the sheet in front of you. If everyone lived by those rules, what kind of school would you have? church? family?

''Take your 10 commandments home and talk about them with your parents. Many of your parents have different feelings about rules; this is a good chance for you to find out how they feel.

''Tell them how you feel too. You could discuss any home rules you feel are unfair or propose new rules that would help you begin to set some of your own limits.

''We'll close with a silent prayer asking God to help us make our families better.''

After the prayer, close with a group scrunch—a hearty, huge hug where everyone scrunches as closely together as possible. ∎

39 Sometimes I Hurt

By Paula Mott-Becker

*J*unior highers can't always stop angry and spiteful words or change others' insensitive actions. However, they can control how they interpret and respond when faced with painful situations. It's their responsibility to evaluate their own reactions and determine whether they help or harm themselves and their relationships.

Use this meeting to help young people determine how their actions affect them and the important people in their lives.

OBJECTIVES

Participants will:
- identify experiences that cause them to hurt;
- evaluate ways they respond to their hurts;
- determine whether their personal beliefs and actions tend to increase their hurts or help them positively deal with them; and
- discover helpful actions and thoughts to cope with their hurts.

SUPPLIES

Gather a lot of newsprint; masking tape; markers; six posterboard "reaction signs," each with one of the following written on it: "Laugh," "Strike Back," "Avoid It," "Ignore It," "Talk It Out," "Clam Up"; six 10-inch-square posterboard "money cards," each with one of the following written on it: "$0,"

"$10," "$25," "$50," "$75," "$100"; for every three to six group members, a Bible; and, for each person, a 3×5 card (depending on your choice of method in activity #2), a 5×7 "tally card" with "Response" and "Payment" written across the top and numbers one through six written down the left-hand side, a pencil, a "Does It Hurt or Heal?" handout and a "From Hurting to Healing" handout.

BEFORE THE MEETING

Read the meeting and collect supplies.

Cover a large section of a wall with newsprint for the graffiti wall. At the top center write "Sometimes I Hurt." Divide the sheet into three equal sections. Head each section with one of the following: "Family," "Friends," "School/Teachers."

Place the reaction signs on the walls at various points around the room.

Create a "money line": Place on the floor a strip of tape about 14 feet long (adapt for the size of room and number of people). Tape the money cards onto the line at equal intervals.

NOTES TO THE LEADER

Focus discussion on feelings and reactions, not on blame or specific details.

Junior highers might try to "bait" you into joining their side in family problems. Don't get into arguments over the right or wrong of what a parent does or says. Deal with how kids reacted and whether it hurt or helped the situation.

If someone begins to talk specifically about an intimate experience, suggest he or she see you or an adult sponsor after the meeting to talk more.

THE MEETING

1. *Painful pantomimes*—Gather group members together. Ask them to each think of a time when they were doing a physical activity or were involved in a situation that actually caused them physical pain. The activity could be anything from running a marathon, to painting a house, to falling off a ladder. Tell them to keep their experiences secret and each think of a way to pantomime what happened. Ask volunteers to do their pantomimes, one by one. The rest of the group should guess what happened. Do as many pantomimes as time allows.

Discuss: "Which, if any, of the activities were good for the person even though they caused pain? Could any of the activities have been done in such a way to prevent the hurting? How? How do we know whether the physical pain we feel is good or bad for us? How is physical hurting sometimes like the pain we feel inside?"

Say: "Physical pain lets us know when we've been hurt or when we're hurting ourselves. It's usually obvious and easy to identify. It can be both good and bad for us, depending on how we deal with the pain. To become physically fit and strong, we must face and deal with some degree of pain. Once we've done that we feel better and we're more resistant to injury.

"It's the same with the pain we experience from personal relationships. Close friendships and family togetherness always include some times of hurting. Hurting can become healing through understanding our feelings and responding in good and appropriate ways."

2. Graffiti wall—Direct kids' attention to the graffiti wall. Make markers available. Tell group members you'd like them to write on the wall some of the experiences they've had that have caused them to hurt. For example, parents' divorce, losing a friend, being rejected. The written experiences should be placed under the appropriate headings: "Family," "Friends" or "School/Teachers." Tell kids to keep experiences short and allow each other privacy while they think and write. Say that they shouldn't use any names in what they write. If junior highers have trouble getting started, do some sharing in the whole group. Then send kids to the graffiti wall.

If having your entire group work at the graffiti wall doesn't seem feasible, adapt the idea by handing out 3×5 cards. Kids could privately write on the cards and then tape them onto the wall under the proper headings.

Allow a few minutes for everyone to read what others have written. In the whole group, discuss: "With whom does this group seem to experience the most hurts? What kinds of experiences show up most often?"

Select from the graffiti wall six situations kids would like to discuss. Do this by having kids each choose one hurt from each category. Count the choices and use the ones with the most votes. Label hurts one to six, not necessarily in priority. Write the six hurts on newsprint so group members can read them.

3. *Hurt reactions* — Now have kids focus on how they'd respond to the six situations if they happened to them. This exercise makes junior highers more aware of how their feelings affect their reactions. Use this process:

1. Hand out tally cards and pencils. Draw the group members' attention to the reaction signs and money line.

2. Read the first of the six situations identified from the graffiti wall. (For example, "being rejected.")

3. Instruct kids to stand by the reaction sign that best describes how they would respond to this situation if it happened to them. (For example, "Clam Up.")

4. Ask them to mark their answer under the #1 response on the tally card.

5. Now ask group members to each think about how strongly they feel about this situation. Have them imagine they each have $100 that can be used to get rid of this painful experience. They can use as much or as little as they'd like. (For example, to escape being rejected I'd spend $99.) With each new situation, they'll have another $100.

6. Instruct kids to each move to the location on the money line that best indicates their response. (For example, I'd stand close to the $100 end.)

7. Have them mark their answer on the tally card under the #1 payment.

8. Repeat this procedure for each of the remaining five situations.

Ask an adult sponsor to jot down some of the overall group responses: How does the group seem to respond most often? Which kinds of situations seem to be most painful?

Summarize your observations before you move into the discussion. Have kids form groups of three to six with an adult sponsor in each group. Discuss: "Which of your responses are positive and helpful? Why? Which are negative or hurtful? Why? Compare your response to the amount of money you were willing to spend to get rid of the problem. As the problems gain in importance, did you find your responses to be more or less helpful? Explain. What does this tell you about yourself?"

As kids discuss each situation, ask them to talk about which response would be most likely to bring a positive resolution to the problem. Ask each small group to tell its discoveries to the large group.

4. *Bible discoveries* — Read the story of the lost son in

Does It Hurt or Heal?

● Read Luke 15:11-32.

● Complete the following sentences:
1. The father in this parable probably felt hurt because . . .
2. The hurt of the younger son came from . . .
3. The older son was hurt because . . .

● What reaction did each character have to his painful feelings?
Father: _____
Younger son: _____
Older son: _____

● Read the sentences below. In the spaces on the right, put an "F" by any statements you believe the father would be likely to agree with. Do the same with the younger son, writing "YS," and the older son, writing "OS." Statements may have more than one mark by them.

People who hurt me should be punished for what they've done. _____
My happiness depends on how others treat me. _____
Forgiveness is possible even in the worst of hurtful situations. _____
Angry reactions are good because they let people know just how bad you feel. _____
I shouldn't have to tell people when I hurt; they should know what's wrong. _____
Sometimes it's best to wait and think before you react. _____
It's better to ask people to explain their words and actions, rather than assume you always know what they mean. _____
I'm responsible for my own actions and must face up to the things I do wrong. _____
People should always act the way I expect them to. _____

● In what ways did each character's reaction help to heal or hurt his relationships?

Father: _____
Younger son: _____
Older son: _____

● Read the above sentences again. Apply them to a personal situation in which you were hurt. Which sentences would help you positively deal with the problem? Which sentences would cause greater hurt? Why?

Luke 15:11-32. Say: "The three characters in this drama all experienced pain. The father watched his younger son turn his back on the life and love he'd been given; he must have suffered as he hoped and waited for his boy to return. The son who left home encountered pain when he realized his defeat and returned home in shame. Even the older son felt hurt and unappreciated when he saw his younger, irresponsible brother being lavished with gifts and a celebration. Each one reacted differently to pain. Let's use the handout to discuss and examine how each person responded."

Have kids get back into their groups of three to six. Give each group member a "Does It Hurt or Heal?" handout. Give each small group a Bible. Have kids fill in their answers and discuss them in their small groups.

From Hurting to Healing

Leader: When we look at these torn and tattered crosses;
Group: We think of your pain, Lord, and we remember that you, too, have been hurt.
Leader: When we hold these crosses in our hands;
Group: We can be sure that you know how we feel when we hurt.
Leader: When we remember your cross;
Group: We remember what you did to turn pain into praise.
Leader: Help us bring our pain and hurts to you. Help us learn to forgive even in the hardest of times. Help us replace our anger and resentment with love.
Group: Change our hurting to healing.
All: Show us once again how to love. Amen.

---

5. *Healing*—Take down the graffiti wall and have each person tear a cross from it. Hand out copies of "From Hurting to Healing." Gather kids together in a circle and choose a leader for the reading. Have group members hold the crosses they've torn. Read responsively "From Hurting to Healing."

Close with a hug exchange. Tell junior highers they can't leave until they've each given hugs to five different people. ■

40 Worries, Worries

By Kristine Tomasik

Worry, worry, worry! It makes kids bite their fingernails and tear out their hair. Studies show that kids feel serious anxiety at younger and younger ages.

Use this meeting to help junior highers sort their worries and learn techniques for staying on top of worry-wart-itis.

OBJECTIVES

Participants will:
- identify and express personal worries;
- learn three steps to stop needless worry; and
- experience God's calming presence.

SUPPLIES

Gather a cassette tape or record of screechy, nerve-racking music (most kids probably consider dissonant contemporary classical music nerve-racking); a cassette player or turntable; enough red and orange 4-inch-wide construction-paper circles so each group member gets three; markers; a life-size outline of a human body on newsprint; masking tape; Scotch tape; newsprint; a bunch of 3×5 cards cut in half; a cassette tape or record of soothing, soft music; a Bible; and, for each person, a "RAFT Through Your Worries" handout and a pencil. Optional: a chalkboard.

BEFORE THE MEETING

Read the meeting and collect supplies.

Think about your own anxieties. Practice taking them into Jesus' calming presence and letting them go.

Tape the human-figure newsprint onto the wall.

Practice reading the guided faith experience (activity #6) aloud. Don't read too fast. Pause enough. Speak in a soothing voice.

NOTES TO THE LEADER

According to research reported in the book *Five Cries of Parents* by Strommen and Strommen (Harper & Row), the top 10 worries of young adolescents are (1) school performance; (2) personal looks; (3) how well other kids like them; (4) that a parent might die; (5) how friends treat them; (6) hunger and poverty in the U.S.; (7) violence in the U.S.; (8) that they might lose their best friend; (9) drugs and drinking; and (10) that they might not get a good job. Other fears expressed by young adolescents include nuclear destruction of the U.S., that their parents might divorce, and that they (the young people) might die soon.

Think about what your group members' worries might be.

THE MEETING

1. *Gnaw, chew, churn*—As group members arrive, have the screechy, nerve-racking music playing. Or, scratch your fingernails across a chalkboard a couple of times. Say: "Makes you feel really calm, doesn't it?"

Ask group members to each get into the position they most often worry in. Maybe someone will scrunch up in a ball and hold his stomach. Maybe someone will chew her fingernails. Have kids freeze in their positions. Ask: "What does your body feel like right now? Do you like it? Why or why not?" Have kids continue holding their worry positions.

2. *Worry warts*—Ask kids to think about what worries them.

Let them resume their normal postures. Encourage everyone to take a few deep breaths and shake down.

Give each group member three red and orange circles. Provide markers. Ask kids to each write their three most common worries on the red and orange "warts."

Now have kids tape their worry warts onto the "worrier"— the body outline on the wall. Say: "Worrying a lot gives you worry-wart-itis—a sad and dangerous disease!"

3. "RAFTing"—Have everyone sit in a circle. Say: "I'm going to teach you a process for dealing with worry. It's called 'RAFTing': 'R' stands for 'Reality check' (finding out whether your worry really is something to worry about), 'A' for 'Action,' and 'FT' for 'FaiTh.'" Give each person a "RAFT Through Your Worries" handout and a pencil. Explain the ideas on the handout.

RAFT Through Your Worries

When you start to worry, go RAFTing! Ask yourself the three RAFTing questions:
- How *realistic* is this worry? Do a reality check.
- What *action* can I take to stop this worry?
- How can my *faith* help me with this worry?

Take one of the worry warts from the worrier on the wall and work through the RAFT process with the kids. For instance, suppose someone is worried about not passing a test. Write ideas on newsprint so everyone can see.

- *Reality check:* If you've studied hard, this may not be a realistic worry, and you probably need to just relax. But if you haven't studied much, this probably is a realistic worry!
- *Action:* If the worry is realistic, you need to study more. Maybe finding someone to study with would help.
- *Faith:* Remember that God has given you special gifts and the ability to study. God will help you!

RAFT through several more worries. Encourage the kids to take notes on their handouts. Then give junior highers more practice RAFTing with the following activities.

4. Reality checks—Have kids form groups of three to do reality-check skits. Explain: "One group member will express a worry, and the other two will ask reality-check questions. For example, 'If you don't get invited to the Valentine dance, are you really going to die?' or 'What do you think actually will happen if your worry comes true?' " Small group members should switch roles until everyone's had a chance to be the worrier.

Quickly get kids back into one large circle. Discuss: "How did reality-check questions affect your feelings of worry?"

5. *Action doodles*—Give kids the 3×5-card halves and markers. Tell them to each take a wart off the worrier and doodle any action—except praying—that deals with the worry. Tell them to doodle on the 3×5-card half, not the wart. Point out that this action should be something practical—such as getting a new kind of haircut if he's worried about his looks, or talking to her youth pastor about her fear that her parents will divorce, or getting tutoring to improve math grades.

Once kids have drawn their action doodles, they should tape them onto the warts, then tape the warts back onto the worrier on the wall, and take another wart. Say it's okay to add an action doodle to a wart that already has one. Continue until kids run out of ideas.

Have kids collect their own warts and get into groups of three to discuss the action doodles drawn on them.

6. *Exploring faith*—Form pairs. Have one person be the "pineapple" and the other be the "coconut." Beginning with the pineapples, have partners alternate reading the following passages aloud. After one person reads a passage, the other person must summarize its message about faith. The passages are: Psalm 23:1-4; Proverbs 3:5; Romans 5:1-2; Galatians 2:16; Ephesians 2:8; and Hebrews 11:1-3.

When pairs have reviewed all the scripture passages, have volunteers share their partners' summaries with the whole class.

Then have pairs join together to make foursomes. Have kids take turns completing the following sentence: "One time my faith helped me deal with worries was..."

When kids have all shared in their foursomes, call the whole group together and have them read aloud Psalm 23:1-4 in unison from the same Bible translation.

Say: "Whenever we're faced with troubles, we can put our faith in God and he will lead us."

7. *Closing*—Have kids stand in a large circle. Repeat together the RAFT approach to worries: "Reality check, action, faith." Remind group members to RAFT when they're worrying about something.

Pray for kids to be able to better handle worries, with God's help.

Invite junior highers to take home their "RAFT Through Your Worries" handouts and their personal worry warts and action doodles. ∎

Section Six:

VALUES AND DECISIONS

41 *Being Thankful*

By Barry Gaeddert

S *aying thank you doesn't happen naturally. From an early age, children have to be taught to say "please" and "thank you." Yet often the words are so mechanical they're meaningless.*

But giving thanks to God and others—really giving thanks—brings happiness that many ungrateful people never experience.

Use this meeting to help your group members understand the importance of real thankfulness.

OBJECTIVES

Participants will:
- identify some things they're thankful for;
- discover whether they naturally say thank you;
- run a relay to help them understand Luke 17:11-19's meaning about giving thanks to the Lord;
- explore what the Bible says about thankfulness; and
- give thanks to God with a "Thanks, God" banner and prayer.

SUPPLIES

Gather Christian records or cassette tapes; a turntable or cassette player; a small prize such as a special kind of sucker or notebook; the nine letters of "Thanks, God," each cut from an 11×14 sheet of construction paper; markers; a long piece of yarn; masking tape; for each small group of four to six, a Bible and a blank thank-you note with an envelope; and, for each person, an "Autographs" handout, a pencil and two cookies or candy bars or other snacks.

BEFORE THE MEETING

Read the meeting and collect supplies.

Thank God for the opportunity to do this meeting with junior highers, and ask him to help it make a difference in their lives.

NOTES TO THE LEADER

Remember, young people learn experientially! Your junior highers will learn more by *experiencing* giving thanks than by just hearing about it. So throughout this meeting, thank the kids for their contributions and encourage their efforts at saying thanks.

THE MEETING

1. Greetings—Invite two or three young people to arrive 15 minutes early and be greeters. Also ask the adult helpers to do this. As group members arrive, have the greeters meet them at the door and thank each person for one specific thing. For example, greeters can thank group members for coming to the meeting, for smiling, for being on time or for bringing a friend.

2. Autographs—Play this game just to get energy flowing. Play Christian background music. Give each person an "Autographs" handout and a pencil. Tell group members to move around the room and ask others to sign their autographs beside things they're thankful for. If you have a small group, tell kids they may have others sign their names more than once, but they must get each person to sign at least once. Give a small prize to the first one finished.

3. An early surprise—Tell your group members refreshments will be served early. Tell them to relax and talk among each other as you hand them out. Give one cookie, candy bar or other snack to each person. Secretly count the number of junior highers who say thank you. As soon as everyone has the food, say: "I gave you the refreshments early for a reason: I was counting how many of you said 'thank you.' Are you surprised

---

Autographs

Collect autographs from different group members until your sheet is full.
Find someone who is thankful for . . .

1. Good grades _____
2. His or her own room_____
3. His or her 13th birthday _____
4. The food he or she eats _____
5. The youth group_____
6. His or her stereo _____
7. Good health _____
8. Good looks _____
9. A close family_____
10. A new friend _____
11. Not falling asleep in class _____
12. Recently solving a big problem _____
13. Jesus _____
14. Making the team _____

---

that only (however many) thanked me?'' (If most of your junior highers thank you, thank *them* for this.)

Read aloud Luke 17:11-19. Explain that Jesus expected each of the lepers to say thank you, just as he expects us to.

Hand out another cookie, candy bar or other snack to each person. See how many say thank you this time! Thank them for their politeness.

4. *"Getting the others" relay*—This relay acts out Luke 17:11-19. Divide the group into two teams—or, if your group is large, into teams of 11 people each. Have each team choose a captain, who stands facing his or her team from the opposite side of the room.

Explain that on "Go," the first person on each team runs to his or her captain and shouts "Thank you!" The captain shouts "Where are the others? Go get one!" That person runs back to the team, links arms with the next person in line, and both run back to the captain. They repeat the same words ("Thank you!" "Where are the others? Go get one!") and both run back to the team. This continues, adding one person at a time, until the entire team runs with arms linked to the captain.

At the end, thank everyone for participating and applaud the winners.

5. *Bible thank-yous*—Divide the group into small groups of four to six. Have an adult sponsor in each group. Give each small group a Bible, a blank thank-you note with an envelope, and a pencil. Assign each group at least one of these passages: Psalm 7:17; 92:1-4; 100:1-5; 136:1-3; 138:1; Romans 7:25; 1 Corinthians 15:57; 2 Corinthians 9:15; Ephesians 1:15-16; Colossians 3:17; 1 Thessalonians 5:18; Revelation 11:17.

Tell the groups to look up their Bible passages and write on the thank-you notes what they learned about being thankful. Tell each small group to put its note in the envelope, seal it and write on the return-address corner the name of one group member, who will read the note aloud when it's time.

Collect the thank-you notes in the envelopes. Set them aside.

6. *Saying thank you*—Get kids into nine groups (a group may consist of one or more people). Give each group one of the "Thanks, God" large construction-paper letters, and markers. If you have fewer than nine people, assign more than one letter to individuals as necessary.

Have kids use markers to decorate their letters with words and symbols representing things they want to thank God for. Play background music.

When kids are finished, hang a long piece of yarn (clothesline-style) in a corner of the meeting room. Let group members tape the letters, in order, onto the string.

7. *Closing*—Get everyone together in a circle. From your stack of thank-you notes, randomly choose one at a time. Have the "return-address persons" open and read the notes, then go and tape them onto the "Thanks, God" letters or yarn.

Have everyone hold hands for the closing prayer. Tell group members to each thank God for a person, thing or event if they wish, then squeeze the hand of the person on their right to signal that person's turn. Say it's okay to not pray aloud and just squeeze the next person's hand, if some desire. You begin the prayer, and when the person on your left squeezes your hand, say "Amen." ■

42 Dealing With Temptation

By Steven McCullough

Junior highers daily find themselves in tempting situations. Many worry because they've been tempted, even though they may have done nothing wrong.

Use this meeting to help your kids realize that temptation is normal, and that they can follow Jesus' example to resist temptation.

OBJECTIVES

Participants will:
- play games to experience temptation;
- identify tempting situations in general and for themselves;
- learn that being tempted is not sinning;
- examine how Jesus resisted temptation; and
- discuss how to personally resist temptation.

SUPPLIES

Gather items for a "temptation table": two or three loaded squirt guns, a squeeze bottle filled with water, some change, a cold can of soft drink, small candies, several chocolate chip cookies, a $1 bill, a sign that says "Nude" covering a photo of a "nude" animal, straws in paper wrappings, paper airplanes, a radio and some paper balls next to a sign that says "Do not throw"; newsprint; markers; a sheet of newsprint with each of the 3×5-card instructions written on it; a Bible; a small Styrofoam cup; water; a pitcher; a sheet of newsprint with the questions for discussion from activity #5; a coffee can filled with candies, enough for one for each group member; extra candies; and, for each person, a piece of scrap paper to crush into a ball, a 3×5 card, a pencil, a straw and a "Tempting Discussion" handout.

BEFORE THE MEETING

Read the meeting and collect supplies.

Set up the temptation table. Be creative!

Explain the temptation table to one or two group members, and ask them to go ahead and investigate some items if others don't do so right away.

Meet with adult sponsors. Encourage them to carefully handle the small group discussions about personal temptations. Also ask them to be willing to stay after the meeting to meet with any junior highers who want to talk.

NOTES TO THE LEADER

This meeting may get wild; be prepared for a short period of anarchy. Take advantage of it to point out what happens when we give in to temptation.

THE MEETING

1. *Temptation table*—Begin by saying it'll be a few minutes before the meeting starts. Tell kids they may look at the things on the table, but they can't touch them. Don't be too convincing about your order not to touch. Leave the room.

After about five minutes, come back and announce that you're ready to begin. Have kids sit in front of the temptation table. Ask how many used the things on the table. Say it's okay that they did; you'd simply like to know. Ask two or three more times, each time reassuring them it's okay to admit they gave in.

If there isn't much response, hold up the photo covered with the sign that says "Nude," and ask "Should we look?" Suggest even you are really tempted to look. Then reveal the photo.

Ask: "What is temptation?" Ask for examples of some things that tempt people; for example, drugs, sex, nude photos. List them on newsprint. Also list some places where these temptations occur: home, school, shopping mall.

2. *Paper balls*—Have kids form two teams and stand in lines so that each team member faces a member of the other team, about 15 feet apart. Give each person a piece of paper to crush into a ball.

Tell junior highers they must each try to hit the person they're facing with their paper ball, but they'll only have one chance. They may throw their ball whenever they want, but if they wait, they may end up closer to their target. Also say that you may stop the game at any time, and those who didn't throw their ball by then just miss out.

Tell junior highers they must sit down where they are once they've thrown their ball. Also say you may randomly have some kids sit down and not get to throw.

When kids understand, begin. Randomly instruct the teams to move one step closer and tell a few kids to sit down without throwing. After a few minutes, stop the game.

Discuss: "Why did you throw your ball when you did? Were you tempted to wait or throw sooner? Why? How did you feel during this game? How is this like facing other kinds of temptation?"

3. *What tempts me*—Divide the group into small groups of four to six with one adult leader per group. Give each person a 3×5 card and a pencil. Show your newsprint example of what to write on both sides (see next page: 3×5-Card Instructions).

Have group members each copy the example and fill in three of their temptations and where they most often occur. Then let small groups discuss their temptations.

4. *Animal fights*—Give each small group an animal name: wolves, dogs, bears, lambs, birds. Then bring all small groups together. Ask a group member to read aloud Matthew 4:1-11. Have kids think about Jesus and his temptations as they listen.

Give each group member a straw. Have kids get in a spread-out circle and stand next to people with different animal names. Place a small Styrofoam cup of water in the center of the circle. (Have a pitcher of water nearby.) Tell the group to circle clockwise. Periodically change the direction to counterclockwise and back.

Tell kids when you call an animal name, those "animals" must run to the center of the circle, sip from the cup with their straws and squirt the water out at each other. Give them the game's boundaries: They must stay in the youth room (or in the

3×5-Card Instructions

(Side 1)
Matthew 4:1-11
Jesus' temptations

(Side 2)
I'm tempted by
what   where

1.

2.

3.

parking lot or wherever).
    Begin calling out the names. Increase the pace gradually.
Call two or three animal names at a time. Sooner or later, some-

one will use the cup instead of the straw to get the others really wet. When this happens, simply say not to do that again. (Refill the cup from the pitcher of water.) When the cup of water has been thrown a couple of times, stop the game.

5. *Tempting discussion*—Have kids return to their small groups. Display these questions for discussion on newsprint:
- Were you tempted to throw the cup?
- Why did you or didn't you?
- How did it feel to be tempted?

After a few minutes, reread aloud the passage from Matthew about Jesus' temptations. Again, tell group members the choice is theirs to make. Tell them Jesus was tempted, and since he couldn't do wrong, being tempted isn't sin. But we choose whether to give in to temptation or to resist temptation as Jesus did.

Give each group member a "Tempting Discussion" handout and a pencil. Have small groups discuss the questions.

Tempting Discussion

- How do I recognize temptation?
- Why isn't being tempted the same as sinning?
- How did Jesus resist temptation?
- How can I resist temptation?

---

6. *Closing*—Bring all group members back together. Say everyone will get a prize. Get out the coffee can filled with small candies and say there's only enough for everyone to take one piece. Put the coffee can in the center of the room and tell kids "Go for it!" If you come up short, simply point out that it seems someone was tempted to take more than one. Then distribute the extras.

After everyone has the candy, say if anyone wants to talk more about any personal temptations, leaders are available after the meeting. Close in prayer, asking for God's help and strength as we struggle with temptation in both big and small things.

Encourage kids to take home their 3×5 cards and "Tempting Discussion" handouts. ∎

43 I Can Do as I Please!

By Tom Couser

Junior highers often complain that their parents don't give them enough freedom. However, they don't always realize that with independence comes responsibility. Freedom means responsibility.

Use this meeting to help junior highers consider the responsibility that accompanies freedom.

OBJECTIVES

Participants will:
- experience teamwork through a name game and group task;
- become aware of their growing independence and responsibility; and
- discover what qualities of responsibility God has given them.

SUPPLIES

Gather upbeat music cassette tapes or records; a cassette player or turntable; six to 10 magazine pictures of various professionals (for example, a dentist, mechanic, nurse, musician, athlete, farmer, truck driver, pilot, librarian, homemaker), each attached to blank paper or newsprint; masking tape; a sheet of newsprint with the discussion questions in activity #3 written on it; Bible; large ball of yarn; and, for each person, a pencil, a

"Today I'm Free to . . ." handout, and six to 10 3×5 cards (one for each magazine picture).

BEFORE THE MEETING

Read the meeting and collect supplies.

Tape onto the walls the pictures of professionals attached to blank paper or newsprint.

THE MEETING

1. *It comes with the job*—Have upbeat music playing. Greet junior highers as they arrive. Give them each a pencil and tell them to wander around the room and look at the pictures you've posted. Have kids each write on the blank paper beside each picture a word or phrase describing the pictured person's responsibilities or qualities needed to do the job. For example, for a dentist, a word might be "careful." Or for a truck driver, a phrase might be "likes to travel." Allow time for words to be written by each picture.

2. *The name game*—Divide the group into small groups of no more than six. Have an adult sponsor in each group. Say: "Each of you should introduce yourself to your group by giving your first name with a word in front of it that starts with the same letter as your name. The word must describe you. For example, 'Terrific Tom' or 'Silly Sue.'" Explain that each person must repeat all the previous names and descriptions before giving his or her own name and adjective. Have groups begin with the person whose name begins with or is closest to the letter "A."

When everyone's finished, say: "Now prepare to introduce yourselves as a group to the rest of us. Do this by using a familiar nursery-rhyme tune. Create a song including something about each person in your group. Use your descriptions from the new game. Choose a tune such as 'The Farmer in the Dell,' 'Mary Had a Little Lamb' or 'Old MacDonald.'"

When all groups have completed the task, ask them to share their songs with the whole group.

3. *"Today I'm free to . . ."*—Use this section to get kids thinking about their own personal expanding responsibilities. Give each group member a "Today I'm Free to . . ." handout;

242

Today I'm Free to . . .

For each of the following statements, write your responses in both columns. Choose from these responses:

1—Not at all
2—Only when I have to
3—Sometimes

4—Quite often
5—All the time

	Now	Five years from now
I prepare my own meals.	_____	_____
I clean my own room.	_____	_____
I care for younger brothers and sisters.	_____	_____
I buy my own clothes.	_____	_____
I earn my own spending money.	_____	_____
I wash my own clothes.	_____	_____
I set my own curfew.	_____	_____
I decide when I'll attend church.	_____	_____

have kids each complete the handout and discuss it with their small groups.

Display these questions on newsprint and have small groups discuss:

● Are you satisfied with the responsibility you have now? Why or why not?

● What do you like about having responsibility in each area?

● Which responsibility do you fear most? Why?

● Does having responsibility make you feel more free or more tied down? Explain.

Bring everyone back together. Ask: "What did you discover about yourself?" Talk about answers.

4. *I can be responsible*—Give each person as many 3×5 cards as there are pictures on the wall. For example, if there are 10 pictures, give each person 10 3×5 cards. Have kids each stand in front of a picture (more than one person may be at each picture). Allow about one minute (or whatever time you feel is appropriate) by each picture. During that one minute, kids must copy the words by that picture on one of their 3×5 cards. Then they must each circle on their 3×5 card two words of responsibility that they possess. For example, the dentist picture could say "careful," "patient," "intelligent." Tammi might circle "careful" and "patient" as words that describe her. Be the timekeeper.

When one minute passes, shout "Next responsibility!" Then kids should all move one picture to the right. Play lively background music during this activity. Continue until everyone's made it to all the pictures. Collect the pencils.

5. Free indeed!—Bring group members together for a closing prayer. Make sure they bring their 3×5 cards with them. Have kids sit in a circle, knee-to-knee. (If your group is larger than 20, divide into smaller groups.) Have a young person read John 8:31-36. Say: "We all want independence and freedom, but we need to be responsible too. Jesus said knowing the truth about God's love sets us free—really free! As a symbol of God's love bringing us together, I'll toss this ball of yarn to someone. When you receive the yarn, thank God for all the qualities he's given you to be a more responsible person. Say, 'Thank you God for giving me . . .' and read all the words you circled on your cards. Then toss the ball of yarn to someone else in the circle, only keep holding on to your end of the yarn. We'll keep tossing the yarn and praying until each person has received the yarn. We'll make a giant web of God's love that ties us together as we grow and mature."

After everyone's received the yarn, have group members continue to hold the web together and sing "They'll Know We Are Christians by Our Love." ∎

44 *Make Up Your Mind*

By Ben Sharpton

Junior highers get advice from peers, radio, television, movies, books and magazines. But these sources seldom agree on what they say. So how do kids make up their minds about important questions?

Use this meeting to help junior highers identify tough questions and learn how to find answers.

OBJECTIVES

Participants will:
- identify tough moral and ethical questions; and
- work through one or more questions with a practical decision-making process.

SUPPLIES

Gather newsprint; chairs; markers; Bibles; a concordance; a Bible handbook; a Bible dictionary; a copy of your church or denomination's statement of belief; and, for each person, one of the four "Decision Radio Stations" cards and "A Decision-Maker's Prayer" handout.

BEFORE THE MEETING

Read the meeting and collect supplies.

Place several chairs in a row along one wall of the room.

Make sure you have an equal number of each of the four different "Decision Radio Stations" cards, enough so each group member will have only one card.

Pray for God's guidance.

THE MEETING

1. *The arrival*—Give your young people a warm welcome. Then ask them to each choose a partner and complete this sentence: "A good thing that happened to me this week was . . ." Sing one or two songs that deal with guidance, like "Blowin' in the Wind" and "Day by Day."

2. *A decision-making dilemma*—Get everyone together, then ask three volunteers to leave the room. After they've gone, explain to the remaining kids that you're going to ask the three volunteers to make a hypothetical decision—they'll have to decide which color to paint your meeting room. Tell the kids to give the volunteers conflicting, but firm, suggestions about the color the room should be. For example, kids born in January through April should insist on a pale blue; those born in May through August should strongly suggest yellow and green; and September through December kids should urge the volunteers to keep the room the color it is.

After the kids understand their task, have the three volunteers return. Say: "The group members are trying to decide which color to paint the meeting room. We want you to make the final decision. Feel free to ask the others for opinions or advice." After a few minutes of persuasive discussion, ask the volunteers to tell their final color choice, and how they arrived at that decision.

Then discuss: "In order to make a correct decision, is it also necessary to talk to other church people? Why or why not? Would your decision about the color benefit others who use the room? Why or why not?" Explain: "This exercise was meant to help you begin to think about decision-making. During this meeting we'll look at how to make tough decisions."

3. *A decision line*—Point to the row of chairs along one wall; explain that it's a "decision line." Tell the junior highers to indicate their beliefs about certain topics by sitting in the appropriate chairs. One end of the row represents "God's Concern"; the other end represents "Up to You." As you read one item at a time from the "Important Decisions" list, have kids who think that God wants to offer his guidance regarding that item sit toward the "God's Concern" end of the row. Kids who

Important Decisions

- Your choice of friends
- Your choice of deodorant
- The music you listen to
- Whether to smoke cigarettes
- Your choice of a wife or husband
- The color of your room
- How much alcohol you drink (if any)
- The guys or girls you date
- The slang words you use
- Your career
- Whether to watch music videos

think God has no preference about their decision should sit at the "Up to You" end of the row. If someone's already sitting in a chair that another person wants to occupy, the second person simply sits on the first person's lap. Briefly discuss each item after kids have made their seating choices.

4. Tough questions—Gather group members together and ask them to name some tough questions junior highers have to answer; write them on the newsprint. If they don't mention them, suggest: drinking alcohol, sexual petting, smoking, masturbating, swearing, using drugs, stealing, lying.

After the group has listed numerous topics, have kids vote as to which one is the toughest. Circle that item, then rephrase it as a question that's clear to everyone; for example, "Should a junior higher drink alcohol?" or "Is it okay to steal if you don't get caught?" Write the rephrased question on the top of a second sheet of newsprint. (Don't discard your list of tough decisions.)

Beneath the rephrased question, list the possible decisions junior highers can make about the question. (Don't evaluate the responses at this time.) Several alternatives for drinking might include: (1) Don't drink; (2) Drink whenever and wherever you want; (3) Drink only with your family on special occasions; (4) Wait until you're legally old enough to drink; and (5) Drink moderately with your friends.

5. *God's guidance*—Say: "As Christians, we believe God offers guidance in all decisions. Sometimes he speaks through wise Christian friends; other times he speaks through our experiences or intelligence." Hold a card for each of the four radio stations. Say: "Often we listen to news broadcasts from several different radio stations to see if they agree. Likewise, God speaks through several 'stations': the Bible (show a WBBL card); our experiences (show a WXPR card); our church and its heritage (show a WCHR card); and our own thinking (show a WTHK card). As we seek God's guidance, we should consult several 'stations' to be assured of our decision."

6. *Decisions, decisions*—Give one of the "Decision Radio Stations" cards to each group member. (Be sure to distribute an equal number of each station.) Then divide the group into four task forces by instructing the young people to sit with others who have the same kind of station card. Have an adult sponsor in each group.

Have the groups each focus on the rephrased question from activity #4 and decide which alternative is best, based on *their* point of view. The WBBL group decides the best alternative by searching the Bible, concordance, Bible handbook and Bible dictionary. The WCHR group searches the church or denomination's statement of belief to find out what your tradition says about each option. (This group may want to call a pastor or deacon and ask his or her opinion.) The WTHK group tries to think through a rational decision—why to choose one alternative over the others. The WXPR group focuses on personal experiences about the issue: What happens when friends drink alcohol? Does anything good come from drinking alcohol?

After the task forces have had sufficient time to make their decisions, gather as one large group. Ask each group to tell which alternative it chose and why. Turn to the newsprint listing the question and alternatives and say: "Based on the way God has revealed himself to us through the Bible, church, minds and experience, which appears to be the best alternative for us?" Circle that alternative. If your group chooses more than one alternative, work together to reword them into one response.

Congratulate the kids on a job well done. If time permits, allow the task forces to work through another decision. Rotate kids to other task forces so they can experience others' thoughts and methods about making decisions.

Decision Radio Stations

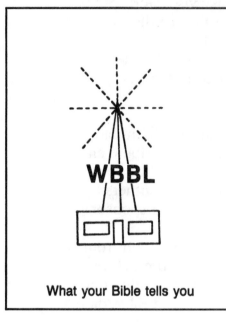

What your Bible tells you

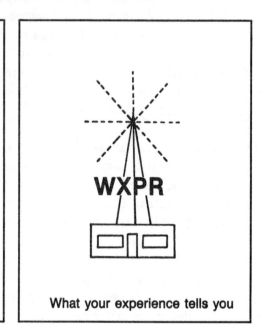

What your experience tells you

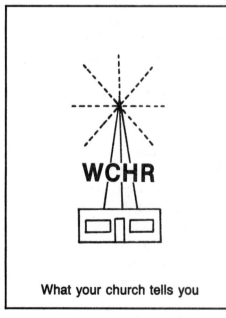

What your church tells you

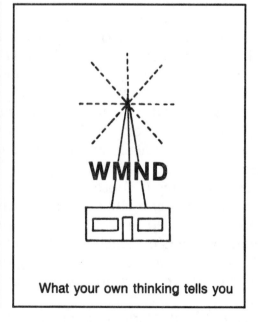

What your own thinking tells you

A Decision-Maker's Prayer

Leader: We live in a demanding and confusing world.

Group: But we're not alone.

Leader: We face decisions at every turn.

Group: You are with us wherever we go, Lord.

Leader: Sometimes it's hard knowing what you want us to do.

Group: But you've given us your Word to show us your way.

Leader: All scripture is inspired by God and is useful for teaching the truth, rebuking error, correcting faults, and giving instructions for right living.

Group: We can observe your work in the lives of those who have gone before us as we study our church traditions.

Leader: It's nice to know others have been there before us.

Group: You have given us minds to be able to discern your truth.

Leader: Thank you, Lord.

Group: You reveal yourself to us daily as we experience you in our world.

Leader: These experiences have helped us grow.

Group: You have promised that you will never leave us or forsake us.

Leader: We live in a demanding and confusing world.

Group: But we're not alone.

Amen.

7. *Closing worship*—Sing the song "Alleluia"; add verses like "Thank you, Father" and "Guide us daily." Read Psalm 31:3 and Isaiah 58:11. Hand out copies of "A Decision-Maker's Prayer"; read it as instructed. ■

45 *Shoplifting*

By Barry Gaeddert

Recent research suggests that more than 40 percent of all teenagers shoplift. And they start young.

Kids may shoplift because they're encouraged or dared by other kids to do so; it's exciting. Or they may shoplift because they want something "everyone else" has. What they don't often think about is how shoplifting affects other people and what could happen to them if they're caught.

Use this meeting to help kids consider the effects of shoplifting and see why the Bible's message makes good sense.

OBJECTIVES

Participants will:
* take ownership of something they created and discover their feelings when it's taken from them;
* hear from authorities how shoplifting affects businesses and what happens to shoplifters who are caught;
* play a game that demonstrates how easy it is to give in to peer pressure; and
* creatively express what they discover the Bible teaches about shoplifting.

SUPPLIES

Gather an equal number of red objects and blue objects (for

example, buttons, small pieces of paper, marbles); enough modeling clay for each group member to have some; four Bibles; four 3×5 cards, each with Deuteronomy 5:19, Romans 12:2, Romans 13:9-10 and Ephesians 4:28 written on it; newsprint; markers; paper and pencils.

BEFORE THE MEETING

Read the meeting and collect supplies.

Invite a couple of congregation members to be guest speakers: Ask a business owner to give an example of what shoplifters do to his or her business. Ask a police officer or security guard to give an example of how he or she catches shoplifters and what happens to who's caught. Help the speakers decide whether they'd prefer to each talk for three to five minutes or to share a 10-minute time slot. Explain the value of their part in the meeting: Kids will see them as authority figures and will be more attentive to the problem. Tell them what your group members are like. Be sure they know when and where you meet.

Think about some crazy faces and sounds to use in activity #4.

Meet with adult sponsors who will attend the meeting. Discuss the information in this meeting's introduction and "Notes to the Leader" section. Explain activity #5 and find out which group task they each prefer to coach. Ask them to stay after the meeting to be available for kids who want to talk.

NOTES TO THE LEADER

This meeting may not be easy for some of your group members. Kids who *have* shoplifted may feel guilty. Or they may have a hard time admitting they did something wrong. Be sensitive to your kids.

On the other hand, kids in your group who *haven't* shoplifted can learn why it's harmful and be influenced to avoid shoplifting altogether. Be candid about the facts.

So forge ahead—with a prayerful combination of sensitivity and candidness.

THE MEETING

1. Steal-it game—Divide the group into two teams. Give one team a bunch of red objects. Give the other team the same number of blue objects. Have the teams hide the objects around the meeting area. Then on the word "Go," let each team's members "steal" as many of the objects hidden by the other team as they can find. After a few minutes, stop the game. Count the number of items stolen by each team and declare a winner.

2. *Create and lose*—Give each group member a portion of modeling clay. Tell kids the clay is now theirs. Say they may build, create or model anything; the clay belongs personally to them. After several minutes, say: "I changed my mind. You can't keep these; I'm going to take them back." Collect the clay and place all the creations into one lump. Have an adult sponsor ask kids how they feel having what belonged to them taken away.

Introduce the topic by saying: "It hurts to have your own property taken from you. Yet every day many kids do that by stealing or shoplifting from stores. Let's hear from some people who know about that."

3. *Guest speakers*—Introduce the business owner and police officer or security guard. Let them tell group members their stories about shoplifting.

Encourage questions from the junior highers. After some discussion, thank and say goodbye to your speakers.

4. *Zany and crazy things*—Have kids line up in one line behind you. Tell them they must do everything you do. Lead the kids outside. Turn and face the kids and make a crazy face: Stick out your tongue, put your thumbs in your ears, or whatever. After the kids repeat it, move to another spot in full view of cars driving by and make a crazy sound for the kids to repeat. Continue with crazy faces and sounds for several minutes, then lead the group back inside.

Ask: "Were you embarrassed doing any of these things? Why? Would you have done these things if no one else in the group did them? Why or why not?" Point out that people do a lot of things, including shoplifting, because other people are doing them and not necessarily because they want to.

5. *A creative look at the Bible*—Get kids into four groups, with an adult sponsor in each group. Give each group a Bible and one of the 3×5 cards with the Bible references written on them.

Have kids in the groups take turns looking up and reading

these passages. Tell groups they'll each create something to explain what the Bible says about stealing or conforming.

According to the adult sponsors' preferences, instruct the groups as follows.

Group #1: Make an object that explains the Bible's message. For example, a square peg and a round hole could illustrate not squeezing into the world's mold. (Give group #1 modeling clay.)

Group #2: Draw a mural that shows the Bible's message. For example, a series of illustrations could tell a story of someone thinking about shoplifting, but then seeing the store owner and deciding to not hurt him. (Give group #2 newsprint and markers.)

Group #3: Write a news story that includes the Bible's message. For example, a made-up story about shoplifting could tell what happened to a shoplifter because he or she broke the law. (Give group #3 paper and pencils.)

Group #4: Make a skit that portrays the Bible's message. For example, a junior higher who really wants something could choose to do odd jobs to earn the money to buy it.

When all groups are finished, let them present and explain their creations. Discuss the presentations. Emphasize that "loving others" is the best reason to obey the laws of the Bible, including the law not to steal.

6. Closing—Get everyone together in a circle. Say: "Some of you may have shoplifted. God can forgive you. Some of you have thought about it. God can help you decide not to shoplift. God can meet your needs. Let's pray silently for a few moments. Talk to God about your thoughts right now on shoplifting. Ask him to help you want to do what's right." After a minute, say "Amen."

Tell kids that if anyone wants to talk about what's on their mind, you and some adult sponsors will stay after the meeting. ∎

46 *Think Before You Drink*

By Michael Walcheski

Drinking is an issue with junior highers. Search Institute's recent study revealed alarming facts: 85 percent of the eighth-graders surveyed have tried alcohol at least once; 46 percent have attended a drinking party during the last year; and 33 percent of current eighth-graders began drinking in sixth-grade or earlier.

Let your junior high group be a place for kids to face these tough decisions. Use this meeting to help junior highers explore the issue of making "God-decisions" concerning alcohol.

OBJECTIVES

Participants will:
- give advice to someone who's struggling with the decision whether to use alcohol;
- read and discuss scripture that focuses on God's perspective on their choices;
- explore 10 ways to say no; and
- receive positive words of encouragement to stand up to pressure to use alcohol.

SUPPLIES

Gather two colors of yarn cut into an equal number of

2 1/2-foot pieces (enough for each person to have one); markers; a two-sided chalkboard (or two back-to-back chalkboards); chalk; two chalkboard erasers; newsprint; strips of paper with one of these words on each strip: love, joy, peace, patience, kindness, goodness, faithfulness, humility, self-control (prepare enough strips for each person to give one to each other group member; for example, if there are 10 kids in your group, prepare 90 strips); and, for each person, a plastic cup with a hole punched in the rim, a blank address-sticker label, a pencil, an envelope, "A Letter From a Friend" handout, a Bible, and "Making God-Decisions" handout.

BEFORE THE MEETING

Read the meeting and collect supplies.

Create a list of words for chalkboard charades. Choose words unique to your group of junior highers. For example, names of junior high schools, local heroes or landmarks. End your list with the theme words in the sample charade list in activity #2.

NOTES TO THE LEADER

When discussing alcohol among teenagers, expect a wide range of reactions. Some kids might wonder what you're talking about, while others might try to "act cool." Be patient. Remind yourself and them as gently as possible that God does have something to say about this topic, and he cares greatly about the decisions they make.

THE MEETING

1. *Personalized glasses*—As kids arrive, give each of them a plastic cup with a hole punched in the rim. Tell them each to thread a piece of yarn through the hole and create a necklace with the cup hanging like a pendant. Make markers available. Have junior highers each write on a sticker label their name and two words they think of when they hear the word "party." They should each stick the label onto their cup.

After everyone's wearing a personalized cup around his or her neck, bring group members together in a circle. Have each person tell his or her name and the two words associated with "party."

2. *Chalkboard charades*—Divide the group into two teams according to the two colors of yarn. Say: "We're going to play 'chalkboard charades.' The goal is to guess what's being drawn on the chalkboard. The rules: The person drawing the charade on the board must not talk and must not write words, letters or numbers—only pictures or symbols.

"One point will be awarded to the team that correctly guesses an item first. One person from each team must come to me to get the charade word. Then those two will draw it on different sides of the chalkboard while their team members try to guess what it is. Once a word has been correctly guessed, both teams will move on to the next word."

Sample Charade List

- homework
- skateboarding
- recess
- beer*

- six-pack*
- sports
- tacos
- party*
(*theme words)

- drunk*
- pizza
- taking out the trash
- wine*

Use the five theme words to lead into the meeting's topic. When the game is finished, say: "The last five charades point to our meeting's topic. We're going to talk about alcohol and ways to decide about it."

3. *Friendly letters*—Have group members form small groups, no larger than six. Have an adult sponsor in each group. Say: "Imagine you just got this letter." Give "A Letter From a Friend" to each person, plus a pencil and an envelope. Have a volunteer read the letter aloud. Continue: "Now write your reply on the back of the letter. Write whatever you feel would most help your friend in this situation. Don't sign your name. When you're finished, seal it in the envelope."

After group members have completed their letters and sealed them in the envelopes, collect the envelopes and redistribute them among each small group. Make sure no one gets the letter he or she answered.

Have members read their letters individually as if they were the ones receiving the advice. Then discuss: "How did you feel about the advice? If you were given that advice, would you follow it? Why or why not? What are three main things to consider when you make a decision about drinking?"

A Letter From a Friend

I'm writing to you because there's no one else to talk to. I'm not saying who I am, because I'm too embarrassed about my situation.

The other night I went to a party with some friends. Toward the middle of the party, some of the kids broke into Jerry's dad's liquor cabinet. Then everybody started drinking.

I wasn't sure what to do. I didn't really want to drink, but they kept asking and asking. One girl said I was chicken. Another said they shouldn't have invited me to the party.

I like going to parties with my friends. I don't want to be left out. But I don't feel like I want to drink. I don't know what to do. Can you help me?

Write soon,

Frustrated

Making God-Decisions

Read Philippians 4:8-9.
- What decisions lead to good things for me, my friends and family?

Read John 3:19-21.
- Am I willing to let others know I'm living by "God-decisions"? Why or why not?

Read Philippians 2:1-5.
- How is drinking harmful to me? Is it ever helpful? Explain.
- How is drinking harmful to others? Is it ever helpful? Explain.

Read 1 John 3:1.
- What advice would God give you, his child, if you were faced with a decision about drinking? Why are God-decisions hard to make sometimes? How can God-decisions become easier to make?

When the small groups have finished, ask each to give a brief report. List on newsprint each group's answers to the last question. Don't hesitate to add "main things" such as drinking's illegal for people their age, or the Bible warns against alcohol abuse (Proverbs 20:1; 23:29-35; Romans 12:1-2; 1 Corinthians 6:19-20; Ephesians 5:18).

4. *Making God-decisions*—Hand out "Making God-Decisions" and Bibles and have junior highers discuss the handout in their small groups. Have each group designate one person to record the responses.

Bring the whole group together and ask for discoveries from the Bible study.

Read the 10 ways to avoid a difficult situation (see diagram).

Have kids rank the top two ways of saying no to drinking that best demonstrate a Christian attitude. Talk about their choices.

---

10 Ways to Avoid a Difficult Situation

1. Say no
2. Leave
3. Ignore it
4. Make an excuse
5. Change the subject

6. Make a joke
7. Act shocked
8. Use flattery
9. Offer a better idea
10. Return the challenge

(From *Peer Pressure Reversal* by Sharon Scott, Copyright © 1985. Human Resource Development Press, 22 Amherst Rd., Amherst, MA 01002, 1-800-822-2801. All rights reserved. Reprinted with permission of the publisher.)

---

5. *A cupful of care*—Say: "God wants the best for us. His Spirit wants to work in us—especially during times of tough decisions." Read Ephesians 5:18 and Galatians 5:22-23. Say: "To help one another, let's fill each other's cups with reminders of God's Spirit."

Display the strips of paper in piles according to words. For example, have a "love" pile, a "self-control" pile, and so on. Tell kids each to choose a word as a gift to give each other person in the group. They must choose one word for each person, fold it and put it in each person's personalized glass hanging around his or her neck. Make a rule: No peeking!

When the group's finished, gather everyone together in a circle and join hands for a prayer. Read Galatians 5:22-25. Pray for God's Spirit to control your lives.

Let junior highers read their cupfuls of care on the way home. ∎

47 Which One Will I Choose?

By Ben Sharpton

Young people are bombarded with more time-demanding options than any previous generation was. How do they decide what to do? All too often they make decisions hastily, based on "gut" feelings. Or their decisions are heavily influenced by peer pressure.

Use this meeting to help junior highers learn a decision-making process.

OBJECTIVES

Participants will:
- identify major decisions that junior highers face; and
- examine practical steps in making personal decisions.

SUPPLIES

Gather newsprint; markers; for every four or six group members, a Bible, a copy of one of the three case studies; and, for each person, a 3×5 card, a pencil, a "Decision-Making Aids" handout and a copy of "The Decision-Making Process."

BEFORE THE MEETING

Read the meeting and collect supplies.

Read each scripture passage in activity #5 and identify who the decision-maker was and what he or she had to decide.

260

THE MEETING

1. *Greetings*—As young people arrive, greet each one with an "I-care-about-you" handshake. (Using the right hands, backs of the hands facing each other, wrap thumbs around each other. With a downward motion, release the thumbs and shout "Hey!") Ask about the kids' week and *listen* to their answers.

2. *So much to do*—Pass out 3×5 cards and pencils to your young people. Ask them to jot down *everything* they must do between the end of your meeting and their next session of school. For example, do homework, sleep, shower, feed a pet, dress for school and call a friend. Next, have them each place a star (★) by the items that involve making decisions.

Next, ask group members to circle those items that involve tough, hard-to-decide-about issues. Have kids each share their list with a partner.

3. *Decisions, decisions*—Brainstorm as a group and list on newsprint as many decisions that your group can identify that junior highers face. Some that your group may suggest:
- what to wear to school;
- whether to drink alcohol;
- which TV programs to watch;
- whether to smoke;
- who to "go with";
- whether to try out for a sport;
- whether to do "extra credit" work for better grades;
- whether to join certain groups;
- which radio station to listen to;
- what to do on the weekend.

When you have a substantial list, ask the kids to read the items and name the day-to-day decisions. Ask: "What makes certain decisions 'easy'?" As the group names them, cross out the "easy" items.

Next, study the list one item at a time and, as a group, rank each item according to its popularity among junior highers. For instance, if "whether to smoke" is the most common decision junior high kids face, rank it "1." If your group considers "whether to join certain groups" to be the second most common decision their peers face, rank it "2."

4. *Tools to help*—Give each person a "Decision-Making

Aids" handout. Explain that these "tools" can be used during different steps in the process of making a decision. Next, give a copy of "The Decision-Making Process" to each young person. Point out the decision-making aids in the left-hand column; each tool works best with the accompanying step. Use the example to talk through this process with your group. In the example, the decision-maker must decide how to spend a gift of $50.

5. Bible decisions—Have each group member get back with his or her partner from activity #2. Instruct the pairs to find one or two other pairs and form groups of four or six. Have one adult sponsor in each small group. Write these column heads across the top of a sheet of newsprint: "Scripture Passage," "Person," "Problem," "Possible Decisions," "What We Would Have Decided" and "Grade." Hand out a Bible to each

Decision-Making Aids

Brainstorming: List as many things as you can, regardless of the quality. Avoid evaluation until you've listed as many items as you can.

Rating:  Give each item a numeric rating that best describes how it compares to the others. Rate items according to cost, popularity, time, etc. Lower numbers ususally reveal a higher priority.

Category: Examine your items, choices or criteria to see if any fit into smaller categories. This can be helpful in understanding your choices and making compromises.

Advice: Contact mature, wise people and ask their advice on a subject. Explain your reasoning and seek their suggestions regarding your decisions.

262

The Decision-Making Process

Use these decision-making aids to help you choose!

The following steps outline a model of decision-making that you may use in your personal choices. Notice that these four items spell out the word "STEP."

ADVICE

State your problem. Be specific. What are you trying to decide? Why is a decision necessary? What do you want?

BRAINSTORMING   **RATING**

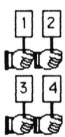

Think of your alternatives. List them all. Aim for quantity.

ADVICE   **CATEGORY**

Evaluate your options. Which one seems best?

ADVICE

Perfect your decision. Choose one alternative.

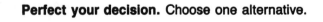

The Decision-Making Process Example

Use these decision-making aids to help you choose!

The following steps outline a model of decision-making that you may use in your personal choices. Notice that these four items spell out the word "STEP."

ADVICE

State your problem. Be specific. What are you trying to decide? Why is a decision necessary? What do you want?

How should I spend $50⁰⁰?
My parents want me to save it.

BRAINSTORMING   **RATING**

   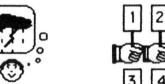

Think of your alternatives. List them all. Aim for quantity.

⑤ *save it*
① *Save part of it*
⑥ *take parents out to dinner*
③ *buy 3 pairs of jeans at Factory Outlet*
④ *buy 1 pair of jeans in mall*
② *tithe part of it*

ADVICE   **CATEGORY**

Evaluate your options. Which one seems best?

Parents say
  save it
Bible says
  tithe
Friend has
  new outfit

Save or
spend all
_____
Save it
Take
parents
to dinner

Save or
spend part
_____
Shop
factory
outlet
Save part
Tithe

ADVICE

Perfect your decision. Choose one alternative.

Place $25⁰⁰ in savings account,
tithe $5⁰⁰ and shop factory
outlet

Case Studies

Case Study #1

You're an eighth-grade girl. You enjoy swimming, cheerleading, making new friends, traveling and horseback riding. Summer is near and you want to do something special this year. Several different camping programs are available for people your age and you think you might like to attend one this summer. You receive a $5 allowance each week. A friend of yours is going to "Camp Richkids" in the mountains, where she'll canoe, climb mountains, go to dances, etc. Its cost is $749. Other camping opportunities:

- a weekend backpacking trip—$39;
- a YMCA week-long camp with swimming and horseback riding—$79;
- computer workshops at school—$40;
- horseback-riding classes at a local stable—$125;
- church camp—$65; and
- Camp Whatsit (swimming, crafts, hiking)—$250.

Research the options and report back to the group.

Case Study #2

After a great deal of struggle, counseling and prayer, your parents have decided to divorce. They regret having to make this decision, but feel that it's necessary. They've asked you to decide where you want to live—in your dad's new apartment or here with your mother. Your dad will live in another part of the city (in a new school district). You love both parents and you know they both love you. The school in that part of town is new and the student body seems to have a lot of spirit. Regardless of your choice, you'll be able to spend weekends and a summer month with the other parent.

Be prepared to report your options and decision to the group.

Case Study #3

You are a bright student, but your grades recently have taken a nose dive. Your parents believe you're too involved in extracurricular activities and need to cut back. You now enjoy being in the band, two service clubs, your church choir and your church youth group. Your parents want you to participate in weekday tutor sessions (after school each day for an hour). Among other things, this would mean you'd have to drop out of the school band.

Evaluate your choices and report your decision to the group.

small group and assign each group one or more of the following
scripture passages:

- Genesis 42:3-29
- Matthew 14:3-11
- Luke 22:54-60

- 1 Kings 3:16-27
- Matthew 27:11-26

Tell small groups to read their passages and find the information listed on the newsprint. As they make their discoveries,
have them write the information on the newsprint under the
appropriate columns. Finally, each group should give its
decision-maker a grade ("A" to "F") regarding his or her decision. If the individual made a good decision, he or she would
deserve an "A." If the individual blew it, the group should give
him or her a failing grade ("F"). Have groups report their findings to the large group and explain why they gave the grades
they did.

6. Making decisions—Now, give your group a chance to
practice using the decision-making process. Hand out one case
study to each small group. Tell group members to use the steps
outlined in "The Decision-Making Process" handout to help
them find solutions to the problems. There is room on each
handout for responses. Tell group members to *use the process*
and not just think of a solution; the important thing is to focus
on *making decisions*— not just on a decision. Have group members report their findings to the large group.

7. Closing—Have a circle prayer thanking God for his
guidance and love and for providing people with skills to make
decisions.

Encourage the kids to take home their copies of "The
Decision-Making Process" for personal use. ∎

Section Seven:

SERVICE

48 *Being Disabled*

By Cindy Parolini

Junior highers have trouble seeing beyond phys-ical disabilities. They want so much to fit in themselves that it's hard to accept people who ap-parently don't fit in at all.

Use this meeting to help your junior highers ex-plore the facts and feelings of being disabled, and what their Christian response can be.

OBJECTIVES

Participants will:
- experience and (or) observe a variety of physical disabilities;
- get in touch with feelings a disabled person might have;
- see how Jesus responded to disabled people;
- evaluate your church's sensitivity to disabled people; and
- choose appropriate responses to disabled people.

SUPPLIES

Gather cassette tapes or records of Christian music; a cas-sette player or turntable; construction paper; markers; scissors; straight pins; finger-food refreshments such as brownies or fruit, and punch; newsprint; a wheelchair (to be hidden in a van in the parking lot); and, for every six group members, an envelope of beginning relay directions on six slips of paper (see activity #2), three stopping-point slips of paper with instructions (see ac-tivity #2), three blindfolds, six pencils, six pieces of paper, six crackers, six inflated balloons, a "How It Felt" handout, a roll of masking tape, a Bible, and a slip of paper with either Luke 14:1-5 or John 9:1-11 written on it.

268

BEFORE THE MEETING

Read the meeting and collect supplies.

If possible, arrange to have a physically disabled junior higher attend this meeting. If you don't know a disabled junior higher, call local junior high schools and ask about such a person. Talk with him or her and explain the meeting. Ask him or her to think about and be willing to answer the questions in activity #7. Encourage him or her to bring a friend.

Choose the stopping places for each team of six in the disabled relay. Each team should stop at a different location, with about the same distance between each stopping place. Place the relay supplies and instruction slips at the proper places.

Find someone who has a van that can accommodate a wheelchair, then borrow a wheelchair. Have the van driver wait in the church parking lot with the wheelchair in his or her van until the group comes out, ready to use the wheelchair.

NOTES TO THE LEADER

During the disabled relay, have adult sponsors stationed at the stopping places and en route to ensure team members' safety. These adults should intervene if someone's in danger, and set the team(s) on the right track.

If you or these sponsors, however, see some team members who don't follow through with their role (of blindness, for example), don't interrupt the relay. Rather, address that problem in the discussion that follows.

If a disabled young person comes, make sure he or she gets the "able-bodied" role in the disabled relay.

THE MEETING

1. *Name tags*—Have Christian music playing as kids arrive. Make construction paper, markers, scissors and straight pins available. Direct kids to create name tags and pin them on.

2. *Disabled relay*—Tell group members they're going to run a relay of simple tasks, but they'll have special instructions. Divide the group into teams of six. Give each team its envelope of beginning directions, containing six slips of paper. Tell teams each member must take one slip and obey its instructions. Also say all team members must stay together during the relay. Of the

six slips:

● *two slips say:* You can't see for the duration of the relay. You can speak but you can't see. From now on you are blind. (Distribute blindfolds to all team members who are now blind.)

● *two slips say:* You can't talk for the duration of the relay. You can see but you can't talk. From now on you are mute.

● *one slip says:* You are able-bodied for the whole relay. You can't acquire any disabilities. You also can't assist your team members in any way.

● *one slip says:* Lead your team to the first stop for the relay. Go to _____. There you'll find your next instructions.

▶ At the first stopping points, each team finds six pencils and six pieces of paper and a slip of paper that says:

Two members of your team can no longer walk and must be carried for the duration of the relay.

Your task at this stop: Everyone must write his or her name without using hands.

When you've all completed the task, go to _____.

▶ At the second stopping points, each team finds six crackers and a slip of paper that says:

One more member of your team can't walk and must be carried for the duration of the relay. Another member is suddenly mute and can't talk for the duration of the relay.

Your task at this stop: Everyone must eat a cracker.

When you've all completed the task, go to _____.

▶ The third stopping points should be back near where the relay began.

At the third stopping points, each team finds a blindfold, six inflated balloons, and a slip of paper that says:

One more member of your team is blind for the duration of the relay.

Your task at this stop: Everyone must pop a balloon.

When you've all completed the task, return to the place where you began this relay.

3. *How it felt*—When all teams have finished the relay, have them rid themselves of the disabilities and sit in "team circles." Have one adult sponsor in each small group. Give a "How It Felt" handout to each group. Have group members discuss the questions.

How It Felt

Have your small group discuss:
- What did you think of the relay? Did you find it frustrating? silly? Explain. How did your team do?
- If you were one of the disabled team members, how did you feel being disabled? What did you learn? Did your able-bodied team member laugh at you? If so, how did that make you feel? How do you think people who are really disabled feel when someone makes fun of them? Did you "cheat" on your disability, for example, talk when you weren't supposed to? If so, why? How do you think people who really have that disability feel, knowing they can't ever "take a break" from it?
- If you were one of the able-bodied team members, how did you feel? Did you laugh at the other team members? Why or why not? Did you help them, even though you knew you weren't supposed to? If not, did you want to? Explain.
- Did your team members stay together the whole time? Why or why not? Was staying together hard or easy? Why? What are some real-life situations where disabled and able-bodied people can't stay together? (For example, a wheelchair-confined person couldn't join able-bodied friends at a place without wheelchair facilities.) How do you think the able-bodied friends feel about that? the disabled friends?
- In real life, what are some situations where you or others you know make fun of someone else? How do you handle such situations? How do you think the person who is made fun of handles it? Are *you* ever the brunt of someone else's fun? How do you feel when that happens? What would you like to happen instead?
- How do you react when you're around someone who's disabled? If you were (or are) a disabled person, what would you want to tell people?

4. Snack break—Give a roll of masking tape to the adult sponsor in each small group. Have the adults tape together the thumb and forefinger on both hands of all the kids.

Let group members enjoy the refreshments, but they must not remove the tape from their hands.

5. Jesus and disabled people—After the snack break, have kids get back into their small groups. They may remove the tape from their hands. Give each group a Bible and a slip of paper with either Luke 14:1-4 or John 9:1-11 written on it. Tell groups to each have someone read their passage aloud, and then discuss how they think Jesus felt about the disabled person in the passage.

When groups have finished, gather members together in a large group circle and have one person from each group report. List on newsprint the ways they think Jesus felt.

6. *The church and disabled people*—Take your group out to the church parking lot, where a van is waiting with a wheelchair in it. Have one person get in the wheelchair.

As a whole group, pretend to "walk through" a typical Sunday at church with the wheelchair-confined person. From the parking lot, go to the classrooms, to the sanctuary, to the bathrooms, to the fellowship hall—whatever route would be typical.

Along the way, notice and discuss: "Is there a 'handicapped parking' place? Is the church building easy for the wheelchair-confined person to enter? Are there ramps alongside staircases? Is there adequate space to maneuver in the hallways? Do the bathrooms have facilities for wheelchair-confined people?"

If the answers are no and the excursion through the church is difficult with your wheelchair-confined group member, let others lift him or her (in the wheelchair). When finished, have kids return to your meeting area and sit in a circle.

Discuss whether the kids think the church welcomes disabled people. If the building itself prevents such people from attending, as a group write a letter or plan to talk with the Board of Church Properties (or the appropriate person or board). Request changes.

7. *Choosing how to respond*—Ask group members how their feelings about disabled people have changed during this meeting.

If a disabled young person is present, encourage him or her to answer:

● What attitudes do you see most in other people? Which do you like and dislike?

● When do you like to have help doing something? Why? When do you prefer to be left alone? Why? (For example, ask the disabled person to describe the mechanics of eating out, and how he or she would and wouldn't want help.)

Now write in big letters on a sheet of newsprint "How to Respond." On another sheet write "How Not to Respond." Have everyone brainstorm ideas, and list them. For example, under "How to Respond" you might list "ask if the person wants help''; under ''How Not to Respond'' you might list ''stare at the person's wheelchair (crutches, dark glasses).''

Evaluate the lists. Throw out ideas that won't work. Keep helpful ones.

Close with a prayer asking for God's help in caring for disabled people and seeing beyond their disabilities. ■

49 God's Good Earth

By Ed McNulty

*J*unior highers are interested in the world around them. They notice God's gift of creation, as well as our misuse of it.

Use this two-part meeting to help kids create a slide show focusing on God's need for us to be stewards, or caretakers, of his creation.

OBJECTIVES

Participants will:
- explore the scriptural basis for creation;
- take slide pictures and arrange them for a presentation;
- search for songs related to creation and record them for the sound track; and
- gain a sense of accomplishment by preparing their presentation to share with others.

SUPPLIES

Gather records of songs about Earth and creation (songs by John Denver or hymns such as "Joyful, Joyful, We Adore Thee" work well); a turntable; a wire cutter; a sheet of newsprint with Genesis 1—2, Psalm 8, 19:1-6, 24:1-6, Psalm 93, Psalm 96 and Psalm 104 written on it; several cameras and rolls of slide film; nature magazines and picture books published by National Geographic or the Sierra Club; paper; pencils; a blank cassette tape; a cassette player; a slide projector and slide trays (needed the second time the group meets); a connecting jack for recording directly from the turntable to the cassette player; and, for each person, several inches of colored telephone wire (get this from a telephone company or get similar wire from a craft store) and a Bible.

BEFORE THE MEETING

Read the meeting and collect supplies.

Ask some adult sponsors to help with driving, choosing slides and taping songs.

Plan two meeting times for this activity. One meeting to take pictures and choose songs; another meeting to choose the slides and prepare the presentation.

Schedule a date and time to present your slide show to the congregation. This gives the junior highers a goal to aim for.

THE MEETING

1. Sculpture creations—As the group gathers, play songs about Earth and creation. Distribute several inches of telephone wire to each person. Ask kids to listen to the words of the songs and each sculpt a symbol of the message; for example, a fragile flower, a shining sun, a lightning bolt. Discuss the wire sculptures and the messages they represent, then combine them into one large "Earth Creation." Set this aside. Ask: "How do you define Earth? our environment? pollution? What do you think of our misuse of God's creation? Describe the pollution in our community. What can be done about it?"

Tell the junior highers that many people aren't aware of the problems of pollution. By putting together and showing a slide presentation, they'll make others aware of God's need for caretakers of his Earth.

2. Scripture search—Divide the group into small groups of four to six and give each kid a Bible. Display the newsprint with the scripture references on it. Ask group members to look up the scripture references. Have them answer: "What do these passages say about our world? our Creator? ourselves"? After 15 minutes, gather as a large group and share discoveries.

Ask group members what natural beauty they see in the community; for example, trees, flowers, gardens, hills, fields, lakes, seashore. Then ask group members what pollution or destructive use of the environment they see in the community; for example, belching smokestacks, trash along the road, littered vacant lots, gaudy signs and billboards, waste material from strip mining, dirty streams.

3. Camera patrol—Say: "To prepare our slide show on

creation—God's wondrous gifts, and our misuse of them—some of you will stay here to listen to albums and find songs for a sound track. Others will take cameras and film and go out to photograph scenes of nature's beauty and scenes of pollution and neglect.''

Choose who will stay and who will go. Tell photographers to take pictures of things you've discussed: flowers, trees, fields, littered roads, spilled trash cans, and so on. Tell them to return in one hour and give you the rolls of film. Distribute the cameras and film; ask the adult sponsors to take the photographers to various locations around the city.

Keep one camera and roll of film at the church. The group there may choose songs requiring scenes impossible to photograph "live"; for example, the mountains if you are in Kansas! So ask a young person to photograph pictures from nature magazines and books. (Photograph large pictures so a close-up lens won't be necessary.)

4. Sound track review crew—Ask the kids who stayed to listen to albums and choose three or four songs for the sound track. Have the kids develop a connecting narrative using their own words and a few scripture verses (such as those studied earlier). The presentation should last 10 or 15 minutes.

Distribute paper and pencils and have the kids write out the script in the exact order of the narrative, scripture and lyrics. If time permits, record the sound track. Assign one person to type the script and make several copies for the next meeting.

Making Slide Shows

One junior high group created a slide show with this equipment: instamatic cameras, one carousel slide projector and one filmstrip projector with a slide attachment. The filmstrip projector was slow, but by stacking the slides carefully, the operator could keep up with the carousel projector. This group even received an invitation to show their presentation at a local ecology conference!

For more information on the "how to" of slide making and tape recording, see *The Basic Encyclopedia for Youth Ministry* by Benson and Wolfe (Group Books), or *Gadgets, Gimmicks and Grace: Multimedia in Church & School* by Ed McNulty ($2.50 from Visual Parables, First Presbyterian Church, 49 S. Portage, Westfield, NY 14787).

5. *Closing*—When the photographers return, collect the film. Discuss some scenes they photographed. Were the kids surprised by what they saw? Why or why not? Have the sound track crew fill in the other group on its progress. Tell kids that at the next meeting they'll be "putting it all together"—actually creating the slide show.

Gather everyone around the wire "Earth Creation." Ask each person to complete this sentence: "I thank God for his gift of . . ." Sing a hymn such as "For the Beauty of the Earth"; and close with a prayer asking for help in completing the slide show.

6. *Putting it all together*—At the next meeting, bring all the developed slides and copies of the script. Divide the group into small groups. One small group can record the sound track if this wasn't done at the previous meeting. Give the other small groups portions of the script and ask them to find slides to match key words in each line. They should circle the words to indicate the slide changes. One slide per line is a good rule of thumb, unless the song is unusually slow.

Load the slides into trays, and run through the presentation with the sound track. There may be a few places where slides need to be added or taken away. Make these adjustments and finalize the presentation. You're now ready to share it with others! ■

50 Good Things to Do for Others

By Bill Stearns

Most Christians seem to think doing good comes naturally. But junior highers know better.

The me-first cruelty, competitiveness and back-biting of the junior high world is evidence that doing good doesn't come naturally.

Use this meeting to help kids understand the importance of doing good things for others.

OBJECTIVES

Participants will:
- admit that on a human level doing good doesn't seem valuable and isn't exactly a popular pastime;
- search the scriptures for God's emphasis on doing good;
- share personal needs as areas where others can do good; and
- do some good individually and as a group this coming week.

SUPPLIES

Gather a podium; banner and poster-making supplies (such as scrap material, posterboard, string, construction paper, scissors, glue); a few current newspapers; newsprint; markers; a gavel; two or three prizes or fun activities; for every two group members a Bible; and, for each person, a pencil, a copy of the check and a "Scripture Search Crossword Puzzle" handout.

278

BEFORE THE MEETING

Read the meeting and collect supplies.

For the auction, arrange two or three prizes or fun activities. For example: Arrange a ride in a local police patrol car. Have a parent bake a spectacular fudge cake. Borrow somebody's video-camera equipment and offer a make-your-own-video opportunity. Get permission from a popular radio station to let a kid introduce a song or two as a guest disc jockey. Or spend a little money and offer a poster or free-hamburger coupon or admission to something.

Find two or three people who need help that junior highers could provide. This could be housework, yardwork or errand-running. Also find a good time during the coming week for each project, if the group can do it.

THE MEETING

1. *Arrival activities*—Use early birds to:
● set up the podium;
● make banners and hoopla for the auction; and
● browse through newspapers and begin tallying how many stories there are about people doing good vs. doing bad.

2. *"The Poor Kid's Auction"*—This event can have as much razzle-dazzle as your noise limitations and maturing dignity allow. Stand at the podium. Announce: "Ladies and gentlemen, step right up for 'The Poor Kid's Auction'! Yes, folks, that's right; we provide the money. (Hand out a check and a pencil to each person.) We provide the amaaaaazing prizes! Step right up!"

Explain: "We have three items to bid for tonight. You may bid for any of them, but your check is good for a measly $5,000! Now, who'll start the bidding on this fine . . .?"

As you auction off the two or three prizes or fun activities you prepared earlier, have the highest bidder write the amount he or she bid, sign the check and hand it in. Kids will catch on that if they pool their checks, they can bid much higher than an individual's limit of $5,000—although only one person can take the prize. Move things along quickly.

Then say: "And now, ladies and gentlemen! What am I bid for a fine opportunity to do some good, to scrub a grimy bathroom, mop a kitchen floor, do a load of dirty laundry, and vacu-

Check for "The Poor Kid's Auction"

195

Jill or Joe Junior Higher
16543 Whatadrag Drive
Mass Nowhere, USA 12345

_____ 19 ____   64-89/2710

GOOD FOR UP TO $5,000

$ _____

Pay to the
order of _____ Dollars

_____

BB Bucksville Bank   Signature _____

998234798734   98734876655   676   00000000079837   987

um and dust an entire house for a lady? How much will you pay for this privilege of doing this glamorous good deed?" Play with the expected moans, groans and lack of bidding.

If you get a bid, remind the bidder that he or she will actually get to *do* these fine activities.

Before things slow down too much, bang your gavel and announce that the fitting end of any auction is a prayer. Ask for God's help in wanting to do good things for others.

3. Newspaper stories—Have kids sit in small groups of three to six. Make sure there's an adult sponsor in each group. Give the small groups the current newspapers and ask them to find stories about people doing good and stories about people doing bad. After a while, ask: "What is your count of stories of good vs. bad?" Add the results; the implications should be clear. Write a big "DOING GOOD ISN'T VERY POPULAR" on newsprint.

4. *Scripture search*—Hand out the crossword puzzles. Have kids find partners. Give each pair a Bible. Have partners work together on the "Scripture Search Crossword Puzzle" to find out what God says about doing good. Expect questions and problems with the puzzle; use them as informal discussion points to emphasize biblical ideas on goodness. When the first pair finishes, announce that time's up and those who didn't finish can take the puzzle home.

Conclude the activity by writing on newsprint: "GOD SAYS DOING GOOD IS IMPORTANT."

5. *Talk time*—Ask: "It seems obvious, but what exactly *is* doing good? I think you'll discover the answer in our next activity."

Have group members return to their same small groups. Have the sponsor in each group explain: "Everybody needs help in some way. If somebody would do a good deed in your life, what would it be? Maybe if somebody hired you for a Saturday job, it'd be a good thing; maybe somebody would help you with your homework; maybe somebody would pray for you to get along better with your brother or sister. Let's each finish this sentence: 'A good deed somebody could do for me is . . .' I'll give you exactly 47 seconds to come up with something you really need in your life."

The adult should then be first to share, setting the honest, personal tone of the sharing. If your kids would be more comfortable writing their sentences, fine. (If so, make sure you have paper.) If some groups finish early, they can help finish members' crossword puzzles and (or) pray for the needs just shared.

From the center of the room, get the small groups' attention by saying: "So we've caught on by now that if somebody did something good for us, it'd be something that met a need, that helped us. Did you notice in the auction that some people 'did good' by sharing their checks to help another person bid? (Write on the board: "DOING GOOD IS MEETING PEOPLE'S NEEDS.") This is one reason God says doing good is so important; it's his way of meeting people's needs. It feels great to have somebody help you just because they want to, not because they have to or because you're paying them."

6. *Wrap-up ideas*—The wrap-up can be quick. Review the three points on the chalkboard: "Although doing good isn't very popular, it's God's way of meeting people's needs—our own in-

Scripture Search Crossword Puzzle

Across

1. Matthew 7:21-23. "_____"
everyone who does good deeds
knows Christ; but everyone who
knows Christ will do good deeds.

5. Psalm 14:1; Romans 3:12. What
person always does good?

6. Matthew 25:34-40. When we help
feed others, it's as if we've "_____"
Jesus.

7. Acts 9:36. Woman full of good
works.

9. 1 Corinthians 3:12. On the foundation of knowing Christ, doing good
is compared to building with gold;
but selfish, worthless actions are
compared to building with "_____."

10. Romans 1:18. God's "_____"
hits evildoers.

11. Acts 10:38. Hometown of this
man who went around doing good.

12. 1 Timothy 2:1-2. What's a good
thing you can always do for everybody?

14. Matthew 5:16. Good works are
seen like a light that "_____."

16. Proverbs 12:14; 13:21. What will
come back to you when you do good
for someone else?

Down

2. Ecclesiastes 9:18. How many
evildoers does it take to mess up
something good?

3. Proverbs 3:27-28. When should
you do good to your neighbors?

4. Ephesians 2:10. Christians are
created in Christ to do "_____" (two
words).

8. 1 Timothy 6:17-18. A rich man
does good if he does what?

9. Romans 2:10. What's something
you can expect for doing good?

10. 2 Corinthians 9:8. When does
God help you abound in good
works?

13. Titus 3:1. How many types of
good deeds should we be prepared
to do?

15. Is it easy or hard to act out Romans 12:21?

cluded, as others return good for the good we've done for them. There's a good feeling that goes along with doing good deeds; the person helped feels good, and—as we'll soon discover—the person doing the good deed feels good too!''

Explain that the housecleaning you tried to auction off was a serious need of an elderly person; detail the need. Personalize one or two more needs that would be good candidates for a group good deed. Then ''auction'' the projects, using hand votes as ''bids,'' to choose a group good deed project for the coming week. Immediately announce the time and place and any equipment needed for the project.

Have a time of silent prayer when each junior higher can pray—which is doing good—for the needs expressed in the sharing session. Then pray for God to help each person simply to do good. ∎

Scripture Search Crossword Puzzle Answers

51 The Joy of Giving

By Jerry Martin

Kids need the chance to give to people less fortunate than themselves. Provide them with the opportunity. Instead of feeling powerless about the plight of hungry people thousands of miles away, junior highers can focus on the food needs in your community.

Use this meeting to let junior highers help hungry people within reach.

OBJECTIVES

Participants will:
- learn what the Bible teaches about caring and giving;
- distribute food to families in need; and
- discuss the before and after feelings of giving.

SUPPLIES

Gather donated food items; maps with directions to delivery locations; paper; pencils; markers; scissors; a loaf of bread; for every five or six group members, a box for delivering food in, a "Team Work" handout, a "Food Delivery Discussion" handout; and, for each person, a 3×5 card with a food item written on it (for forming teams; use five or six food items that can be grouped together—for example, five fruits, five vegetables, five cereals, five dairy products), a straight pin, a chair and a Bible.

BEFORE THE MEETING

Read the meeting and collect supplies.

284

At least four weeks before the meeting, inform the congregation of your food-delivery project. Ask for donations. Use the church newsletter, bulletins and posters. Include this information:

Information for the Congregation

● *When:* The date by which all food items must be donated.

● *What:* Food-item suggestions (for example, canned fruit and vegetables, canned soups, tomato sauce, peanut butter, oatmeal, dry cereals, rice, powdered milk, sugar, flour, shortening, all-in-one packaged dinners).

● *Where:* The place to take donated items.

● *Who:* The name and phone number of someone to contact with questions.

Secure the names and addresses of local people in need of food donations. (Ask your pastor or a local social-welfare agency.) Get the same number of homes as the number of youth group teams (five or six kids to a team) you expect to have.

Make individual maps with directions to the homes so drivers can easily find them. Include the name(s) of the resident(s) and any special information the food-delivery team should know. For example, elderly, handicapped, unemployed, single parent. This information helps teams prepare for their visits.

Recruit an adult sponsor/driver for every five or six young people. (If necessary, adjust the size of the teams to the size of the vehicles.) The adults will help the kids prepare the food boxes, share in the team discussions and transport the teams for food delivery.

THE MEETING

1. *Food guessing game*—As kids arrive, pin the food-item cards on their backs. Make sure no one peeks! Say: "Find out what food item you are. You may ask only yes or no questions. You have only a few minutes. Go!"

After everyone's discovered what food item he or she is, have everybody sit in a circle, on chairs.

2. *Upset the food basket*—Choose one person to be "It." Remove his or her chair from the circle. "It" stands in the center and calls out the name of a food category represented on people's backs (for example, cereals or vegetables). Those who have items in that food category pinned to their backs must change seats without "It" taking a seat. If "It" succeeds in getting into one of the chairs, then the person whose chair was taken becomes "It." The person who's "It" may also call out "Upset the food basket!" Then everybody must change seats before "It" gets into an empty seat.

3. *What God says about giving*—Divide the group into teams according to the food items pinned on kids' backs. Make sure each team has an adult sponsor/driver. Say: "We've played fun games concerning food, but we're *really* here to do something important with food. We're going to deliver groceries to people in our community.

"Each team is going to someone's home to deliver a box of food. But before we leave, it's important to understand *why* we're doing this. Let's look at God's point of view."

Assign each team one of the following scripture passages: Acts 20:35; 2 Corinthians 9:10-15; James 2:14-17; 1 John 3:16-18. Give team members Bibles. Allow them about five minutes to read the passage and prepare a non-verbal skit showing what it means. Bring everyone together to enjoy the skits.

4. *Time for teams*—Give each team a "Team Work" handout. Have the team members do what it says. Make food items, boxes, paper, pencils, markers and scissors available.

5. *Food delivery*—Give all adult drivers their maps and directions to the homes. Depending on your area, allow 30 to 45 minutes for the deliveries. Ask the adults to watch the time and encourage team members to talk with the resident(s) at each home if there's time. Make sure everyone knows the designated time to return to the church.

6. *Back at the church*—Ask team members to sit together knee-to-knee. Give each team a "Food Delivery Discussion" handout. After the teams have discussed, have each team choose one spokesperson to briefly share with the whole group one special moment from the food-delivery experience.

286

Team Work

1. Fill a box with an assortment of food.

2. Design a special card to accompany the food. Sign your names and add a message of Christian love.

3. Discuss:
- What does our scripture passage have to do with delivering food?
- What's exciting about doing this?
- What's scary?
- What other feelings do we have about doing this?
- What other actions will show the person(s) we care?

Food Delivery Discussion

- What did we enjoy most about this experience?
- What bothered us?
- What surprised us?
- How have our feelings changed since the beginning of the meeting?
- Which is more fun—giving or receiving? Explain.

7. ***The "Bread of Life"***—Get all the teams together in a big huddle. Hold a loaf of bread in the center of the circle. Say: "This is a reminder that Jesus came to be our 'Bread of Life'" (John 6:35). As an act of encouragement for giving and to remember the hungry, pass the loaf around the huddle. Have each person take a small piece of bread to eat. Give a prayer of thanks for the opportunity to give. ■

52 A Junior High Trash Bash!

By Joani Schultz

Junior highers like to know they can make a difference. They need reminders that they're valuable and God can use them right now.

Use this service-centered meeting to help kids see their worth as God's people and make a difference in the community by picking up garbage.

OBJECTIVES

Participants will:

● experience activities that create a sense of teamwork and cooperation;

● make an impact on the community by picking up garbage; and

● receive awards and celebrate making a difference.

SUPPLIES

Gather a piece of paper; pen; inexpensive trash bags for the games (you'll need one stuffed with newspapers for the garbage volleyball game, and three or four for each group of six); a volleyball net; masking tape; sturdy trash bags for garbage pickup (at least one or two per person); a Bible; a cassette tape of the song "We Can Make a Difference" by Tom Franzak; a cassette player; and, for each person, a "Trash Bash Award." Optional: prizes for the "Trashin' Fashion Show" and Trash Bash T-shirts for everyone.

288

BEFORE THE MEETING

Read the meeting and collect supplies.

Realize that this meeting takes special advance planning and organization. But it's worth the effort in terms of helping junior highers feel good about themselves. Get another adult to co-coordinate this meeting with you.

If you'd like, design your own special version of the "Trash Bash Award." Ask a few artistic junior highers to help. Make the awards look as official as possible. You could make a crazy "official seal" using a newspaper ribbon attached with a sticker or star. Try to find a volunteer calligrapher to be the "name grabber" and write group members' names on the certificates the day of the meeting.

Select a garbage pickup site. Choose an area that's heavily littered—one kids can tell they've cleaned when they're done. Some possibilities are freeway interchanges, ditches, downtown streets, parks, school lots, empty lots, elderly people's yards. After you've chosen your site, make sure it's safe for your junior highers. You might need to inform city officials of your plans.

Plan about 35 to 40 minutes for the opening games and 10 to 15 minutes for the closing celebration. Keeping in mind your area and the job you choose, calculate the time needed for transportation and garbage pickup. Plan accordingly. Publicize the meeting time (beginning and ending) and tell everyone to wear old clothes and bring gloves. How about designing a poster that's a trash bag with Trash Bash information pouring out of it?

Recruit supervisors and drivers for vans, pickups or trailers—vehicles that can haul kids and full trash bags. Check into the possibility of city or county officials planning a special garbage pickup near the spot you plan to clean up. That'd save you needing to transport the garbage to a dump.

Find a couple volunteer parents to run a "Munchie Mobile." Especially if it's hot, junior high workers will appreciate cold drinks and refreshments. How about a sign on a car advertising it as the Munchie Mobile? Willing parents can drive around and give kids refreshments—cookies, watermelon, energy snacks, juice. Make sure junior highers put their own trash in the bags!

Arrange for photographs to be taken. Maybe the newspaper or local TV station would be interested in covering such a fine endeavor by junior highers. That's one more way of raising junior highers' self-worth.

If your closing celebration will be outside, make sure your

cassette player will provide enough volume.

If possible, go all out and design special T-shirts for the kids to wear while they pick up trash. Have junior highers help with this. T-shirts could say "I'm picky! Trash Bash survivor," "I survived the great Trash Bash" or "I can make a difference!"

THE MEETING

1. *Name grabber*—As kids arrive, have one adult or high school young person write each person's full name on a piece of paper. During the opening games or after everyone leaves for the garbage collecting, have this person prepare a "Trash Bash Award" for each person. You'll need the awards delivered to you at the garbage pickup site if your closing celebration will be there. Make sure no one is left out.

2. *Garbage volleyball*—As junior highers filter in, form two teams. Kids can join the activity as they arrive. Have everyone sit on the floor with a low volleyball net dividing the two teams. No poles are necessary—just two sets of strong arms. Then play regular volleyball, except no one can move around. Use a trash bag stuffed with newspapers as the volleyball.

3. *"Trashin' Fashion Show"*—Divide the group into teams no larger than six. Give each team masking tape and three or four cheap garbage bags, and these instructions: "Use the trash bags to design an original fashion creation for the 'Trashin' Fashion Show' contest. One person must model your creation for the whole group. You must also come up with a team cheer for collecting garbage. For example, 'Stash that trash!' or 'We're not trash! Hey! We're not trash!'"

Allow 10 to 15 minutes. When everybody's ready, have a "narrator" from each team describe his or her teammate's apparel. Have fun with it! Wrap up the contest by hearing each team's cheer. (If you'd like, offer prizes for the craziest fashions.)

4. *Pick up "icks"*—Introduce your Trash Bash project. Say: "Sometimes we feel like we don't really matter very much. But today we're going to make a big difference. We're going to clean up _____. We're going to show our community we really care!"

Have drivers transport junior highers to the garbage collection site. Make sure you have plenty of adult supervisors and lots of trash bags. Depending on your cleanup project, choose the best procedure: You could break into smaller Trash Bash troops, or form one big line and clean a large area as you march across. Remind kids to pick up all trash—nothing that's alive.

5. "We can make a difference!" celebration and awards ceremony—When the group's completed the garbage pickup, meet together around the full trash bags for the final celebration.

Have a young person read Psalm 8:3-9. Say (in pep-talk style): "We're so special, God put us in charge of his creation. Sometimes we blow it, but when we do, we know we can pick up the pieces and start over again. We're special! We're loved! *We're* not trash! We can make a difference!"

Call kids forward one by one to receive their "Trash Bash Awards." Get the group involved: You can read the person's full name, "Joe Fleming," then have the group members shout "Joe makes a difference!" Make this a special celebration.

Have group members form a circle around the garbage they've collected and join hands. Pray: "Lord, see what we've done. Thanks for giving us the opportunity to serve you in this way. We've made your world a little brighter by giving of our-

Trash Bash Award

This award hereby certifies that

_____

has made a difference today,

_____

By giving unselfishly of time, energy and service, the recipient of this auspicious "Trash Bash Award" is hereby thanked and declared a valuable person, loved by God!

selves. Thanks for loving us and making a difference in our lives. Amen.''

Have junior highers turn sideways, place their hands on each other's hips and form a line to ''snake dance'' to the song ''We Can Make a Difference'' by Tom Franzak. Weave around the collected garbage. Coach kids to sing along whenever the phrase ''We can make a difference'' appears in the song.

Transport group members back to the church so they can be picked up. And, if necessary, transport the full trash bags to a dump. ∎

Section Eight:

SEASONAL AND SPECIAL EVENTS

Be My Valentine

By Katie Abercrombie

Valentine's Day celebrates love. Junior highers think about love a lot. They fall in and out of love many times. But they wonder: What is love? How do I express it?

Use this Valentine meeting to help junior highers explore and celebrate the characteristics of real love according to 1 Corinthians 13:4-7.

OBJECTIVES

Participants will:
- express what love means to them;
- discuss the characteristics of love described in 1 Corinthians 13;
- write loving characteristics they see in each other; and
- celebrate loving friendships.

SUPPLIES

Gather a large sheet of newsprint with "Love is . . ." written at the top; masking tape; markers; a sheet of newsprint with the incomplete sentences from activity #4 written on it; a Bible; scissors; decorating supplies such as crepe paper, glue, pipe cleaners, glitter and stickers; for every two group members, an 8 1/2 × 11 construction-paper heart cut in half to form a unique puzzle; and, for each person, an 18-inch piece of yarn, a pencil, a "Love Survey" handout, an 11 × 17 sheet of construction paper (red, pink or white) and enough 2-inch construction-paper hearts to have one for each other group member.

294

BEFORE THE MEETING

Read the meeting and collect supplies.
Find some kids to:

● decorate the meeting room with Valentine's Day decorations;

● prepare refreshments to fit the theme (red punch, heart-shaped cookies, pink-frosted brownies); and

● plan party games to fit the Valentine's Day theme. A good resource is *Holiday Ideas for Youth Groups* by Rice and Yaconelli (Zondervan).

If possible, find someone with experience in clown makeup to paint hearts on people's faces.

Tape the "Love is . . ." newsprint onto the wall.

THE MEETING

1. *Love is*—Greet junior highers and ask them to write their definitions of love on the "Love is . . ." wall. Provide markers. If you have someone to paint hearts on faces, have him or her do that now.

2. *Name tags*—Say that, because this party is about love, you'd like each person to think of a loving characteristic he or she possesses that begins with the same consonant or vowel *sound* (not necessarily the same letter) as his or her name. For example, Cindy might be "sweet Cindy"; Kevin might be "caring Kevin"; and Suzanne might be "supportive Suzanne." Provide heart-halves and markers and have kids each write their name and descriptive word on their heart-half to make a Valentine name tag. Give each person a piece of yarn to hang the name tag around his or her neck.

3. *Valentine name game*—Have everyone sit in a circle. (If you have more than 20 group members, make more than one circle.) Explain that you're going to play a game where group members will learn what everyone wrote on the name tags. You begin by sharing your name tag (your adjective and name) and then turning it around so no one can see what you wrote. The person on your right then shares his or her name tag, turns it around and repeats your Valentine name tag. And so on. Let the group help out when someone has a hard time remembering.

4. *To me, love means*—Tell junior highers to think about what love means to them. Ask them to think about all kinds of love: the love of parents, other family members, friends, in guy-girl relationships, and God's love. Ask them to think about special relationships, people they love a lot and times they felt loved.

After a few minutes, display the newsprint with the following incomplete sentences. Hand out pencils. Ask kids to number 1 to 6 on the back of their name tags and write how they'd complete each sentence:

1. The best two-word description of love I can think of is . . .

2. When I love someone, I . . .

3. I feel loved by my parents, family or friends when . . .

4. God's love means . . .

5. An essential ingredient of love is . . .

6. The most loving thing a person can do for someone else is . . .

When everyone has finished writing, ask junior highers to get into pairs by finding the person whose heart-half fits theirs to form a complete heart. Give pairs a few minutes to discuss their sentence completions. Remind kids that if they don't feel comfortable talking about something, they may pass.

5. *"Honey, If You Love Me"*—Have everyone sit in a circle. Ask for a volunteer to be "It." This person will go up to any other person, look him or her in the eye, and say "Honey, if you love me, won't you please smile?" The other person must respond "Honey, I love you, but I just can't smile," *without* smiling or laughing. They should do this three times. If the responding person smiles or laughs, he or she becomes "It." If he or she keeps a straight face, "It" must choose another victim and try again. If your group isn't too large, keep going until everyone has had a chance to play.

6. *1 Corinthians 13*—Read 1 Corinthians 13:4-7 slowly to the group. Ask group members to close their eyes and concentrate on the passage.

7. *Love survey*—Give each person a "Love Survey" handout. Have kids find their pencils. When kids have completed the survey, have them sit with their partners again and another pair to form groups of four. Have small group members each tell

Love Survey

For each characteristic of love, write the name of a person you know who has it, how he or she expresses it and how it affects you.

Love characteristic	Who has it	How he or she expresses it	How it affects me
Love is patient. I don't have to have everything just the way I want it right now. I give people plenty of time to accomplish tasks or understand what I'm saying.			
Love is kind. I look for the best in other people and try to build them up rather than put them down.			
Love does not envy. I'm happy with who I am and what I have. I'm happy for someone else who has something I don't have, even if I'd like very much to have it.			
Love does not boast. I don't brag constantly about my accomplishments, abilities or possessions, but I'm quick to congratulate others on their accomplishments.			
Love is not proud. I'm willing to be friends with all kinds of people. I'm not afraid to make the first move in a friendship. When I've hurt someone, I'm willing to admit I was wrong.			
Love is not rude. I treat others with the same respect I'd want.			
Love is not self-seeking. I don't always put myself first. I'm aware of and considerate of the needs of others.			
Love is not easily angered. It takes something really big to make me angry. I don't "fly off the handle" over little things.			
Love keeps no record of wrongs. I find it easy to forgive others. I look for the positive things that happen in my relationships rather than the negative.			
Love does not delight in evil. I don't enjoy doing things that are wrong. I feel bad when I see people doing things that hurt others.			
Love rejoices in the truth. When I see people treating each other with respect, kindness and honesty, I feel great!			
Love always protects. I feel I should help and protect those who are weak.			
Love always hopes. Even when things aren't going well in my relationships, I work hard to help them get better.			
Love always perseveres. When things aren't going well in my relationships, I hang in there.			

about two survey items: who has the characteristic, how this person expresses it, and how it affects the group member sharing.

8. *Personal hearts*—Give each person an 11 × 17 sheet of construction paper. Provide pencils, scissors and decorating supplies. Have each group member draw and cut out a large construction-paper heart. Tell kids to be creative and to use any of the materials provided to decorate their hearts. Each junior higher should write on the heart his or her name and three characteristics of love from 1 Corinthians 13 that he or she has or would like to develop. Have the groups of four brainstorm ways to develop the desired characteristics. As the kids finish, have them tape their construction-paper hearts onto the wall.

9. *Heartfelt appreciation*—Give each person enough small hearts to give one to each other person in the room. Tell the group members they're going to give valentines by telling the loving characteristics they see in each other. Each person should tape one of the small hearts onto each group member's large heart on the wall. On the small heart, he or she should write one of the characteristics of love in that person and how it's expressed. For example, Amy might write on Jennifer's little heart: "kindness, because she reaches out to people who are different or who are being left out." Encourage everyone to think of a characteristic for each other person. You and your adult sponsors should watch for anyone who isn't receiving many valentines and give them some.

10. *Valentine celebration*—Close the meeting with the special refreshments and games. Before anyone leaves, gather together for a prayer and a group hug. ■

54 *It's Easter!*

By Leo Symmank

The high point of a Christian's year is Easter. Christ's triumph over death is the once-for-all-times victory.

For young people, Easter can be a memorable day because of the celebration of new life—Christ's and their own.

Use this Easter meeting to involve young people in your group with each other, exploring biblical accounts of new life and in a creative Easter celebration.

OBJECTIVES

Participants will:
● explore biblical accounts of Christ's Resurrection after experiencing a Bible Easter egg hunt;
● discuss the importance of resurrection stories for their daily lives; and
● celebrate their own and Christ's Resurrection.

SUPPLIES

Gather materials for the art projects you choose to do in activity #4 (see activity #4 for a listing of materials); songsheets or hymnals with favorite Easter songs; for every four to six group members, a large sheet of newsprint, a marker, a roll of masking tape, an ''Easter Bible Study Instructions'' handout, four to six slips of paper with Matthew 28:1-15, Mark 5:35-43, Mark 16:1-8 or 1 Thessalonians 4:13-18 written on them (the Bible passages will divide the group into small groups; if you have more than 24 group members, repeat the same verses on different-colored slips of paper); and, for each person, a Bible and an egg-shaped container (plastic or tin).

BEFORE THE MEETING

Read the meeting and collect supplies.

Ask someone to bring refreshments.

Prepare the eggs: Insert the slips of paper with the Bible passages into the eggs—one per egg. Make sure you have enough eggs for each person to have one, and that the Bible passages (and perhaps colors of paper) will divide the group into small groups of four to six.

Hide the eggs.

THE MEETING

1. *A Bible Easter egg bunt*—When your junior highers have arrived, invite them to hunt for the hidden Easter eggs. Each person is to pick up only one egg. After everyone has found an egg and removed the scripture passage, ask kids to get into small groups by finding other group members who have the same scripture passage (or color of paper). Make sure there's an adult sponsor in each group.

2. *Easter Bible study*—Hand out Bibles for everyone. Give each small group a large sheet of newsprint, a marker, a roll of masking tape and an "Easter Bible Study Instructions" handout. Tell kids to do what the handout says.

3. *Large group reports*—Once each small group has completed its scripture study, bring everyone together. Ask each small group to take turns sharing the following information with the large group:

● An outline of the events in the scripture passage.

● The most important phrase or sentence in the scripture passage.

● Two important meanings the scripture passage has for young people's lives.

4. *Easter celebrations*—Point out that the junior highers have been sharing their faith orally in both the small and large group. Next they can share their faith visually.

Have kids get back into their small groups. Encourage small groups to use the passages they just studied as the springboard for the visual presentation of the Easter theme. Ask groups to first discuss what they want to say through their art form before they begin creating it. Some options:

● *A mobile of resurrection symbols or pictures.* Materials: Wire coat hangers, doweling, string or thread, balsa wood or cardboard for symbols, Easter pictures with cardboard backing, glue, old Sunday school leaflets, a single-edged razor blade for balsa wood, pliers for coat hangers, scissors for cardboard and pictures.

● *An Easter banner.* Materials: A large piece of felt or other material for the banner; a piece of doweling for the top of the banner; pieces of felt, colored yarn, glue, needle and thread, scissors.

● *An Easter collage.* Materials: Photo magazines, Sunday school leaflets, worship service bulletin covers, a large piece of cardboard, glue, scissors, poster paper.

● *An Easter hymn.* Kids could use an existing melody or compose their own music to fit original lyrics.

Easter Bible Study Instructions

● Look up your scripture passage in the Bible and read it.
● Tape your sheet of newprint onto the wall.
● Outline the events in the story on newsprint. Ask someone in your group to tell the story to the whole group later.
● Decide which is the most important phrase or sentence in your scripture passage. Choose someone in your group to read it to the whole group later.
● Have each person again quietly read the section of scripture and consider what meaning this scripture has for his or her personal life. (How does it encourage comfort or reassure you?) Have each person share his or her thoughts in the small group.
● As a group, complete this sentence to share with the total group: "Two important meanings this scripture has for our lives are . . ."
● Choose someone to report your sentence completion to the total group.

5. *Closing*—Bring the groups together. Ask each small group to share its art with the other groups and explain its meaning. Invite prayers from the group relating to the Easter theme. Sing favorite Easter songs. Serve refreshments.

6. *Artwork display*—Consider displaying the art forms in the church. Incorporate the art forms into the congregation's Easter worship services. ■

55 *A Bike Hike Special*

By Cindy Hansen

Get junior highers together for a bike day! Use the time to work together not only on physical fitness, but on spiritual fitness as well.

OBJECTIVES

Participants will:
- experience a fun biking adventure; and
- stop three times along the route to touch, taste, see, hear and smell God's gifts.

SUPPLIES

Gather two chairs; two dice; a piece of posterboard with the "Bike-Day Relay" instructions written on it; a piece of posterboard with the Bible paraphrase in activity #1 written on it; masking tape; a Bible; one copy of the poem "Grass"; a pair of nose plugs; and some cookies. Everybody should have a bike and helmet and bring a sack lunch and plenty of water.

BEFORE THE MEETING

Read the meeting and collect supplies.

Place two chairs a few feet apart at one end of your meeting room. Place one of the dice on each chair. Tape the "Bike-Day Relay" instructions onto the wall between the two chairs. Tape the Bible paraphrase onto the wall too.

Plot the bike-trip course and create the schedule for the bike ride. For example, you could plan three to four miles between each stop. Begin at the church at 9 a.m., stop midmorning at a grassy hill, stop for lunch at a picnic area or park, stop midafternoon at a field or wooded area, then return to the church.

Pack the nose plugs, cookies and poem to carry with you for use during the bike-hike stops.

Publicize the event with posters that say "Gear Up for Bike Day!" Have junior highers announce the event in church or Sunday school by wearing their helmets, wheeling in their bikes and telling the bike-day details.

NOTES TO THE LEADER

This event is a leisurely, one-day bike trip. No matter what the distance, it's important to stress the following guidelines with your junior highers well before the event.

● Be sure your bike fits you and is in good condition.

● Equip your bike with a good rack, a bright light and reflectors.

● For safety's sake, wear a helmet.

● Ride with the traffic

● Ride single file.

● Ride defensively—don't expect cars to see you.

● Signal your turns.

● Carry plenty of water.

● Practice building up your endurance; gradually increase your mileage.

THE MEETING

1. Bike-day beginnings—Have everyone warm up for the bike trip by playing a relay. Divide the group into two teams. Instruct them to line up on the end of the room opposite the two chairs, with one of the dice on each chair, and the poster with the relay instructions.

Tell team members to, one at a time, run to the chairs, roll the dice, do the corresponding activities, run back to their line and tag the next person on their team. The first team done wins. The winners get to lead the pack of bikers when they begin to peddle.

Gather group members together and say: "Just as a bike trip strengthens our bodies for good health, so do praise, adoration and thanksgiving strengthen us as Christians in daily living." Encourage them to look for God's gifts on the trip from the moment they get on their bikes.

All together, look at the second poster and read the paraphrase of 1 Corinthians 9:23 and Hebrews 12:1: "All the bike-

Bike-Day Relay

[•] Run around the chair twice while humming "A Bicycle Built for Two."

[•.] Lie on your back and peddle while you count to 10.

[•.•] Go to a person on the other team and say "Have fun on the bike trip!"

[::] Do 10 jumping jacks.

[•:•] Run to a person on your team, shake his or her hand and say why you're glad he or she is coming on the trip.

[:::] Stand on the chair and yell "Hooray! Bike day is here!"

trip training and preparation we do for the gospel's sake, in order to share in its blessings. Let us ride with determination the course that lies before us."

Have everyone hop on the bikes and follow the leader (single file) to the first stop. Enjoy the ride!

2. First stop—Ask bikers to stretch out on their backs and relax. Say: "Look up. Call out the gifts you see that you're thankful for." For example, clouds, the color blue, trees.

Next say: "Roll over on your stomachs and look down. Tell some of God's gifts you see from this perspective." For example, grass, ants, shiny stones.

Ask group members to sit up. Have them each place their forefingers and thumbs together to form a peephole. Say: "Look through the window you've made. Call out other gifts you see that God has given us." For example, people, transportation, water.

Have a volunteer read Matthew 6:25-33. Allow a moment for everyone to consider the grass, flowers of the field and birds of the air.

Ask everyone to find a long, wide blade of grass. Have group members each place their blade of grass between their thumbs to form a reed. Give them a few minutes to practice blowing into the grass. Let kids "make a joyful noise unto the

Lord,'' thanking him for the grass and lilies of the field.

Ask junior highers to listen as you read the poem "Grass" by Don Theye. Have them be prepared to sound their grass instruments when they hear the cue.

Say: "All aboard the bikes and to the next stop! Remember to keep looking for the good things God gives."

Grass

It seems there must be
A lot of good reasons
Why there's so much grass,
But most of them are
When the grass grows green.

There's house grass for mowing,
Tall grass for flowing,
Thick grass for hiding and
Slick grass for sliding.

Then there's, of course,
Bluegrass (which is really green)
And crab grass (not at all mean).

Any grass will stain your knee
Or cover insects you can't see.
Fresh grass is for animal-munching.
Soft grass for picnic-lunching.
Morning grass, kissed with dew,
That I like. Do you too?

Oh, winter-brown old grass is okay.
It holds the earth together and keeps
Feet from getting too muddy
When the snow melts. But, of
Green grass one fact I sure know.

It's only with a blade
Of limp green grass
That you can hold it just so . . .
Put it carefully to your lips . . .
To send forth the sound of . . .
Eagles and crows with . . .
    Just
        The
            Right
                Size . . .
                Blow!!!!!!!!

Don Theye

---

3. Second stop—Have everyone hop off the bikes and stretch legs by going on a "good smell" hunt. Allow a few minutes for everyone to locate something especially fragrant. Depending on the area, it might be a flower, a ponderosa pine or simply the fresh air. Gather junior highers back together. Then number off and start with the highest-numbered person leading the group to his or her find. Follow each person to his or her spot and share the good smell. End with person #1.

Gather group members in a circle and discuss the sense of smell. Ask: "What would life be like without noses? What gifts would we miss if we couldn't use our sniffers?'' Ask for a volunteer, then bring out the nose plugs. Have him or her wear the nose plugs and eat a cookie. Let others try it. Say: ''Our sense of smell affects our sense of taste. God knows we need our nose! Let's thank him for our sense of smell so we can taste our food. Let's thank God for our sack lunches!''

As you eat, have a continuous lunch-time prayer. Have everyone, one at a time, tell of his or her all-time favorite food. Then have everyone say why he or she would be thankful for his or her neighbor's lunch.

Before leaving the area, have group members pack their trash in their bags and pick up other trash they see. Leave the area cleaner than it was when you came.

Bike to the next stop and keep looking, smelling and listening for God's gifts.

4. *Third stop*—Ask the bike riders to find a comfortable spot, lie down, close their eyes and listen. Have them each hold up a finger for each sound they hear. They may hear wind, bugs, people, cars, animals. Have group members sit in a circle and tell about what they heard. Then ask them each to choose one sound to help make a progressive ''sound track.'' Explain that you'll point to them one at a time and they are to sound off and continue doing so until everyone is sounding off at the same time. Once everyone is involved, you'll be an ''orchestra director.'' Increase or decrease the volume with hand and arm signals. Then point to individuals to stop, until the last one is finished.

Replay the sound track by letting different members direct. They can raise and lower the volume. For fun, imagine the sound track can be fast-forwarded and reversed.

Next, give kids a few minutes to each find two rocks. Have group members form a circle, then discuss what the rocks feel like. Ask: ''Are they rough? smooth? jagged? solid?'' Ask group members to compare the rocks to themselves. You could start by saying something such as ''This rock reminds me of the stability my family gives me.''

After everyone has shared, say: ''We'll now have a 'rock concert.' Jesus said, 'These stones will shout if you don't.' So we're going to lift up our praises to God with the rocks.'' Have kids create rhythms and verses. For example, clap out a rhythm to this verse:

Oh(x) give(x) thanks(x)

Un(x)to(x) the(x) Lord(x)
For(x) he(x) is(x) good(x)
And(x) his(x) mer(x)cy(x)
En(x)dur(x)eth(x) for(x)ev(x)er(x).
Say: "All aboard the bikes and to home base!"

5. *Homeward bound*—Once you reach the church, lead the troop in a few exercises to stretch out the stiffness from biking all day. Have kids touch their toes, reach to the sky, twist at the waist.

As a closing activity, play "Bike Wheel of Blessings." Tell kids to take off their shoes. Have junior highers form a bike wheel and spokes by sitting on the floor in a circle with their feet touching in the center and their arms stretched out in front. Ask for volunteers. Have volunteers, one at a time, stand in the middle, fold their arms across their chest and fall into the others' outstretched arms. The other group members catch them and pass them around. The trick is for the volunteer to stay stiff and trust the others. The other group members have to keep their arms out in front of them at all times to catch the middle person.

As each volunteer is passed around, have kids yell out why they're thankful for that person. For example, if Stan's in the center, they could shout, "He's full of fun"; "He never gave up"; "Stan kept us going."

Let everyone have a chance to be in the center of the bike wheel.

Read to group members the poster paraphrase of 1 Corinthians 9:23 and Hebrews 12:1, only change it to past tense: "All the bike-trip training preparation we did for the gospel's sake, in order to share in its blessings. We rode with determination the course that was before us." Have all the bike riders join in shouting a loud "Amen!"

6. *Variations*—Other twists to this meeting:
● Plan a bike-day fund raiser. Have kids each get money pledges for each mile they ride.
● Increase the time to two or more days.
● Organize a bike progressive dinner. Bike to different junior highers' homes for salad, soup, main course and dessert.
● Hike instead of bike. ∎

56 *Preparing for High School*

By Ron King and Karen Sherrill

Making that big jump into high school often brings a flood of fears. It's scary, traumatic, threatening.

But starting high school can also be exciting and challenging—the beginning of a wonderful growing-up experience.

Use this meeting to help junior highers prepare to have a positive experience in high school.

OBJECTIVES

Participants will:

● clarify the major fears behind the transition into high school;

● discuss needs brought on by entering a new school environment;

● discover characteristics of God that address their needs and fears; and

● have the opportunity to choose to support each other in high school.

SUPPLIES

Gather high school paraphernalia such as pennants, letter jackets, jerseys, posters, banners, mascots; a whistle; one bat; one lopsided plastic ball; two softball bases; one 2 1/2-foot cloth strip for every two group members; a VCR and TV monitor (and necessary cables and extension cords); a videotape of *Back to the Future* or *The Last Starfighter* (or other current movie that shows various emotions that come in new situations); a "Video Questions" handout for each small group of four to six; six Bibles; six slips of paper, each with one of these references written on it: Psalm 90:2; Psalm 102:25-27; Isaiah 40:6-8; Romans 8:31, 38-39; Hebrews 7:25; Hebrews 13:8; newsprint and markers; an indelible marker; masking tape; a cassette recorder or turntable; a cassette tape or record of "Great Is Thy Faithfulness," "Raining on the Inside" or "Everywhere I Go" (the last two are Amy Grant songs); a couple of typical "cafeteria ladies" uniforms (don't forget the plastic shower caps); and, for each person, a "Commitment Contract" handout and a pencil. Optional: an obnoxious buzzer.

BEFORE THE MEETING

Read the meeting and collect supplies.

Get a few group members to decorate the meeting room with the high school paraphernalia.

On newsprint, write and post the meeting schedule; make it look like a high school class schedule.

Choose an adult sponsor to wear coach-type clothes and direct the Siamese softball game.

Choose a game area for Siamese softball (this works well indoors or outdoors).

Prepare the videotape. If you have *Back to the Future*, cue up the segment that shows Michael Fox arriving in the past. If you have *The Last Starfighter*, cue up the segment that shows "Alex" being taken from Earth to the Frontier Station, and plan to fast-forward the tape past the back-home segment and play it again where the starfighter training begins. Find a good point to stop the tape after seven to 10 minutes, or when you feel the impact of being in a new environment has been made.

Select a couple of group members to wear the cafeteria garb and serve refreshments.

Have someone prepare refreshments to be served cafeteria-line-style; for example, strawberry shortcake: shortcake, strawberries, whipped cream.

NOTES TO THE LEADER

The main needs and fears to address during this meeting are

acceptance and rejection; loss of status, sense of worth and belonging; and loneliness. Keep the focus on God's ability to meet the variety of needs brought on by entering a new school.

THE MEETING

1. *The arrival*—Allow a few minutes for messing around.

Open the meeting by having an adult sponsor dressed in coach-type clothes blow a whistle and instruct group members to participate in the game.

2. *Siamese softball*—Divide the group into two teams. Have team members choose partners; tie partners' legs together (like for a three-legged race) with the cloth strips. Each pair of ''Siamese'' partners will act as one player in the game. Have a ''leftover'' group member or Siamese pair pitch for each team. The plastic ball is pitched underhand and may be hit in any direction; there are no foul balls. Runners go between two bases: first and home. As many runners as possible may stay on first base, and all may score at once. Runners are ruled out when the opposing team catches a fly ball, forces out the runners at first, tags the runners between bases, or throws the ball at the runners and hits them while they are off a base. Each team gets four outs. Any time runners get to first and then back to home safely, they score.

3. *Introducing the topic*—Have group members untie themselves and gather in the meeting room.

Introduce the video segment by explaining that people experience many different thoughts and emotions in new situations. Illustrate this by giving a brief example from your own life (for example, your first time on the high dive, your first kiss, your first visit to a youth group).

Ask group members to watch the video and think about what thoughts and emotions the main character is experiencing. Show the video segment.

4. *New situations*—Divide the group into small groups of four to six with an adult sponsor in each.

Give each small group a ''Video Questions'' handout. Allow time for groups to discuss the questions.

Let small groups each choose one member to tell all group members about his or her funny new-situation experience.

Video Questions

What do you think the main character was thinking in the video segment? Why?

Have you ever had those thoughts in a new situation? If so, describe the situation.

What do you think the main character was feeling in the video segment? Why?

Have you ever felt the same way in a new situation? If so, describe the situation.

Tell about a time when you didn't know many people around and something funny or embarrassing happened to you (for example, at a dance, on a vacation, in a new class).

5. *A personal example*—While group members are still in small groups, stand up and illustrate the fears and needs you experienced in adjusting to high school. Do this by sharing a short story about an embarrassing situation. Communicate that being concerned is a natural and normal reaction to a new environment, but the anxiety doesn't need to continue.

For fun, have some junior highers quickly act out the embarrassing situation you described.

6. *New fears*—Now ask the small groups to list fears that someone might have about entering high school. Hand out newsprint and markers and have each group write those fears.

Have the small groups think of the *need* that causes each fear and write it next to that fear. For example, the fear of being rejected; the need for acceptance.

7. *How God meets needs*—Have all group members get back together. Ask for six volunteers to look up and read aloud scripture passages. Hand out Bibles and slips of paper, each with one of these references: Psalm 90:2; Psalm 102:25-27; Isaiah 40:6-8; Romans 8:31, 38-39; Hebrews 7:25; Hebrews 13:8. After each passage is read, have the group clarify the verse. Ask: "What's being said? What's being said about God? What's important about this characteristic of God?''

Explain that God is fully capable of meeting our fears and needs. Take the newsprints listing fears and needs, and over the top of the fears and needs write the characteristics of God that offer help. Use an indelible marker for this. Have some group members tape the sheets of newsprint onto the walls.

Ask group members to listen to the cassette tape or record you've chosen to wrap up your meeting. Play the song. Close by emphasizing that God will always be there to help.

8. *Helping each other*—Say that high school can be a great experience if group members support each other. Suggest they agree to say hi to each other in the halls, be willing to listen to someone's bad-day story on the way home, never put down each other, etc.

If you have group members who will attend different high schools, separate them into groups according to the schools. Have kids brainstorm more ways they can support each other in high school.

Hand out the "Commitment Contracts" and pencils. Have

Commitment Contract

I, the Undersigned, do hereby promise you, the party of the first part,

_____, that I will give faithful support as the party of the first part moves up to high school. I will endeavor to do this by listening to, laughing, crying, sharing and talking with the party of the first part,

_____, on a consistent basis to the best of my ability. I, the Undersigned, do also agree to share ice cream, corn dogs, and especially my friendship with you. I'm committed to see you through!

Party of the second part,
the Undersigned

_____

each person sign his or her name in the two blanks. Then encourage everyone to indicate support by signing the bottom of each other's contracts. Encourage your adult leaders to sign the bottom of these contracts as well. Suggest that group members take their contracts home and display them in their bedrooms.

9. *Cafeteria fun*—Announce that the "cafeteria" is now open (you might want to use an obnoxious buzzer for this purpose). Have group members line up when your "cafeteria ladies" are ready to serve the refreshments. Enjoy! ■

57 *The Big Gift*

By Larry Keefauver

Each Christmas we give and receive gifts. But
one gift surpasses all others—the gift of God's
son, Jesus. The mystery of God's love for us becomes real at Christmas. God who is Spirit becomes Flesh. The challenge: How do we communicate the Incarnation (the Word becoming Flesh) to
junior highers?

Use this Christmas meeting to let the familiar
(and concrete) gift-giving serve as an analogy to
communicate the Incarnation.

OBJECTIVES

Participants will:
- share with the group past Christmas experiences and gifts
that are meaningful to them;
- explore a Bible passage about the Incarnation;
- discuss the uniqueness of God's gift to us; and
- be encouraged to share their understanding of the Incarnation as a Christmas gift with their families.

SUPPLIES

Gather Christmas carols on cassette tapes or records; a cassette player or turntable; an instant-print camera with enough
film and flashbulbs to take a photo of each group member; five
different-size Christmas-wrapped boxes, each with one of the
following items inside: a dollar bill, a clock, a pair of gloves, a
dictionary, a piece of sheet music; a cassette tape or record of

"All Good Gifts" from *Godspell*; small candy canes for all kids except three to six (depending on the size of your small groups); newsprint; markers; masking tape; a specially wrapped, large empty gift box—much nicer than the other packages—with a lid that may be easily removed without tearing the wrapping paper; Christmas wrapping paper and ribbon; scissors; Scotch tape; a table to serve as an altar or worship center; for every three to six group members, a set of three to six 3×5 "scripture cards," each with a phrase from John 1:1 written on it ("In the beginning," "was the Word," "and the Word was with God" and so on—each set of cards needs to have the complete verse), three to six large candy canes; and, for each person, a small jewelry-type box and a pencil.

E THE MEETING

 the meeting and collect supplies.
 the specially wrapped empty gift box out of sight.

ETING

eetings—Play Christmas carols as kids arrive. Take a
 each person as he or she enters. Have everyone sit in
 und the five gift boxes. Ask group members to guess
 ach package. Let them handle the presents, but not

avorite Christmas and Christmas gift—
 ese sentences yourself: "My favorite Christmas was
 was (age) and what happened was . . ." "The best
Christmas gift I ever received was . . ." From your photos of the group members, select a photo at random and hold it up. Ask that junior higher to complete the same two sentences. Continue this until all group members have completed the sentences.

3. *Giving good gifts*—Play "All Good Gifts." When the song is over, explain that the greatest gift that God gave us was his son, Jesus.
    Divide the group into small groups of three to six. Give each group a set of scripture cards. Say: "Your group's set of cards contains a verse from the Gospel of John. The first group to unscramble its verse and arrange the cards in correct order

wins a special prize. The game ends only when all teams correctly unscramble the verses. Keep working until your team finishes. Ask me (or another adult) to check your work. Go.''

Play ''All Good Gifts'' or carols in the background. Give the first group to finish the larger candy canes, and give the rest the other candy canes.

4. *Unique gifts*—Have kids get back into the circle. Explain: ''A gift tells us much about the giver. You shop for that one special gift that no one else can give. People who have everything are hard to shop for—nothing you can give them seems special, unique or one-of-a-kind. The five gifts in the center of this circle represent special gifts you might choose for someone you love.''

Have the group vote for the gift to be opened first, second, and so on. Open each gift and lead a brief discussion with a question such as: ''How does money (or a clock or gloves or a dictionary or music) represent something unique or special we might give someone we love?''

The discussion might go something like this: ''Money represents our ability to buy whatever gift we choose.'' Or, ''A clock represents the time we might spend thinking of just the right gift, or perhaps that we might give a gift of our own time and energy—shoveling snow, for example.'' Or, ''Gloves represent something we might make with our hands like a painting, needlepoint, woodcraft.'' Or, ''The dictionary represents words we might use to write a letter, poem or card to tell a person how special he or she is to us.'' Or, ''The music represents a talent we might use to create a gift for the person we love.''

There are no right answers. Don't force discussion. As soon as one item plays out, go to the next.

Then, ask: ''How do each of these gifts represent a way that God gave of himself?'' List the ideas on newsprint. You might need to offer an idea or two to start the discussion. For example:

● money—God created the wealth of the universe;

● clock—God acted in history to show us what he is like;

● gloves—God created the universe to show us his power and glory;

● dictionary—God used language to speak to us through the law and the prophets; and

● music—God spoke through songs—Psalms—to tell us of his majesty and his love for us.

5. *The Christmas gift*—Place the specially wrapped, empty gift box in the center of the circle. Say: "This gift represents the most unique, costly gift that God could give those he loves. The other gifts we talked about weren't enough. This represents his unique gift of love. What do you think is in this box?"

Your junior highers will guess many items: a cross; a picture of Jesus; a Bible; a Nativity scene. Accept each answer. Then say: "All of you guessed correctly. The unique gift God gave us was himself in the form of a human being, Jesus. I could have selected any of the things you guessed to place in the box, but I chose . . . "

Open the box and show the group that *it's empty*! Pass the box around the circle so everyone can touch it and look inside.

Ask: "How does this empty box represent God's unique gift of himself in Jesus?" This is a tough question. A few in the group may come up with some interesting comments. Remember, the purpose of the meeting is to make an abstract concept, the Incarnation, as concrete as possible.

After the group tries some answers and struggles a bit, suggest this: "The empty box represents the empty tomb. *Christmas isn't Christmas without the Resurrection.* Jesus is here right now in the Spirit. We can't see him, but he is in this room."

Have each young person take a small box and wrap it as a Christmas gift to take home and place under his or her Christmas tree. Then say: "This small gift box should remind you of the gift of Jesus who is with you now."

6. *Closing worship*—Play Christmas carols in the background. Give each junior higher his or her picture and a pencil. Have each person complete the following sentences on the back of his or her own picture: "One gift I can give to God this Christmas is . . . " "One way I can show love to (a person's name) this Christmas is . . . "

As the group sings "Silent Night," have each person place his or her picture on a table serving as an altar or worship center.

Form a circle, have the group members join hands and repeat after you the following prayer: "God, thank you for your gift of yourself in Jesus. Amen."

Remind the group members to each take their Christmas gift home to place under their Christmas tree and to share its meaning with their family on Christmas day. ∎

58 *Christmas Corners: A Babysitting Service*

By Catherine Simmering

Christmas is a time for sharing gifts. Use this babysitting service project to let junior highers share their "gifts": their talents, their lives, their energies. They'll in turn receive "gifts" from the young children. And the parents of young children in your congregation will appreciate some free time for Christmas shopping.

OBJECTIVES

Participants will:
- learn what kinds of activities young children like to do;
- work together to prepare for those activities;
- experience leadership as they carry out the activities with young children; and
- be appreciated by church families for giving time and energy.

SUPPLIES

Gather stick-on name tags; markers; notebook; pen; baby-care supplies (if not already in the nursery)—extra disposable diapers, tissues, washcloths; if you can't use the church nursery, playpens and/or portable cribs, and toys and small tables and chairs; and a special treat such as pizza and soft drinks for junior highers after the event.

Depending on your choice of "corners," also gather the following supplies.

The Play Corner: toys, the pretend boat made from a refrigerator box, the beanbag-game cardboard box and beanbags.

The Quiet Corner: soft rugs, pillows, children's books and puzzles.

The Music Corner: turntable, children's records, rhythm instruments, plain paper, crayons, pen and masking tape.

The Cookie-Decorating Corner: tables to work at, paint shirts or aprons, plain sugar cookies, small paintbrushes, bowls of various colors of thin frosting, and wax paper.

The Gift-Making Corner: newsprint or old plastic tablecloths for the floor, 11 × 14 pieces of colored construction paper or lightweight cardboard, Christmas cards, pictures cut out from magazines, colorful stickers, crayons, scissors, paste, clear Con-Tact paper, various kinds of beads (large bags of beads may be purchased at craft supply stores) and painted macaroni that can be strung together, string, Christmas wrapping paper, tape, gift-wrap ribbon, pen and masking tape.

The Christmas-Story Corner: flannelgraph figures of the Christmas story, flannelgraph board, empty egg cartons, cotton balls, plastic miniature babies, 2-inch-square pieces of flannel, pen and masking tape.

BEFORE THE MEETING

Read the meeting. Carefully do all these preparations.

● Get together with your junior highers and decide when the group will provide the babysitting service. The first or second Saturdays in December are good times.

Arrange to use the church nursery and other areas for the activity corners. Make sure it's okay to use the kitchen for the children's sack lunches and snacks.

Decide how long you'll provide this babysitting service. From 9 a.m. to 2 p.m. works well. Also decide on the age of the children; I recommend preschoolers, up to 5 years old.

● Publicize the event! Use the church newsletter and Sunday bulletins. Have junior highers make posters and give creative announcements during worship and other family gatherings. Have group members make "tickets" and send them to church families with young children. (See the "Ticket Example"). The parents don't need the tickets to admit their kids; they're just a fun way to publicize the event.

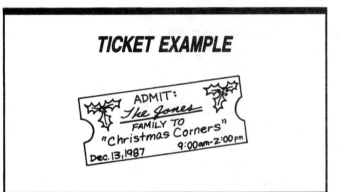

TICKET EXAMPLE

You might want junior highers to call church parents the week before "Christmas Corners" to remind them of the free babysitting. Have the callers remind parents to send along sack lunches and snacks with their children. Also have the young people ask the parents whether they expect to be leaving their kids, so you'll have an idea of the attendance.

● Choose junior highers to be responsible for each corner, and also for the nursery. Depending on the size of your group, have one to six young people for each area.

The following corners need special preparation. Have the kids in charge do this. Help them find supplies, and give guidance. Let them do these preparations at their convenience. Give them these instructions:

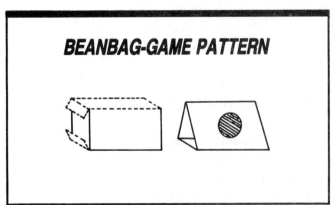

BOAT PATTERN

BEANBAG-GAME PATTERN

The Play Corner: Make a pretend boat by using a refrigerator box (available from an appliance store). Cut out the shape of a boat (see the "Boat Pattern"), but don't cut off the end flaps. Tape the end flaps together so the boat will keep its shape and stand up. Cut out windows, and paint the boat if you'd like.

Also, make a beanbag game: Cut off the ends and one side of a box so you have a triangle shape. Then cut out a large hole in one side. Tape the cardboard together so it stands alone (see the "Beanbag-Game Pattern").

Make beanbags by sewing

lightweight cloth to make sacks, inserting dry beans and hand-stitching the sacks together. Or buy beanbags.

The Cookie-Decorating Corner: Make or buy plain sugar cookies. The night before "Christmas Corners," make a variety of colors of thin frosting.

The Gift-Making Corner: Cut out pictures from magazines. Choose pictures young children would like: colorful designs, family pictures, animals, toys. Also cut individual sheets of Con-Tact paper to the same size as the 11×14 construction paper or cardboard.

Spray paint uncooked macaroni noodles.

Cut string into 25-inch lengths and wrap Scotch tape around both ends of each piece so it won't unravel.

The Christmas-Story Corner: Practice telling the Christmas story using flannelgraph figures. Cut egg cartons so that the individual egg holders are separate. Cut 2-inch-square pieces of flannel.

● Have all junior highers responsible for the corners and the nursery gather the supplies they need ahead of time. Also have them create posters or signposts to label the corners. They'll have fun decorating their areas too (see the "Signpost Example").

Plan ahead, on paper, where the corners will be located. Keep the quiet area away from the play areas.

● In a notebook, prepare a few pages like the example.

● Choose a junior higher to stay by the entrance to greet parents and children and ask the parents to sign in the children using the notebook. Also have the junior higher check out children when parents pick them up.

● Choose another junior higher to be the "name-tagger." He or she should stay by the entrance and provide markers and name tags, and make sure all the children wear name tags.

● Choose three or more group members to escort parents and children around the corners and help the kids get settled when their parents leave. The escorts should wait by the entrance when they're not busy.

SIGNPOST EXAMPLE

NOTEBOOK PREPARATION

CHILD'S NAME AND AGE	ANY SPECIAL INFO ABOUT CHILD	WHO TO CALL IN AN EMER-GENCY	TIME CHILD IS PICKED UP BY PARENT

NOTES TO THE LEADER

"Christmas Corners" puts junior highers in positions of leadership. All your young people may not want to take part in this, but encourage those you feel would benefit from the experience.

THE MEETING

1. *Getting ready*—Have all group members and adult sponsors meet together an hour before "Christmas Corners" opens. Let junior highers put up their posters and signposts and decorate their corners. Make sure everything is in order.

Have all adult sponsors and junior highers wear name tags.

2. *The arrival*—As parents and children arrive, have the greeter greet and ask parents to sign in the children; have the name-tagger make sure kids wear name tags with their names clearly written; have the escorts take parents and children around to the corners.

3. *The corners*—Let the fun begin! Children move around to the corners as they wish. Junior highers guide and play with the children at the corners they're responsible for. As children want their snacks or lunch, any junior higher may help them.

● ***The Play Corner:*** Here children just play. They enjoy the boat, the beanbag game and toys.

● ***The Quiet Corner:*** Here children take naps on the rugs and pillows, read, work puzzles or quietly talk.

● ***The Music Corner:*** Here children listen to records and play along with rhythm instruments. They also draw as they listen to the music, or even dance.

Have the junior highers here use a pen and masking tape to mark the kids' names on their drawings.

● ***The Cookie-Decorating Corner:*** Here children wear paint shirts or aprons, sit at tables, and use paintbrushes to decorate sugar cookies with colored frosting.

Have the junior highers here wrap the cookies with wax paper after the frosting has dried a bit. Junior highers should encourage the children to take the cookies home and give them away rather than immediately eat them.

● ***The Gift-Making Corner:*** Here children sit on newsprint or old plastic tablecloths and make place mats, or string beads or macaroni.

For the place mats, they have pieces of lightweight cardboard or 11×14 sheets of construction paper. They can paste on Christmas cards, pictures from magazines and colorful stickers to make designs. They can add crayon decorations too. Then the junior highers should put clear Con-Tact paper over the designs to complete the place mats. Also, the junior highers should use a pen and masking tape to mark the kids' names on their place mats.

For stringing beads and macaroni, children fill the string pieces enough to be either necklaces or Christmas tree decorations. Have the junior highers help by tying the string ends together on the creations.

At this corner kids can also wrap their gifts. Sometimes they enjoy this as much as making the presents!

Have the junior highers here use a pen and masking tape to mark the kids' names on their gifts.

● *The Christmas-Story Corner:* Here the children listen to junior highers telling the Christmas story with a flannelgraph. Then they each make their own tiny manger using an egg carton cup for the manger, a cotton ball for the hay, a plastic miniature baby for Jesus and a small square of flannel for the swaddling clothes.

Have the junior highers use a pen and masking tape to mark the kids' names on their mangers.

4. *The closing*—When parents pick up their children, the junior highers responsible for the music corner, the cookie-decorating corner, the gift-making corner and the Christmas-story corner should make sure the kids remember to take their drawings, cookies, gifts and tiny mangers.

Be sure the junior high greeter is at the exit to check out the children.

5. *Debriefing*—When all the children have gone, give your junior highers a special treat such as pizza and soft drinks. Let everyone talk about the experiences with the children. Ask: "How did you feel about today? How did you feel about being so responsible? What did you learn about children? about yourself?"

Before leaving, have junior highers clean up all the corners and the nursery, and rearrange the furniture and toys. ■

CREATIVE PROGRAMMING RESOURCES FROM GROUP

Group's Best Jr. High Meetings

Here's the answer to your junior high programming needs. You'll get 35 complete meetings that focus on topics important to young people helping junior highers...
- cope with peer pressure,
- communicate with parents,
- build self-confidence,
- improve decision-making skills,
- make room for God,

...and more! You'll challenge your kids to grow in faith by getting them involved in activities, games, and Bible studies. Plus, you'll get...
- helpful objectives and preparation hints,
- easy-to-use instructions and supply lists,
- loads of photocopiable handouts,

...and other information to make meeting planning easy. Programs are ideal for junior high meetings, Sunday school classes, or Bible study groups. And they're easily adapted for small groups.

Group's Best Jr. High Meetings, Volume 2
ISBN 1-55945-009-6

Jr. High Retreats & Lock-Ins

Karen Dockrey

Plan easy, creative retreats and lock-ins for junior highers with step-by-step help from **Jr. High Retreats & Lock-Ins**. Unleash your middle schoolers' zeal for God with this collection of six exciting retreats and six fun-filled lock-ins. Use these retreat and lock-in plans to creatively address important junior high issues...
- self-esteem,
- family relationships,
- peer pressure,
- friendship,
- loneliness and looks,
- life after death,

...and more. In addition, you'll find detailed retreat and lock-in planning models. You'll learn how to choose a site, recruit volunteers, plan a budget—everything you need to lead an effective junior high retreat or lock-in.

Plus, each event design saves you time with easy-to-follow program instructions. Each retreat and lock-in includes...
- introduction and objectives,
- well-planned event schedules,
- complete supply checklists, and
- fun, faith-building activities.

ISBN 0-93152-973-5

Order today from your local Christian bookstore, or write: Group Publishing, Box 485, Loveland, CO 80539.

DEVOTIONAL RESOURCES FOR YOUR MINISTRY...

Devotions for Youth Groups

Get 52 quick devotions in each book that need little or no preparation—on important topics such as...

- love,
- friendship,
- rumors,
- peer pressure,
- faith,
- accepting others,
- grades,
- peace,
- service,

...and more. Each is complete with Scripture reference, attention-grabbing learning experience, discussion questions, and closing. Bring teenagers closer to God with these refreshing devotions!

10-Minute Devotions for Youth Groups
J.B. Collingsworth
ISBN 0-931529-85-9

More 10-Minute Devotions for Youth Groups
ISBN 1-55945-068-1

10-Minute Devotions for Youth Groups, Vol. III
ISBN 1-55945-171-8

The 13 Most Important Bible Lessons for Teenagers

Build a strong foundation of basic Bible understanding with these active lessons that make learning fun. You'll get 13 complete programs on topics like...

- Who is Jesus?
- What is the Bible?
- Why does life hurt?
- Why the church?

...plus, you'll teach lessons on prayer, witnessing, practical service, and end times. Perfect to help new Christians understand their faith or to refresh mature believers. The 13-week format works well for Sunday school or youth meetings.

ISBN 1-55945-261-7

Order today from your local Christian bookstore, or write: Group Publishing, Box 485, Loveland, CO 80539.

FUN RESOURCES FOR YOUR JUNIOR HIGH MINISTRY...

Fun Group-Involving Skits

Use these quick, no-rehearsal dramas as opening crowdbreakers, short devotionals, or to introduce a theme for a whole meeting. Skits are based on familiar Bible stories such as...
- David and Goliath,
- Creation,
- Jonah and the big fish,

...and topics such as...
- peer pressure,
- sexuality,
- fears,

...and many more, all in a variety of pantomime and acting situations. There's no memorization needed, and each skit is followed by discussion and follow-up activities.

ISBN 1-55945-152-1

Boredom Busters

Cindy S. Hansen

Packed with 84 low- and no-cost activities for kids of all ages, this book will help you turn any blah meeting into a blast! Keep your kids' attention by...
- playing human-size tick-tack-toe,
- organizing an orchestra without any instruments,
- deciphering a scrambled Scripture,
- batting a balloon through an obstacle course, and
- working together to lift a teammate over a net.

Don't let boredom keep your youth group from growing in faith. Keep them involved with **Boredom Busters**!

ISBN 0-931529-77-8

Have-a-Blast Games for Youth Groups

Here are 101 quick and easy games that will grab kids' attention and require only a few minutes of preparation. Guaranteed to keep your youth group on the ball and energized with icebreakers for meetings, retreats, lock-ins, or wherever your group is having a good time. You'll find...
- Crazy Competitions—to build teamwork in your group,
- Remarkable Recreations—to help kids build friendships, and
- Dynamic Diversions—for just plain fun.

Be a creative whiz—the easy way—with **Have-a-Blast Games for Youth Groups**.

ISBN 1-55945-046-0

Order today from your local Christian bookstore, or write: Group Publishing, Box 485, Loveland, CO 80539.